# American Civil Rights Biographies

# American Civil Rights Biographies

Phillis Engelbert

**Betz Des Chenes, Editor**

AN IMPRINT OF THE GALE GROUP

DETROIT · SAN FRANCISCO · LONDON
BOSTON · WOODBRIDGE, CT

**Phillis Engelbert**

**Staff**

Elizabeth Des Chenes, *U•X•L Senior Editor*
Carol DeKane Nagel, *U•X•L Managing Editor*
Thomas L. Romig, *U•X•L Publisher*

Shalice Shah-Caldwell, *Permissions Associate (Pictures)*

Rita Wimberley, *Senior Buyer*
Evi Seoud, *Assistant Production Manager*
Dorothy Maki, *Manufacturing Manager*

Pamela A. E. Galbreath, *Senior Art Director*
Cynthia Baldwin, *Product Design Manager*

LM Design, *Typesetting*

**Library of Congress Cataloging-in-Publication Data**

Engelbert, Phillis.

American civil rights: biographies/Phillis Engelbert.

p.cm.

Includes bibliographical references and index.

Summary: Biographies of major civil rights figures, including sidebars covering related events and issues.

ISBN: 0-7876-3173-6 (hardcover)

1. Minorities—Civil rights—United States—History Juvenile literature. 2. Civil rights workers—United States Biography Juvenile literature. 3. Civil rights movements—United States—History Juvenile literature. 4. United States—Race Relations Juvenile literature. 5. United States—Ethnic relations Juvenile literature. [1. Civil rights workers. 2. Civil rights movements. 3. Race relations.] I. Title.

E184. A1E594 1999
305.8' 00973—dc21

The front cover photographs were reproduced by permission of Corbis-Bettmann, AP/Wide World Photos, and Charlene Teters.

Printed in the United States of America

10 9 8 7 6 5 4 3

# Contents

Advisory Board . . . . . . . . . . . . . . . . . vii

Reader's Guide . . . . . . . . . . . . . . . . . ix

Timeline . . . . . . . . . . . . . . . . . . . . xi

Words to Know . . . . . . . . . . . . . . . . . xix

## Biographies

James G. Abourezk . . . . . . . . . . . . . . . . 1
   The Killing of Alex Odeh (box) . . . . . . . 7

Susan B. Anthony . . . . . . . . . . . . . . . 10
   Elizabeth Cady Stanton (box) . . . . . . . 15

Anna Mae Aquash . . . . . . . . . . . . . . . 23
   "Daughter of the Earth: Song for
   Anna Mae Aquash" (box) . . . . . . . . . 27

Ella Jo Baker . . . . . . . . . . . . . . . . . 31
   Bayard Rustin (box) . . . . . . . . . . . . 34

César Chávez . . . . . . . . . . . . . . . . . 39
   Luis Valdez and Teatro Campesino (box) . . . 43

Septima P. Clark . . . . . . . . . . . . . . . 47

**Rosa Parks.**
*Photograph by George Dabrowski. Reproduced by permission of Archive Photos.*

Rodolfo "Corky" Gonzales . . . . . . . . . . 55
    *I am Joaquín* (box). . . . . . . . . . . 57
    The Poor People's March on
    Washington (box). . . . . . . . . . 59
Fannie Lou Hamer . . . . . . . . . . 62
Harry Hay . . . . . . . . . . . . . 71
Myles Horton . . . . . . . . . . . . 79
    Rosa Parks (box) . . . . . . . . . 84
Dolores Huerta . . . . . . . . . . . . 88
    Jesse De La Cruz (box). . . . . . . . 93
Elaine H. Kim . . . . . . . . . . . . 96
Martin Luther King Jr . . . . . . . . . . . 102
    "Letter from a Birmingham Jail" (box). . . . 107
Yuri Kochiyama . . . . . . . . . . . . . 115
    "A Praise Song for Yuri" (box). . . . . . . 120
John Robert Lewis . . . . . . . . . . . . . 123
    The March on Washington (box) . . . . . . 128
Malcolm X . . . . . . . . . . . . . . 135
    Malcolm X and Martin Luther King Jr. (box) . 141
Robert Parris Moses . . . . . . . . . . . 144
    Moses's Opposition to the
    Vietnam War (box) . . . . . . . . . 151
Leonard Peltier . . . . . . . . . . . . 153
    Hank Adams (box). . . . . . . . . . 158
Ed Roberts . . . . . . . . . . . . . 162
Charlene Teters . . . . . . . . . . . . 169
John Trudell . . . . . . . . . . . . . 177
Sojourner Truth . . . . . . . . . . . . 187
    Harriet Tubman (box) . . . . . . . . 191
    "Ain't I a Woman?" (box) . . . . . . . 193
Philip Vera Cruz . . . . . . . . . . . . 197
    "Profits Enslave the World" (box) . . . . . 202

**Index** . . . . . . . . . . . . . . . . . . xxxiii

**John Trudell.**
*Reproduced by permission of AP/Wide World Photos.*

# Advisory Board

S pecial thanks are due for the invaluable comments and suggestions provided by U•X•L's American Civil Rights Reference Library advisors:

- Eduardo Bonilla-Silva, Professor of Sociology, Texas A&M University, College Station, Texas

- Frances Hasso, Assistant Professor of Sociology, Antioch College, Yellow Springs, Ohio

- Annalissa Herbert, Graduate student, American Culture program, University of Michigan, Ann Arbor, Michigan

- Patrick R. LeBeau, Assistant Professor of American Thought and Language, Michigan State University, East Lansing, Michigan

- Premilla Nadasen, Assistant Professor of African American History, Queens College, New York City

- Kamal M. Nawash, Esq., Director of Legal Services, American-Arab Anti-Discrimination Committee, Washington, D.C.

- Diane Surati, Teacher, Crossett Brook Middle School, Waterbury, Vermont

- Jan Toth-Chernin, Media Specialist, Greenhills School, Ann Arbor, Michigan

# Reader's Guide

**A**merican *Civil Rights: Biographies* presents profiles of twenty-three men and women from various racial, ethnic, and nonethnic groups who worked to advance the cause of civil rights in the United States. Each of the people featured in the volume—including artists, educators, labor organizers, ministers, and politicians—contributed to the development of civil rights in a unique way. The volume includes not only biographies of readily recognizable civil rights figures, such as Martin Luther King Jr. and women's rights advocate Susan B. Anthony, it also includes profiles of lesser-known people, such as pioneering gay rights activist Harry Hay and Myles Horton, founder of the Highlander Folk School in Tennessee. The full-length biographies are accompanied by seven sidebar portraits, including Bayard Rustin, coordinator of the 1963 March on Washington, and Jesse de la Cruz, a crusader for farm workers' rights.

## Other Features

*American Civil Rights: Biographies* features additional sidebar boxes that highlight related civil rights events, issues, and documents. Black-and-white illustrations, cross references to other entries in the text, and a sources section accompany each entry. The volume also includes a timeline, a glossary, and a cumulative index.

## Dedication

These books are dedicated to the heroic women and men of all races who have championed civil rights throughout United States history, and to the young people who will work to expand civil rights in the next millennium.

## Special Thanks

Special thanks goes to Elizabeth Des Chenes, Senior Developmental Editor at U•X•L, for her support and guidance; to copyeditor Nancy Dziedzic, for her careful attention to detail; to all members of the advisory board for reading long manuscripts and offering thoughtful suggestions; to James W. Sullivan for providing access to his extensive private library; to Alfonso H. Lozano for answering questions about Mexican history and translating Spanish terms; to the reference librarians at the Ann Arbor Public Library for assistance in locating obscure resources; to William F. Shea for his unique insights; and to Ryan Patrick Shea for his inspiration.

## Comments and suggestions

We welcome your comments on this work as well as your suggestions for topics to be featured in future editions of *American Civil Rights: Biographies*. Please write: Editors, *American Civil Rights: Biographies*, U•X•L, 27500 Drake Rd., Farmington Hills, MI 48331–3535; call toll-free: 1–800–877–4253; fax: 248–414–5043; or send e-mail via www.galegroup.com.

# Timeline of Events in the American Civil Rights Movement

**1826**    Sojourner Truth escapes from slavery.

**1865**    Slavery is abolished with the passage of the Thirteenth Amendment.

**1890**    U.S. military forces massacre between 150 and 370 Native Americans at Wounded Knee in South Dakota.

**1890**    The National American Woman Suffrage Association (NAWSA) is formed by the merger the National Woman Suffrage Association and the American Woman Suffrage Association. The NAWSA's purpose is to fight for the passage of a constitutional amendment guaranteeing women the right to vote.

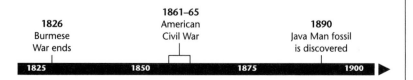

**1826**
Burmese
War ends

**1861–65**
American
Civil War

**1890**
Java Man fossil
is discovered

1825                1850              1875             1900

**Harry Hay.**
*Reproduced by permission of Daniel Nicoletta.*

**1920** The Nineteenth Amendment is passed, granting women the right to vote.

**1932** Myles Horton founds the Highlander Folk School—the South's only integrated educational institution at the time—in the Appalachian Mountains near Monteagle, Tennessee.

**February 19, 1942** President Franklin D. Roosevelt signs Executive Order 9066, authorizing the internment of 120,000 Japanese Americans in camps from 1942 through 1945.

**March 20, 1946** The last of the detention camps for Japanese Americans, Tule Lake in California, is closed.

**1950** Harry Hay founds the Mattachine Society, the first gay rights organization in the United States, in California.

**1954 to 1961** Highlander Folk School staffers Septima Clark and Bernice Robinson establish thirty-seven "citizenship schools" throughout the deep South. At the citizenship schools, African American adults learn to read, write, and fill out voter registration applications.

**December 5, 1955–December 20, 1956** Black residents of Montgomery, Alabama, stage a boycott of city buses, resulting in the racial integration of the bus system. The boycott is coordinated by the Montgomery Improvement Association, of which Martin Luther King Jr. is president.

**January 10 and 11, 1957** The Southern Christian Leadership Conference (SCLC) is founded in Atlanta, Georgia. Martin Luther King Jr. is named president and Ella Baker is hired as acting executive director and office manager.

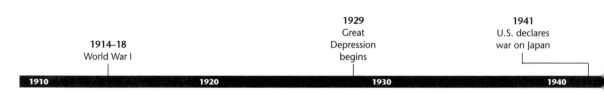

|  | 1914–18 World War I | 1929 Great Depression begins | 1941 U.S. declares war on Japan |
|---|---|---|---|
| 1910 | 1920 | 1930 | 1940 |

**April 16–18, 1960** The Student Nonviolent Coordinating Committee (SNCC) is founded at a conference organized by Ella Baker in Raleigh, North Carolina.

**1961** Civil rights activists conduct Freedom Rides throughout the South, testing the enforcement of Supreme Court rulings outlawing segregated seating on interstate (crossing state lines) buses and trains.

**July 1961** Robert Moses initiates the Student Nonviolent Coordinating Committee's voter-registration campaign in Mississippi.

**April 1963** Martin Luther King Jr. writes his "Letter from a Birmingham Jail."

**August 23, 1963** More than 250,000 people participate in the March on Washington for Jobs and Freedom. Martin Luther King Jr. delivers his "I Have a Dream" speech and John Lewis delivers an impassioned address on behalf of the Student Nonviolent Coordinating Committee.

**March 1964** Malcolm X forms a black-nationalist group called the Organization of Afro-American Unity (OAAU).

**June–September, 1964** One thousand college student volunteers descend on Mississippi for a program called Freedom Summer. The students register voters, run freedom schools, and organize the Mississippi Freedom Democratic Party (MFDP).

**August 1964** Fannie Lou Hamer testifies on behalf of the Mississippi Freedom Democratic Party before the credentials committee at the Democratic Party national convention in Atlantic City, New Jersey.

**Charlene Teters.**
*Reproduced by permission of Charlene Teters.*

**1953**
Russian leader
Josef Stalin dies

**1958**
Arab Federation
is created

**1964**
Malta gains
independence

1950       1955       1960       1965

**Martin Luther King Jr.**
*Reproduced by permission of AP/Wide World Photos.*

**1965** The Crusade for Justice, a Chicano rights organization, is founded by Rodolfo "Corky" Gonzales in Denver, Colorado.

**1965** The National Farm Workers Association, which changes its name to United Farm Workers (UFW) in April 1966, is founded by César Chávez and Dolores Huerta in Delano, California.

**February 21, 1965** Malcolm X is assassinated in Harlem, New York.

**September 1965–July 1970** Grape pickers, represented by the United Farm Workers, conduct a strike in the fields around Delano, California.

**March 7, 1965** On this day, later called "Bloody Sunday," state troopers in Selma, Alabama, viciously beat civil rights demonstrators trying to cross the Edmund Pettus Bridge en route to Montgomery. John Lewis suffers a fractured skull.

**April 4, 1968** Martin Luther King Jr. is assassinated in Memphis, Tennessee.

**July 1968** The American Indian Movement (AIM) is founded in Minneapolis, Minnesota.

**November 1968–March, 1969** Students of color conduct "Third World Strikes" at the University of California, Berkeley, and San Francisco State College, demanding the offering of courses on the history and accomplishments of non-Europeans in the United States.

**November 20, 1969–June 11, 1971** The Indians of All Tribes group occupies Alcatraz Island in San Francisco Bay, California, demanding that the land be returned to Native Americans.

**1966** Guyana gains independence

**1967** First heart transplant performed

**1968** Tet Offensive in Vietnam

**1969** Neil Armstrong walks on Moon

| 1966 | 1967 | 1968 | 1969 |

**November, 1970** James Abourezk is elected to the House of Representatives.

**1972** Ed Roberts founds the Center for Independent Living in Berkeley, California.

**September 1–4, 1972** The La Raza Unida political party, an organization representing the interests of Mexican Americans, holds its national convention in El Paso, Texas.

**November 2–8, 1972** Members of the American Indian Movement occupy the Bureau of Indian Affairs (BIA) building in Washington, D.C., and demand the restoration of tribes' treaty-making status, the return of stolen Indian lands, and the revocation of state government authority over Indian affairs.

**February 27–May 8, 1973** Members of the American Indian Movement and other reservation residents occupy the village of Wounded Knee on the Pine Ridge Reservation in South Dakota, in protest of the corrupt tribal government of chairman Dick Wilson.

**February 24, 1976** The body of Anna Mae Aquash is discovered on the Pine Ridge Reservation in South Dakota. Although the initial autopsy names exposure as the cause of death, a subsequent autopsy shows that Aquash's death was due to a bullet to the back of the head.

**1977** Philip Vera Cruz, vice president of the United Farm Workers, resigns from the union, citing philosophical and political differences with union president César Chávez.

**June 1, 1977** Following a controversial trial and questionable conviction, American Indian Movement activist

**Yuri Kochiyama with her husband Bill.**
*Reproduced by permission of Yuri Kochiyama.*

**1971**
China joins
United Nations

**1973**
World-wide
energy crisis

**1975**
Egypt's Suez
Canal reopens

1970    1972    1974    1976

**James G. Abourezk.**
*Reproduced by permission of
AP/Wide World Photos.*

Leonard Peltier begins serving two life sentences for the murder of two FBI agents.

**February 1979** An arson fire claims the lives of Native American activist John Trudell's wife, Tina Manning, and the couple's three children.

**1980** James Abourezk founds the American-Arab Anti-Discrimination Committee.

**1984** The World Institute on Disability (WID), a public-policy organization that sponsors research into disability issues and promotes the integration of people with disabilities into every aspect of society, is founded in Oakland, California.

**October 11, 1985** Alex Odeh, Southern California regional director of the American-Arab Anti-Discrimination Committee, killed by a pipe bomb in Santa Ana, California.

**November 1986** John Lewis is elected to the House of Representatives. He is reelected six times, most recently in 1998.

**1988** Congress passes the Civil Liberties Act, thereby authorizing the payment of $20,000 to each Japanese American survivor of the internment camps and issuing an apology to all former detainees.

**1980**
Indira Ghandi
regains power
in India

**1983**
Argentina
returns to
civilian rule

**1985**
Mexico City hit
by earthquake

1978    1981    1984    1987

**January 1992** The National Coalition on Racism in Sports and Media protests the use of Native American nicknames and mascots by sports teams at the Super Bowl in Minneapolis, Minnesota.

**April 29–May 3, 1992** Riots erupt in south-central Los Angeles in the wake of "not guilty verdicts" for the police officers whose vicious beating of black motorist Rodney King was captured on videotape. The rioting claimed fifty-two lives and caused upwards of one billion dollars in damage.

**April 23, 1993** United Farm Workers leader César Chávez dies in San Luis, Arizona.

**January 1999** Malcolm X is honored by the U.S. Postal Service with a 33-cent stamp.

**May 1999** The New Hampshire state House passes a bill officially recognizing an annual Martin Luther King Jr. day. Versions of the bill had been presented to state lawmakers for consideration every year since 1979.

**César Chávez.**
*Reproduced by permission of AP/Wide World Photos.*

**1991**
Operation
Desert Storm

**1993**
Canada elects
first female
prime minister

**1999**
Cuba seeks
war damages
from U.S.

| 1990 | 1993 | 1997 | 2000 |

# Words to Know

**A**

**Abolitionism:** The belief that slavery should be immediately terminated; the social movement to eliminate slavery.

**Abolitionist:** A person who works for the elimination of slavery.

**Abortion:** The expulsion or removal of an embryo or fetus from the womb.

**Affirmative action:** A set of federal government policies, primarily in education and employment, that give preferential treatment to racial minorities and women (groups that have historically been victims of discrimination).

**Agribusiness:** Farming processes—for example, the storage and distribution of produce—operated on large, industrial scale.

**Alianza Federal de Mercedes:** This organization (whose name is Spanish for Federated Alliance of Land Grants) was formed in 1963 by a group of Mexican Americans in New Mexico. The Alianza sought to reclaim lands that had been taken from Mexican American farmers following the end of the U.S.-Mexico War (1846–48).

**Allotment:** The U.S. government policy, implemented in the late 1800s and early 1900s, of dividing up reservation lands and parceling them out to individual Native Americans.

**American Indian Movement (AIM):** The best-known and most militant Native American rights organization of the 1960s and 1970s.

**Americans with Disabilities Act (ADA):** Federal legislation, passed in 1990, that prohibits discrimination against people with disabilities in the areas of employment, government-run programs and services, public accommodations (such as hotels, restaurants, and movie theaters), and telecommunications.

**Anglo:** Term used by Hispanic Americans to describe a person of European descent.

**Anti-coolie clubs:** Organizations in California in the 1850s and 1860s that sought to drive Chinese laborers from the workforce and to expel Chinese immigrants from the communities in which the clubs were located.

**Asiatic Exclusion League:** An organization founded in California in 1905 that used violent tactics and legal maneuvering to remove Japanese and Korean laborers from the work force.

**Assimilation:** The process of becoming like, or being absorbed into, the dominant culture.

# B

**Black Cabinet:** A group of influential African Americans that served as informal advisors to President Franklin D. Roosevelt (1882–1945; served as president from 1933 to 1945).

**Black Codes:** Laws developed after the Civil War (1861–65) that denied black Americans the right to vote, the right to own property, and the right to pursue employment or otherwise advance their economic status.

**Black nationalism:** Movement to create political, economic, and social self-sufficiency among black people.

**Black Panther Party (BPP):** Organization founded in Oakland, California, in 1966 by black activists seeking to stop police abuse and provide social services (including a free breakfast program and a free health clinic). BPP members carried arms in public and came into frequent conflict with the police.

**Black power:** Social movement and rallying cry of radical black activists in the mid-1960s through mid-1970s. To many African Americans, the slogan stood for racial pride and the belief that blacks held the power to create a better society for themselves.

**Blockbusting:** Literally meaning "busting apart a block," blockbusting was a practice used by Realtors to maintain housing segregation. Realtors would move a single black family onto an all-white block and pressure whites to sell their homes at low prices. Realtors would then sell those homes to middle-class blacks at much higher prices.

**"Bloody Sunday:"** March 7, 1965—the day on which state troopers in Selma, Alabama, viciously beat civil rights demonstrators trying to cross the Edmund Pettus Bridge on their way to Montgomery, Alabama.

**Boycott:** The refusal to purchase a product or use a service. A boycott gives an oppressed group economic leverage in their struggle for social change.

**Bracero Program:** U.S. government program from 1942 to 1964 to bring Mexican workers to the U.S. to work in factories, and on farms and railroads ("bracero" is Spanish for "manual laborer").

**Brown Berets:** Activist group of young Chicanos in the late 1960s who carried arms to protect themselves and their community from police brutality.

***Brown v. Board of Education of Topeka, Kansas*:** Supreme Court decision in 1954 that declared school segregation unconstitutional.

# C

**Chicano:** Term used by politically active Mexican Americans to describe themselves; the word symbolized their pride in their cultural heritage.

**Civil disobedience:** Nonviolent action in which participants refuse to obey certain laws, with the purpose of challenging the fairness of those laws.

**Civil Rights Act of 1964:** The most expansive civil rights policy in American history, this act outlawed a variety of types of discrimination based on race, color, religion, or national origin.

**Communism:** A political and social system based on sharing goods equally in the community and owning property collectively.

**Congress on Racial Equality (CORE):** Civil rights organization formed in 1942 that promoted nonviolent direct action.

**Counter-Intelligence Program (COINTELPRO):** A Federal Bureau of Investigation (FBI) program whose official purpose was to combat domestic terrorism. In actuality, COINTELPRO was used to weaken the anti-Vietnam War and civil rights movements, the Black Panther Party, AIM, and other militant organizations of people of color.

**Crusade for Justice:** Chicano-rights and social-service organization, founded in 1965 in Denver, Colorado, that worked to end police brutality and discrimination in the public schools.

# D

**Desegregation:** The elimination of laws and social customs that call for the separation of races.

**Disability:** A restriction or lack of ability to perform an activity considered part of the range of normal human behaviors.

# E

**Enfranchisement:** The granting of the right to vote.

**Executive Order 9066:** Decree issued by President Franklin D. Roosevelt in 1942 that led to the internment of 120,000 Japanese Americans in camps during World

War II. The first internment camp opened in 1942, and the last camp closed in 1946.

# F

**Fair Housing Act:** This legislation—Title VIII of the Civil Rights Act of 1968—forbid racial discrimination by private individuals or businesses in housing and real estate transactions.

**Fascism:** A political philosophy that places nation and race above the individual. Fascist governments are run by a single, dictatorial leader and are characterized by extreme social and economic restrictions.

**Fish-in:** A form of civil disobedience in which Indian activists fished in violation of state laws in order to assert their treaty rights. This tactic was frequently used in the 1960s and 1970s in Washington and Oregon.

**Freedom Rides:** Journeys made throughout the South by integrated groups of people to test the enforcement of a pair of Supreme Court rulings striking down the constitutionality of segregated seating on interstate (crossing state lines) buses and trains.

**Freedom Summer:** Mississippi civil rights campaign in the summer of 1964, in which about 1,000 northern college student volunteers registered voters and operated educational and social programs.

# G

**Glass ceiling:** An invisible barrier in private and public agencies that keeps many women and racial minorities from holding top positions.

**Grandfather clause:** A policy that exempted white people from literacy tests to qualify to vote. The clause stated that all people entitled to vote in 1866, as well as their descendants, could vote without taking a literacy test. All descendants of 1866 voters were white, since blacks only gained the constitutional right to vote in 1870.

**Great Depression:** The worst economic crisis to hit the United

States, the Depression began with the stock market crash in 1929 and lasted until 1939.

# H

**Handicap:** A physical or mental condition that prevents or limits a person's ability to lead a normal life.

**Hate Crimes Prevention Act (HCPA):** Proposed federal legislation that would amend current federal law—which permits federal prosecution of a hate crime based on religion, national origin, or color—to include real or perceived sexual orientation, sex, and disability.

**Heterosexuality:** Sexual desire or behavior exhibited between persons of opposite sexes.

**Highlander Folk School:** A civil rights and social justice institute in founded in 1932 in Tennessee. Highlander was unique in the pre-civil rights South because it was a racially integrated facility.

**Hispanic American:** A person living in the United States who was born in, or whose descendants were born in, a Spanish-speaking country (synonymous with Hispanic or Hispano).

**Homosexuality:** Sexual desire or behavior exhibited between persons of the same sex.

# I

**Indian Civil Rights Act:** Legislation passed by Congress in 1968 to guarantee the civil rights of Native Americans living on reservations.

**Indian Removal Act:** Legislation signed in 1830 by President Andrew Jackson, mandating the relocation of Native Americans living east of the Mississippi River to a tract of land called "Indian Territory" (present-day Oklahoma).

**Indian Reorganization Act:** Legislation passed in 1934 that put an end to allotment, returned "surplus" reservation lands to the tribes, recognized tribal governments, and recommended that Indian nations adopt their own constitutions.

**Integration:** The combination of facilities, previously separated by race, into single, multiracial systems.

**Internment:** The act of being confined against one's will.

**Involuntary servitude:** Any situation in which a person is made to perform services against her or his will.

# J

**Jim Crow laws:** A network of legislation and customs that dictated the separation of the races on every level of society.

# K

**Ku Klux Klan:** Anti-black terrorist group formed in the South in the aftermath of the Civil War (1861–65) that has for decades intimidated and committed acts of violence against black Americans and members of other racial and ethnic minorities.

# L

**La Raza Unida:** Mexican American political party (pronounced la RAHssa oonEEDa; the name means "The People United") founded in 1969 that embraced bilingual education, the regulation of public utilities, farm subsidies, and tax breaks for low-income people.

**Latino:** Person living in the United States who was born in, or whose descendants were born in, the geographic region of Latin America.

**Literacy test:** Selectively administered to black applicants, the test required would-be voters to read and/or interpret a section of the state Constitution to the satisfaction of the registrar.

**Lynching:** Execution-style murder of a person (usually an African American), often by hanging, by a white mob.

# M

**Manifest Destiny:** The belief that the United States had a "God-given right" to all the territory between the Atlantic and Pacific oceans. This doctrine served to justify the United States' westward expansion during the 1800s.

**Mexican American Legal Defense and Education Fund (MALDEF):** Organization formed in 1968 to promote the civil rights of Mexican Americans through the legal system.

**Mississippi Freedom Democratic Party (MFDP):** Multi-racial political party created in Mississippi in 1964 that served as an alternative to the all-white Democratic Party.

**"Model minority":** The stereotypical belief that the majority of Asian Americans have blended into the dominant American culture and met with greater educational and economic success than any other racial or ethnic group. The "model minority" concept masks the needs of a large portion of the Asian American community (particularly recent immigrants) for social service programs; it also places enormous pressure on young Asian Americans to excel.

# N

**Nation of Islam (NOI):** Organization of Black Muslims that advocates prayer, self-discipline, separatism, and economic self-help for African American communities.

**National American Woman Suffrage Association (NAWSA):** Organization, founded in 1890, that fought for the passage of a constitutional amendment guaranteeing women the right to vote.

**National Association for the Advancement of Colored People (NAACP):** Civil rights organization formed in 1909 that promotes racial equality and the end of racial prejudice.

**Nativist:** A person who opposes the presence of foreigners and works for foreigners' removal.

**New Deal:** Set of programs instituted by President Franklin Delano Roosevelt (1882–1945) in the mid-1930s aimed at ending the Great Depression (1929–39).

**Nonviolence:** The rejection of all forms of violence, even in response to the use of violence by one's adversaries.

# O

**Organization of Afro-American Unity (OAAU):** A black-nationalist group formed by Malcolm X (1925–1965), the OAAU advocated that African Americans practice self-defense, study African history and reclaim African culture, aspire to economic self-sufficiency, and become active in their communities.

# P

**Passive resistance:** The quiet but firm refusal to comply with unjust laws, passive resistance involves putting one's body on the line, risking arrest, and attempting to win over one's foes with morally persuasive arguments.

***Personal Justice Denied*:** Report published in 1983 by the congressionally appointed Commission on Wartime Relocation and Internment of Civilians. The report explored the harm caused by the exclusion, evacuation, and internment of Japanese Americans during World War II (1939–45).

**Plenary powers:** The authority of Congress to revoke treaties with Indian tribes, as defined by the Supreme Court in 1913. In the early 1900s, plenary powers served as a justification for government invasion into virtually every aspect of Native Americans' lives.

***Plessy v. Ferguson*:** An 1896 Supreme Court decision upholding the constitutionality of the Jim Crow laws. *Plessy* specifically upheld a Louisiana law mandating separate railroad cars for black and white passengers.

**Poll tax:** A tax that blacks were required to pay in order to vote. Once at the voting booth, voters had to provide proof of that they had paid the tax.

**Poor People's March on Washington:** Protest march to the nation's capital by poor people of all races, from all parts of the country, in May 1968. The march had been initiated by Martin Luther King Jr. before his death.

# R

**Radicalization:** The process of moving toward drastic, fundamental change.

**Reconstruction:** The post-Civil War era in which emancipated (freed) slaves were granted civil rights and the Southern states reincorporated into the nation.

**"Red Power:"** American Indian rights movement of the 1960s and 1970s.

**Redlining:** Discriminatory practice used by banks and insurance companies that involved drawing red lines on city maps between black and white neighborhoods and only granting mortgages, or selling insurance to, prospective homeowners in the geographic zones on the "white" side of the red lines.

**Relocation:** U.S. government policy, beginning in 1949, by which American Indians were encouraged to move from reservations and into cities.

**Reservation:** Tract of land set aside by the U.S. government for use by an Indian tribe.

***Roe v. Wade:*** Landmark 1973 Supreme Court case that resulted in the legalization of abortion throughout the United States.

# S

**Scabs:** Workers hired to take the place of, and weaken the resolve of, striking workers.

**Segregation:** The separation of the races, as dictated by laws and social customs.

**Segregationist:** A person who promotes or enforces the separation of the races.

**Separatism:** The rejection of the dominant culture and institutions, in favor of a separate culture and institutions comprised of one's own minority group.

**Sharecropper:** Landless farmer who works a plot of land and in return gives the landowner a share of the crop.

**Sit-in:** Form of civil rights protest in which black students, sometimes joined by white students, requested service at segregated lunch counters and refused to leave when denied service.

**Southern Christian Leadership Conference (SCLC):** Organization of black ministers, formed in 1957, that coordinated civil rights activities in the South in the 1960s and continues to work for racial justice today.

**Southern Manifesto:** Denunciation of the Supreme Court's 1954 school desegregation ruling by 101 southern congressional representatives and senators.

**Sovereignty:** State of being independent and self-governed.

**Spanish-American War:** War, in 1898, between U.S. forces and Spanish forces in Puerto Rico. At the war's end Spain ceded (gave up) to the U.S. its possessions of Puerto Rico, Cuba, and the Philippines.

**Stereotype:** Simple and inaccurate image of the members of a particular racial or ethnic group.

**Student Nonviolent Coordinating Committee (SNCC; pronounced "snick"):** Student civil rights organization that engaged in voter registration activities and nonviolent protests in the 1960s.

**Suffrage:** The right to vote in public elections.

**Suffragist:** A person who works for the right to vote in public elections.

**Sweatshop:** Factory in which workers are paid low wages and toil in unpleasant and often dangerous conditions.

# T

**Termination:** U.S. government policy in the 1950s of terminating (ending) the standing relationships, governed by treaties, between the United States and Native American tribes.

**Third World Strikes:** A series of demonstrations by students of color in 1968 and 1969 at University of California, Berkeley, and San Francisco State College. The students demanded that courses on the history and accomplishments of non-Europeans in the United States be included in the curricula.

**Trail of Broken Treaties:** Protest by the American Indian Movement (AIM) at the Bureau of Indian Affairs (BIA) in Washington, D.C., in the fall of 1972. AIM demanded the restoration of tribes' treaty-making status, the return of stolen Indian lands, and the revocation of state government authority over Indian affairs. AIM demonstrators occupied the BIA building for six days.

**Treaty:** Agreement between two independent nations, usually defining the benefits to both parties that will result from one side ceding (giving up) its land.

**Treaty of Fort Laramie:** Treaty drawn up in April 1868 between the Sioux nation and the United States in which the U.S. government promised to return to the Sioux all lands in South Dakota west of the Missouri River, including Mount Rushmore and the rest of the Black Hills.

**Treaty of Guadelupe Hidalgo:** Treaty signed in 1848 that ended the United States-Mexico War (1846–48). The treaty transferred more than 530,000 miles of Mexican land to the United States. It also guaranteed U.S. citizenship to Mexicans living on that land, and promised the Mexicans the right to retain their property.

# U

**United Farm Workers (UFW):** Union of farm workers, led by César Chávez, formed in Delano, California, in 1966.

**United States-Mexico War:** Armed conflict from 1846 to 1848 in which the United States captured much of the northern territory of Mexico (that land is today the southwestern region of United States).

## V

**Vietnam War:** War lasting from 1954 to 1975 in which the United States sided with South Vietnam in the fight against communism in North Vietnam.

**Vigilante:** Member of a citizens' group that uses extra-legal means to intimidate a certain group of people, for example, foreigners or people of color.

**Voting Rights Act:** Legislation enacted in 1965 that outlawed all practices used to deny blacks the right to vote and empowered federal registrars to register black voters.

## W

**White Citizens' Council:** Organization of white businessmen and professionals that worked to forestall the political and economic advancement of African Americans in the South from the 1950s through the 1970s.

**White primary:** Practice adopted by southern states in the late 1800s that excluded blacks from Democratic Party primaries. Since the Democratic Party held a virtual monopoly over political power in the South, the only meaningful votes were cast in the primaries. White primaries effectively denied blacks the right to vote.

**White supremacist:** A person who believes in the inherent supremacy of the white race above all other races.

**Wounded Knee:** Tiny village on the Pine Ridge Reservation in South Dakota. In 1890 Wounded Knee was the site of a massacre of between 150 and 370 Indians by U.S. military forces; in 1973 the village was occupied by members of the American Indian Movement (AIM) and other reservation residents for ten weeks, in protest of the corrupt tribal government of chairman Dick Wilson.

## Y

**Yellow Power movement:** The struggle for racial equality and social justice by Asian American activists in the late 1960s and 1970s.

**Young Lords Party:** Organization of young Puerto Ricans, formed in 1966, that engaged in armed self-defense of their communities and held protest actions (such as strikes, sit-ins, and boycotts) over living conditions in poor neighborhoods.

# James G. Abourezk

**Born February 14, 1931**
**Wood, South Dakota**

**Lebanese American civil rights activist,
attorney, former U.S. senator**

As a senator, an attorney, and a political activist, James G. Abourezk has been a tireless advocate for the civil rights of Arab Americans and Native Americans. While his commitment to Arab American rights is rooted in his own Lebanese American heritage, Abourezk's commitment to Native American rights comes from his years of living on and around the Pine Ridge Sioux reservation in South Dakota.

Abourezk was elected to the U.S. House of Representatives in 1970 and to the U.S. Senate in 1972. As a senator, he spearheaded the creation of the Senate Select Committee on Indian Affairs and became its first chair. In the 1970s Abourezk authored three pieces of Indian rights legislation that transferred control of Indian institutions from the federal government back to the tribes.

In 1980 Abourezk founded the American-Arab Anti-Discrimination Committee (ADC), a 25,000-member civil rights organization that defends the rights of people of Arab descent and promotes their cultural heritage. Today Abourezk serves as honorary chair of the ADC.

Attorney and political activist James G. Abourezk founded the American-Arab Anti-Discrimination Committee.

## Youth and education

Abourezk was born in 1931 on the Rosebud Sioux Reservation in Wood, South Dakota. His father, Charlie Abourezk, had immigrated to the United States from Lebanon in 1898 and then returned to Lebanon to find a wife. He came back to South Dakota with Lena Abourezk, James's mother, in 1920. Charlie Abourezk first worked as a peddler and eventually opened two general stores.

James Abourezk attended grade school and high school in Wood and nearby Mission. Upon high school graduation, Abourezk enlisted in the navy. He served from 1948 to 1952 and repaired machinery and transported soldiers and equipment during the Korean War (1950–53). In 1957 Abourezk enrolled in the South Dakota School of Mines and Technology. He graduated with a degree in civil engineering in 1961.

After working on a construction project in California, Abourezk returned to South Dakota and decided to study the subject he had always found most interesting: law. He enrolled in the South Dakota University School of Law, from which he graduated with honors in 1966. Abourezk practiced law in Rapid City, South Dakota, until 1970. Although he had a general practice representing victims of personal injury and criminal defendants, he represented many Indians free of charge. Abourezk demanded that South Dakota law enforcement officials treat Indians fairly and seriously investigate charges of foul play against Native Americans.

## Begins political career

In 1970 Abourezk was elected to the U.S. House of Representatives as a Democrat on a platform of gaining Indian rights, ending the Vietnam War (1954–75), and protecting consumers. Two years later Abourezk won a seat in the Senate. He used his freshman maiden speech (the first speech of a senator's career) to attack President Richard Nixon's (1913–1994; served in office from 1969 to 1974) escalation of the war in Vietnam. Abourezk proposed cutting off salaries to all White House officials until Nixon began operating within the confines of the law.

During Abourezk's single term as a senator (1973 to 1979), he sat on the Interior (later Energy) Committee, the Judiciary Committee, the Senate Select Committee on Indian

Affairs, the Budget Committee, and the Space and Aeronautics Committee. (Abourezk was appointed to the latter committee despite his lack of interest in space exploration.) He introduced three pieces of groundbreaking Indian rights legislation in the 1970s: the Indian Self-Determination Act (1975); the Indian Religious Freedom Act (1978); and the Indian Child Welfare Act (1979).

## Supports unpopular initiatives

In 1978 Abourezk led a filibuster (an extremely long speech intended to obstruct regular proceedings) to prevent the deregulation of natural gas. Abourezk believed, correctly, that deregulation would lead to a sharp increase in natural gas prices to the consumer. While deregulation laws eventually passed, Abourezk had succeeded in exposing the self-serving interests of the utility companies. At the same time, Abourezk promoted alternative energy sources, such as wind power and solar power (power derived from the Sun). To his dismay, he found that the government was not interested in exploring energy sources that were not certain to yield profits for energy corporations.

Of all Abourezk's unpopular initiatives in the Senate, one was nearly universally shunned: prohibiting senators from earning any outside income while in office. (In other words, senators would have to live on their Senate salaries alone.) Abourezk made this proposal because he felt that the Senate, with its large number of millionaires, was not representative of the American public.

One of Abourezk's final acts in Congress was forcing a government moratorium on the practice of sterilizing Indian women, often without their knowledge. (Between 1972 and 1975, the Indian Health Service [IHS] sterilized almost half of all Native American women of childbearing years. Many of these women were tricked or forced into signing release forms for the surgery; other women were threatened with losing custody of their children or their welfare benefits if they did not agree to the procedure.)

## Does not seek second term

A year after taking office, Abourezk made the decision not to seek a second term in the Senate. His decision was motivated by a desire to devote more time to his family, to civil rights issues, and to his law practice, as well as by a disillusionment with Capitol Hill politics. "I had always thought being a U.S. senator would be the greatest job in the world," wrote Abourezk in his 1989 autobiography *Advise and Dissent.* "It was a chance to have a great many people listen to me, to my ideas about how the world ought to be changed for the better. I was convinced that I could do the job in a different manner from all the others. I soon discovered, to my chagrin, that most people had no interest in ideas, or in changing the world, except for that part of it that might narrowly benefit them."

## Becomes involved in Arab American rights

Abourezk did not fully embrace his Arab heritage until he traveled to his parents' home village in Lebanon in 1973. There he saw bomb craters made by Israeli warplanes and met with political leaders. "I left Lebanon feeling immensely betrayed," Abourezk commented in *Advise and Dissent.* "For most of my adult life I had believed that Israel had been picked on by the Arab countries.... To learn in Lebanon that the truth had been stood on its head was an emotional shock for me."

Abourezk returned to the United States an outspoken critic of Israel and its powerful lobby in Washington, as well as of U.S. foreign policy in the Middle East. He also began speaking out against racism directed at Arab Americans. "The Arab image—either as a high-rolling, spendthrift, woman-exploiting sheikh in flowing white robes," noted Abourezk in *Advise and Dissent,* "or as a bearded, evil looking barbaric terrorist—for years filled America's airwaves, its newspapers, its movie and television screens."

## The Abscam campaign

For Abourezk, the event that demonstrated the extent of anti-Arab racism in the United States—and in particular in the federal government—was the Abscam campaign of the late 1970s. Abscam was a secret FBI operation intended to ensnare corrupt lawmakers. (The term "Abscam" was short for "Abdul Scum.") In the operation, an Italian American agent wore white robes similar to those worn by wealthy, Persian Gulf Arabs and offered lawmakers bribes in exchange for favors.

When the existence of Abscam was exposed to the public, FBI director William Webster stated that the operation used an "Arab" agent because people would believe that an Arab was capable of bribery. Yet no Arab or Arab American had ever even been suspected of bribing an American politician. Abourezk was enraged at the blatant racism of the operation.

The Abscam operation convinced Abourezk of the need to establish an organization dedicated to fighting racism against people of Arab descent. In 1980 he called a meeting of Arab American leaders; at that meeting the American-Arab Anti-Discrimination Committee was formed. "[The] ADC has blossomed into the largest and most politically aggressive American-Arab organization in the United States," wrote Abourezk in his autobiography. "It has brought together Arab Americans as well as non-Arab activists from virtually every part of America."

James Abourezk (right center) participates in a protest rally outside the South African embassy on December 12, 1984. Abourezk and eleven other demonstrators were later arrested for taking part in the rally. *Reproduced by permission of AP/Wide World Photos.*

## Becomes advocate for Native American rights

Although Abourezk grew up among Native Americans, his support for Indian rights did not begin until he began practicing law in Rapid City, South Dakota. "I grew up believing it was permissible, even heroic, to ridicule the Indians of Wood," Abourezk remarked in *Advise and Dissent*. "I never understood the damage my own racism was doing as I joined the community in its uniformly bad treatment of Indians.... I belittled Indians until I left the reservation and attended college, where a friend, Peggy Goodart, figuratively slapped me in the face one day, forcing me to realize how destructive my attitudes were."

In his capacity as chair of the Senate Select Committee on Indian Affairs, Abourezk visited reservations around the country and witnessed the poverty in which Native Americans lived. "In America there are millions of examples of injustice, of the unfair treatment of people who have no power or no money," Abourezk once concluded. "Treatment of Indian people in the United States provides us with a clear illustration of inequitable justice for the poor." Abourezk placed the blame for the terrible condition of Native America on the federal government, for mismanaging Indian resources, and on racist whites, for their mistreatment of Indians.

## Visits the Pine Ridge Reservation

In 1973 Abourezk traveled to the Pine Ridge Reservation in South Dakota, where members of the American Indian Movement (AIM) and the Oglala Sioux Civil Rights Organization were occupying the tiny village of Wounded Knee. The Indian activists had initiated the takeover to protest the corrupt practices of tribal chairman Richard Wilson, and the brutality of his police force, the Guardians of the Oglala Nation (commonly referred to as the "GOON squad").

Abourezk, along with Senator George McGovern, also of South Dakota, met with the occupation leaders and the eleven white residents who had been present since the takeover began. The senators' goal had been to seek the release of the whites, who had been dubbed "hostages" by the national media.

"When we reached the village and told the hostages that they were free to go," wrote Abourezk in *Advise and Dissent*, "we learned for the first time that all of them lived in

## The Killing of Alex Odeh

On October 11, 1985, Arab American rights activist Alex Odeh was killed by a pipe bomb wired to his office door. Odeh was the Southern California regional director of the American-Arab Anti-Discrimination Committee (ADC), a professor at Cal State Fullerton, a father of three, and a poet. He had appeared on the Cable News Network (CNN) shortly before his death, commenting on the Palestinian hijacking of the *Achille Lauro* ocean liner. During the interview Odeh had expressed regret over the killing of Leon Klinghoffer, a hostage aboard the ship, and had condemned the hijacking. Those statements, however, were edited out before the tape was aired. In the televised segment, Odeh stated that it was time for people to "understand the Palestinian side of the story" and appeared to be defending the hijackers.

Odeh's murder was not an isolated act of anti-Arab terrorism in the United States. In August 1985 a similar pipe bomb was wired to the door of the ADC office in West Roxbury, Massachusetts. Two police officers were injured while trying to defuse that bomb. And on December 16, 1985, an arson fire caused considerable damage to the ADC's national office in Washington, D.C.

Odeh's killers have yet to be brought to justice. Early in the investigation, the FBI identified three suspects with links to the extremist Jewish Defense League. The three men were believed to have escaped to Israel. One of the three, Robert Manning, was later extradited (returned) to the United States and convicted of the 1980 mail bomb killing of a California woman. As part of the extradition agreement, Manning cannot be charged with any other crime.

In 1996, more than ten years after Odeh's killing, the FBI offered a $1 million reward for information leading to the arrest and conviction of Odeh's killers. In January 1999 the FBI posted a $1 million reward in Israel, where the remaining two suspects are thought to reside.

---

Wounded Knee and had no interest in leaving." After the takeover ended, Abourezk returned to the reservation to hold hearings into its causes.

## Accepts invitation from Navajo nation

In 1982 Abourezk accepted an invitation from the Navajo nation in the southwestern United States to serve as its first attorney general. Abourezk established a legal department on the reservation, writing the department's operating procedures and hiring its staff. Abourezk accepted no pay for this work; when the department was up and running, he left it in the care of the Navajos.

## Takes goodwill abroad

Abourezk has sought to increase understanding between the United States and other nations, as well as to negotiate solutions to international crises, both during and after his years in the Senate. In 1977 Abourezk attempted to warm the icy relations between the United States and Cuba by arranging for a basketball team exchange. He traveled to Tibet in 1979 with a *National Geographic* photographer. (The duo were the first photojournalists to enter Tibet since China's takeover of the region in 1951.)

Abourezk traveled twice to Iran in 1979, in unsuccessful attempts to negotiate the freedom of American hostages being held by Iranian revolutionaries. Seven years later, Abourezk traveled to Damascus, Syria, in an attempt to gain the release of American hostages being held in Lebanon by the militant religious group Hezbollah (Party of God).

## A varied career

Through the 1980s and 1990s Abourezk has been involved in the making of several video documentaries and books. His first documentary, entitled *Report from Beirut: Summer of 1982,* chronicled the Israeli invasion of Lebanon and siege of Beirut. The year 1987 saw the publication of *Through Different Eyes: Two Leading Americans, a Jew and an Arab, Debate U.S. Policy in the Middle East,* a book that Abourezk cowrote with Hyman Bookbinder, spokesman for the American Jewish Committee. Prior to the book's publication, Abourezk and Bookbinder had met in a series of debates over issues related to the Palestinian-Israeli conflict. Abourezk published his autobiography, *Advise and Dissent: Memoirs of South Dakota and the U.S. Senate,* in 1989.

Abourezk also served as chief adviser and researcher on a series of thirteen one-hour television segments on the history of American Indians, aired on the Turner Broadcasting

Network (TNN), and in 1991 was a contributor to a series of videos, entitled *The Arab World,* hosted by Bill Moyers.

Abourezk still works at his law practice in Rapid City. He is also an adjunct professor of Middle East studies at American University in Washington, D.C. Abourezk remains very active in the ADC and is on the board of directors of Americans for Indian Opportunity and the Fund for Constitutional Government.

# Sources

## Books

Abourezk, James. *Advise and Dissent: Memoirs of South Dakota and the U.S. Senate.* Chicago: Lawrence Hill Books, 1989.

Abourezk, James, and Hyman Bookbinder. *Through Different Eyes: Two Leading Americans, a Jew and an Arab, Debate U.S. Policy in the Middle East.* Bethesda, MD: Adler and Adler, 1987.

Means, Russell, and Marvin J. Wolf. *Where White Men Fear to Tread: The Autobiography of Russell Means.* New York: St. Martin's Press, 1995.

## Periodicals

Barker, Karlyn. "Abourezk Hasn't Broken Stride since Senate Days." *Washington Post.* December 7, 1985.

"Chain of Terror: Arab Americans under Attack." *Time.* December 16, 1985: 19.

Cockburn, Alexander. "News by Spasm." *The Nation.* November 2, 1985.

Lerner, Steve. "Terror against Arabs in America: No More Looking the Other Way." *New Republic.* July 28, 1986: 20.

McMahon, Janet. "James G. Abourezk." *Washington Report on Middle East Affairs.* December, 1990: 19.

Stanglin, Douglas. "A Belated Reward." *U.S. News and World Report.* August 19, 1996: 20.

"Terror Double Standard." *New Republic.* November 4, 1985: 9.

# Susan B. Anthony

**Born February 15, 1820**
**Adams, Massachusetts**
**Died March 13, 1906**
**Rochester, New York**

**American women's suffrage leader, abolitionist, temperance crusader, and teacher**

Susan B. Anthony was instrumental in securing property rights and voting rights for women.

Susan B. Anthony was one of the best-known leaders in the movement for women's suffrage (the right to vote in public elections). At the time of Anthony's death in 1906, women had the right to vote in only four states: Wyoming, Utah, Idaho, and Colorado. It was not until fourteen years later that the Nineteenth Amendment was ratified, granting all women in the United States the right to vote. In 1978 the U.S. Treasury Department honored Anthony by issuing the Susan B. Anthony dollar, a coin bearing her likeness.

## Early years

Anthony was born to Quaker parents, Lucy Read and Daniel Anthony. The second child of eight (two of whom died young), Anthony spent her first six years on a farm in Adams, Massachusetts. In 1826 the Anthony family moved to Battenville, New York, where Daniel Anthony assumed part ownership of a large cotton mill.

Anthony studied in a one-room schoolhouse and helped with the household chores. When she had learned all that she possibly could in the country school, her father added a wing onto their house, hired a teacher, and established a private school for his own children and other young people in the area. In the evenings the school was opened to employees of the cotton mill. The educational opportunities presented to Anthony were unusual in a day when very little value was placed on the education of girls and women.

Anthony was influenced by her father's dedication to the temperance movement (the campaign to ban the sale and use alcohol). Daniel Anthony's opposition to alcohol arose from his concern about the abuse of women and children at the hands of drunken men. In the general store that Daniel Anthony operated next to the cotton mill, alcohol was conspicuously absent from the shelves.

## Begins teaching career

Anthony's father encouraged his daughter's independence by hiring her to teach in his school at the age of fifteen. Anthony then worked as a private tutor in the home of a Quaker family and later at a public school, earning $1.50 a week. In the fall of 1837 Anthony's father sent her to study at the Select Seminary for Females, a Quaker school for girls, in Philadelphia. One year later, when her father's business failed and the family home was sold to pay off debts, Anthony was called back to Battenville.

In 1840 Anthony took a teaching job that paid $2.50 a week. The man she was replacing in that post had made $10.00 a week for the same duties. This injustice did not escape Anthony's attention. Over the next few years, as Anthony continued to teach, she fended off marriage proposals. "Tis passing strange that a girl possessed of common sense should be willing to marry a lunatic," Anthony wrote after the marriage of a friend.

## Introduced to antislavery movement

In 1845 the Anthony family purchased a farm in a Quaker community near Rochester, New York. The farm became a center of antislavery activity, attracting such guests as her father's friend Frederick Douglass (1817–1895), a former slave and abolitionist. (An abolitionist was someone who actively opposed slavery.) Anthony learned about the horrible conditions in which slaves lived, as well as about the Underground Railroad (the elaborate system of safe houses and secret routes through which many slaves escaped to freedom).

From 1846 to 1849 Anthony served as headmistress of the "female department" at Canajoharie Academy in upstate New York. Although hers was a prestigious position, Anthony became disillusioned with teaching. She had risen as high in the ranks as a female teacher possibly could, yet she was still grossly underpaid and severely lacking intellectual challenge. Disheartened, Anthony returned to the family farm in Rochester.

## Speaks out for temperance

Back in Rochester, Anthony threw her energies behind the temperance movement. Like her father, Anthony was motivated by a desire to stop the beatings of wives at the hands of drunken husbands. In that era there were no laws protecting women from spousal abuse. Furthermore, women were bound to their husbands by their lack of property rights. A woman's inheritance, her belongings, and even her children were legally the property of her husband or, if she was unmarried, her father.

The Sons of Temperance was the primary organization behind the temperance movement in the late 1840s. The male-dominated group welcomed women, but would not allow them to participate in decision-making. Female temperance activists primarily participated through an auxiliary organization, the Daughters of Temperance. Anthony joined the Daughters of Temperance in 1849. Before long, she had become one of the group's most effective organizers and persuasive spokespersons.

The Daughters of Temperance selected Anthony to represent them at a nationwide Sons of Temperance conference in early 1852. When Anthony rose during the conference to make a point, she was silenced by the male representatives. "The sisters," Anthony was told, "were not invited here to speak, but to listen and learn." An enraged Anthony led a delegation of women out of the conference.

## Cofounds Women's State Temperance Society

That April Anthony, aided by her friend Elizabeth Cady Stanton (1815–1892), organized a separate women's temperance convention in New York. That meeting, attended by 500 women, hailed the founding of the Women's State Temperance Society (WSTS), an organization that allowed men to be members but reserved offices for women. Stanton was elected the group's first president, and Anthony its first secretary.

For the next year Anthony traveled throughout New York state making speeches and raising funds for the WSTS. Meanwhile, the rift grew between Anthony and male temperance advocates. Anthony was severely chastised when she echoed Stanton's call for the right of women to divorce drunken and abusive husbands. In 1853, at a WSTS conference attended by many conservative men, Stanton was ousted from the presidency. Anthony resigned in protest, ending her career as a temperance activist.

## Friendship with Stanton leads to involvement in women's rights

During her years in the temperance movement, Anthony had deepened her commitment to women's rights. She had read with fascination the news reports of the 1848 national women's rights convention in Seneca Falls, New York. The convention, organized by Quaker abolitionist Lucretia Mott (1793–1880) and Elizabeth Cady Stanton, had addressed many issues of interest to women: property rights, the right to enroll in institutions of higher learning, pay equal to that of men, and suffrage.

Women's suffrage was a radical idea in that day, even to Anthony. In 1848 Anthony discussed the concept of women's suffrage with her father. Daniel Anthony was a firm

Together with Susan B. Anthony, Elizabeth Cady Stanton organized an 1852 temperance convention that led to the founding of the Women's State Temperance Society. The two women later cofounded the National Woman Suffrage Association.
*Reproduced by permission of the National Archives and Records Administration.*

believer that women should have the right to vote and he carefully explained his position to his daughter. Anthony became convinced of her father's arguments; in fact, her convictions in the matter grew with time and she eventually became one of the nation's foremost suffrage champions.

Anthony was further pulled into the women's movement in 1851, after meeting Stanton. Anthony and Stanton quickly became close friends, but more than that, the duo formed one of the most dynamic partnerships for social change in the history of the United States. Stanton was the deep thinker and master strategist of the pair; Anthony was a great organizer. Anthony put Stanton's ideas into action. Stanton wrote speeches and Anthony delivered them; Stanton wrote petitions and Anthony circulated them; Stanton planned conferences and Anthony worked out the logistics to make them happen. The pair worked together, over the coming half century, on temperance, women's property rights, and women's voting rights.

## Works for women's property rights

Following their departure from the temperance movement, Anthony and Stanton turned their energies to women's property rights. With the help of sixty volunteers, the women went door-to-door for a year, collecting 6,000 signatures in favor of granting women control over their belongings and children. Anthony and Stanton then took their petitions to the state legislature in Albany, where they gave moving appeals. Not surprisingly, the all-male legislature rejected the idea of a property-rights law.

Anthony and Stanton continued their efforts. While Stanton, homebound with six children, could do little more than compose speeches and offer encouragement, Anthony traveled the state collecting petition signatures. She also returned yearly to speak at the state capitol. Finally, in 1860, after six years of campaigning, the women's hard work was rewarded with the passage of the Married Woman's Property Act. This legislation gave women control over their wages, property, and inheritances. The act also stated that "every married woman shall be joint guardian of her children with her husband, with equal powers regarding them." Soon thereafter the legislatures of many other states passed similar laws.

**Elizabeth Cady Stanton**

Elizabeth Cady Stanton (1815–1902) was born and raised in Johnstown, New York. As a child, she attended Johnstown Academy—a boys' school—where she excelled in debate and language studies. Since women were not allowed to enroll in colleges in the early nineteenth century, Stanton attended Emma Willard's Troy Female Seminary in Troy, New York. In 1840 Stanton married abolitionist Harry B. Stanton. The couple had seven children.

Stanton and her good friend, Quaker abolitionist Lucretia Mott, frequently discussed the political and social status of women in the United States. In 1848 Stanton, Mott, and several Quaker women decided to call a public meeting to discuss women's rights. Despite very short notice, over three hundred people (including forty men) attended the two-day convention held in Seneca Falls, New York. During the meeting, Stanton read her famous "Declaration of Sentiments" speech, in which she proposed twelve resolutions (including women's right to vote and to retain property) for discussion and adoption. A second convention was held two weeks later in Rochester, New York, where Stanton's "Declarations" were approved by a majority of the attendees.

After the Seneca Falls convention, Stanton became a recognized leader of the women's rights movement. A confident speechwriter and organizer, she helped women throughout the country prepare for their own meetings and assemblies. In 1869 Stanton and Susan B. Anthony founded the National Woman Suffrage Association (NWSA). Stanton served as president of the organization every year until 1890, when the NWSA merged with the American Woman Suffrage Association (AWSA) to form the National American Woman Suffrage Association (NAWSA).

## Years of antislavery activism

In the 1850s and early 1860s slavery was the foremost social concern in America. Due to the powerful pull of the anti-slavery movement, Anthony found it increasingly difficult to locate support for women's rights. Anthony's organizing abilities, however, brought her to the attention of antislavery movement leaders. In 1855 Anthony had rejected a job offer from the American Anti-Slavery Society—the abolitionist organization founded by William Lloyd Garrison (1805–1879)—in order to devote all her time to the passage of the property rights law.

In 1856 Anthony was again approached by the Anti-Slavery Society. That time she accepted the position of activities coordinator for New York state. For the next four years Anthony divided her time between women's rights and abolitionism. In her antislavery job she coordinated speaking events, including the logistics and publicity, for a group of abolitionist spokespersons (herself and Stanton among them). Anthony was frequently treated with hostility by proslavery individuals and groups; her speeches were drowned out by her detractors, and she was pelted with rotten eggs. In Syracuse, a crowd burned Anthony's effigy (a crude mannequin representing Anthony).

## Generates controversy

As Anthony's fame as a speaker and organizer grew, so did the controversy regarding her political stances. For instance, her 1857 proposal of coeducation (education together, in the same institutions) of boys and girls was met with ridicule by male schoolmasters and female teachers alike.

In 1860 Anthony found herself at odds with Garrison because she had come to the assistance of a battered woman and her child. Anthony had led the woman—the wife of a state senator from Massachusetts—and her child to safety in the home of Quakers in New York City. Upon Anthony's return to New York, Garrison asked her: "Don't you know that the law of Massachusetts gives the father ... control of the children?" Anthony replied: "Does the law of the United States not give the slaveholder the ownership of the slave?... And don't you break it every time you help a slave to Canada? Well, the law which gives the father the sole ownership of the children is just as wicked and I'll break it just as quickly."

## Helps form Women's National Loyal League

In 1863, two years after the start of the Civil War (1861–65) between the Union (Northern) states and the Confederate (Southern) states, President Abraham Lincoln (1809–1865) issued the Emancipation Proclamation. As far as Anthony and Stanton were concerned, the proclamation—which granted freedom to slaves in states at war with the Union, but not to slaves in border states (such as Missouri and West Virginia) within the Union—did not go far enough.

To promote a constitutional amendment guaranteeing the freedom of slaves in every state, Anthony and Stanton formed the Women's National Loyal League. In early 1864 Anthony delivered to Congress a petition with 400,000 signatures in favor of such an amendment. Later that year Congress passed the Thirteenth Amendment, abolishing slavery.

After the war ended in 1865, Anthony once again found herself at odds with the male-dominated abolitionist movement. With the slaves freed, the abolitionists' next big push was to secure voting rights for black males. Anthony was dismayed that women—both white and black—were being left off the voting rights agenda.

## Works for women's voting rights

In the post-Civil War period, Anthony and Stanton chose to dedicate their time and energy to voting rights for *all* Americans. At an 1866 women's rights convention, Anthony convinced attendees to focus on universal suffrage and, accordingly, to rename the group the American Equal Rights Society. For the next year Anthony was on the road constantly, lobbying state and federal lawmakers, addressing women's rights groups, and going door-to-door drumming up support for a constitutional amendment guaranteeing voting rights for all.

In 1868 Anthony and Stanton started up a women's rights journal called *Revolution,* in which they publicized the case for women's suffrage. *Revolution* was provided start-up funds by a wealthy, eccentric businessman named George Train. In the pages of *Revolution* Anthony and Stanton ventured beyond voting rights, making controversial appeals for equal education and equal pay for women and the reformation of divorce laws. They also called upon women to join labor unions. Although the paper had a core of loyal subscribers, it closed in 1870 after going $10,000 into debt.

Despite the efforts of Anthony, Stanton, and countless other volunteers, the postwar amendments guaranteeing rights to blacks did not enfranchise (give the vote to) women. The Fourteenth Amendment, ratified in 1868, granted all citizens equal protection under the law (meaning that all people, but interpreted as "all males," were to enjoy the same legal rights and protections). And the Fifteenth Amendment, ratified in 1870, granted all citizens, regardless of race or color, the right to vote (that right, however, would be revoked for blacks by a series of racist laws before the turn of the twentieth century). In 1869 Anthony persuaded one lawmaker to introduce a women's suffrage bill into the House of Representatives; not surprisingly, it failed. That bill was reintroduced every year until its passage in 1920.

## Founds the National Woman Suffrage Association

In 1869 a split occurred within the women's movement, with one camp calling for immediate women's suffrage and the other camp applauding Congress for granting black males the right to vote (as provided by the Fifteenth Amendment) and advising patience in the matter of women's suffrage. In May 1869 Anthony and Stanton founded the National Woman Suffrage Association (NWSA). The NWSA, with members from nineteen states, had as its goal the passage of a constitutional amendment granting women the right to vote. At the time, the NWSA was considered a radical organization: it did not admit men and even criticized churches for their sexist teachings.

The American Woman Suffrage Association (AWSA)—created in November 1869—differed from the NWSA in its more moderate stance. The AWSA was led by noted orator Lucy Stone (1818–1893) and author Julia Ward Howe (1819–1910). The women selected a prominent minister, Henry Ward Beecher, as their president. Rather than push for a constitutional amendment, the AWSA opted to campaign for women's suffrage one state at a time.

Anthony traveled throughout the United States from 1869 to 1871, building support for a constitutional amendment and raising funds to pay off the *Revolution*'s debt. In 1871 alone she logged 13,000 miles across five states, giving 171 lectures and earning $4,318.

## Votes in presidential election

While working for a constitutional amendment, the NWSA also argued for an broad interpretation of the Fourteenth Amendment that would allow women to vote. The

group pointed to the clause in the amendment stating: "No state shall make or enforce any law which shall abridge the privileges or immunities of citizens of the United States." Women, they argued, were citizens, and any state that prohibited women from voting was in violation of the amendment.

In 1872 Anthony and sixteen suffragists put the Fourteenth Amendment to the test by voting in the presidential election in Rochester, New York. For this act of civil disobedience (refusing to obey a law one considers unjust) the women were arrested. The charge against Anthony stated that she had "as a person of the female sex, knowingly, wrongfully, and unlawfully voted ... contrary to the form of the statute and against the peace of the United States of America."

Anthony was freed on bail pending her trial. In the following months Anthony traveled through New York, Ohio, Indiana, and Illinois, speaking before large crowds about her attempt to vote and her upcoming trial. "It was we, the people," Anthony said in reference to the Constitution, "not we, the white male citizens, nor yet we, the male citizens: but we, the whole people, who formed this Union."

In June 1873 Anthony returned to New York to stand trial in *United States v. Susan B. Anthony*. Because of her gender, Anthony was not allowed to testify. Judge Ward Hunt, who was known for his sexist opinions, took the decision out of the jury's hands and rendered a guilty verdict himself. "The Fourteenth Amendment," the judge declared, "gives no right to a woman to vote, and the voting of Miss Anthony was in violation of the law." The judge then asked Anthony if she had anything to say before her sentencing.

"In your ordered verdict of guilty," Anthony replied, "you have trampled underfoot every vital principle of our government. My natural rights, my civil rights, my political rights, are all alike ignored. Robbed of the fundamental privilege of citizenship, I am degraded from the status of a citizen to that of a subject; and not only myself individually, but all my sex, are, by your honor's verdict, doomed to political subjection under this so-called Republican government."

Hunt ordered Anthony to pay a fine of $100 plus court costs. Anthony refused to pay the fine, calling it an "unjust penalty" and arguing that since she was not considered a full citizen, she was not responsible for the fine. Rather than imprisoning Anthony and making her a big news item, Hunt released her.

## Works for constitutional amendment

In 1875 the Supreme Court ruled that the Fourteenth Amendment did not have any bearing on women's suffrage. In response to that decision, Anthony realized that the only hope for women's suffrage was the passage of a constitutional amendment specifically granting women the right to vote.

Anthony spent the next several years giving lectures, collecting petition signatures, and working off her debt, a feat she completed in May 1876. Anthony drew huge crowds wherever she spoke. In 1877 she presented the U.S. Senate with a voting rights petition signed by 10,000 people from twenty-six states. Few senators took Anthony seriously.

In 1880 Anthony and Stanton began collaboration on a book documenting the women's movement. The two women collected reminiscences and news clips from dozens of women activists. The first volume of *History of Woman Suffrage* was published in 1881 and received tremendous critical acclaim. The duo published their second volume in 1882 and their third volume in 1886.

## Women's movement reunites

In 1883, while taking a much-needed vacation in England, Anthony and Stanton met with British suffragists. That visit inspired Anthony to bring together women's activists from around the world. Upon her return to New York, Anthony set about the task of organizing an international women's rights convention to be held in 1888 in Washington, D.C. The gathering, called the International Council of Women, drew representatives from forty-nine countries and fifty-three women's rights groups in the United States. The meeting was most important for its symbolic value, demonstrating that women around the world faced similar problems and could come together to find solutions. Anthony was especially pleased that Lucy Stone, with whom she had parted ways some twenty years earlier, was in attendance.

In 1890 the NWSA and the AWSA put aside their differences and merged to form the National American Woman Suffrage Association (NAWSA). Stanton, then seventy-five years old, was elected the group's first president; Anthony, who was seventy years old in 1890, succeeded her two years later. Over the next eight years, Anthony coordinated and participated in numerous demonstrations in front of the White House and at other locations around the country. In 1900, at the age of eighty, Anthony stepped down as president so that a younger member, Carrie Chapman Catt (1859–1947), could take over.

At Anthony's last public speaking engagement, just one month before her death, she proclaimed, "Failure is impossible." That phrase became a rallying cry for voting rights activists until the passage of the Nineteenth Amendment. In March 1906, at the age of eighty-six, Anthony died of pneumonia. Ten thousand people lined the streets of Rochester in a blizzard to witness Anthony's funeral procession.

## The "Anthony Amendment" passes

It was not until 1919—thirteen years after Anthony's death and ninety-nine years after her birth—that the women's suffrage bill was approved by Congress. The following year it won ratification from the necessary thirty-six states (ratification by three-fourths of all states is necessary for the adoption of any Constitutional amendment). The Nineteenth Amendment, nicknamed the Susan B. Anthony Amendment, guaranteed women the right to vote.

## Sources

### Books

McElroy, Lorie Jenkins, ed. *Women's Voices*. Vol. 1. Detroit: U•X•L, 1997, pp. 107–16.

Schmittroth, Linda, and Mary Reilly McCall, eds. *Women's Almanac*. Vol. 2. Detroit: U•X•L, 1997, pp. 246–51.

Sigler, Jay A., ed. *Civil Rights in America: 1500 to the Present*. Detroit: Gale, 1998, pp. 46–47, 376–78.

Sinclair, Barbara. *The Women's Movement: Political, Socioeconomic and Psychological Issues*. New York: Harper and Row Publishers, 1975.

Weisberg, Barbara. *Susan B. Anthony*. New York: Chelsea House Publishers, 1988.

# Anna Mae Aquash

**Born March 27, 1945**
**Near Shubenacadie, Nova Scotia, Canada**
**Died 1976**
**Pine Ridge Reservation, South Dakota**

**Canadian-born Native American activist**

**A** t the time of her death in 1976, Anna Mae Aquash was a leading organizer of the American Indian Movement (AIM). AIM was a militant Indian rights group founded in 1968 that fought for the return of tribal lands, enforcement of government treaties, respect for the human rights of Native Americans, and greater economic opportunities for Indians. Before joining AIM, Aquash had worked as an educator and social service provider for young Indians in New England.

In 1973 Aquash left her home and job and headed to South Dakota to devote all her time and energy to the pursuit of Indian rights. Beginning with the siege of Wounded Knee, she spent three years at the center of the struggle. For her activities, Aquash, like other radical activists of the day, was placed under surveillance by the Federal Bureau of Investigation (FBI). In February 1976 Aquash's body was found on a cattle ranch— she had been shot at point-blank range. While Aquash's murder remains officially unsolved, the FBI remains high on the list of suspects.

A leader of the American Indian Movement, Anna Mae Aquash was murdered at the age of thirty-one in a crime that remains unsolved.

**Anna Mae Aquash (far right) on her wedding day.** *Reproduced by permission of Kevin Barry McKiernan.*

## Childhood in Nova Scotia

Aquash was born Anna Mae Pictou in 1945 on the Micmac Indian reserve (a reserve land set aside for use by groups of Indians; it is the Canadian equivalent of a U.S. reservation) just outside of Shubenacadie, in Nova Scotia, Canada. For the first four years of Aquash's life, her mother attempted to raise Anna Mae and her siblings alone. The family lived in a small wooden house with no running water. There was only a wood-burning stove for heat, which was barely adequate during the cold winter months. The family survived on the food they hunted or fished, plus what little they could purchase with welfare checks.

When Aquash was four years old, her mother married a Micmac traditionalist named Noel Sapier. (Traditionalists are followers of Native American cultural practices and religions.) Sapier brought a bit more economic stability to the family and taught Aquash about Micmac culture.

In 1956 Sapier died of cancer, and Aquash's mother sent her children to a school in a nearby town. Prior to that, Aquash had attended the reserve school and had excelled in her studies. At the new school Aquash was constantly subjected to racist remarks and lewd comments. Consequently, her grades plummeted. Eventually, Aquash dropped out of school—as was common among Micmac students at the off-reserve school—and went to work as a migrant farm worker. She harvested potatoes and berries throughout Nova Scotia and New England.

## Begins working for Indian rights

At age seventeen, Aquash and a Micmac friend named Jake Maloney moved to Boston, Massachusetts, in search of greater opportunities. Aquash found work in a factory. She married Maloney and gave birth to two daughters. The family divided its time between Boston and a Micmac reserve in Nova Scotia.

In 1968 Aquash began volunteering at the Boston Indian Council, helping young urban Indians avoid alcohol abuse, a serious problem among Indian youth. In the fall of 1970 Aquash learned of a Thanksgiving Day protest at Plimoth Plantation, a living history museum near the site of the original Pilgrims' landing, and decided to attend. The protest was organized by AIM. AIM sought to publicize its version of the true origins of Thanksgiving—that the tradition began as a celebration of the massacre of the Wampanoag Indians by the settlers. Aquash's participation in that demonstration solidified her commitment to Indian rights.

Shortly thereafter, Aquash and her daughters moved to Bar Harbor, Maine (Aquash had separated from her husband). There Aquash taught in, and her daughters attended, an experimental school called Teaching and Research in Bicultural Education School (TRIBES). Included in the curriculum were classes on Indian history and culture.

When funding was cut off and the school closed down in 1972, the family returned to Boston. Aquash enrolled in the New Careers program at Wheelock College, which emphasized community service as well as classroom learning. Through the program, Aquash worked at a preschool in a predominantly African American neighborhood. During that period she met a Chippewa artist and activist named Nogeeshik Aquash, whom she later married.

## Joins AIM

In the fall of 1972 Anna Mae and Nogeeshik went to Washington, D.C., for AIM's Trail of Broken Treaties protest. AIM members from across the United States presented the Bureau of Indian Affairs (BIA) with a list of demands, including the restoration of tribes' treaty-making status, the return of stolen Indian lands, and the revocation of state government authority over Indian affairs. When the demonstrators were turned away at the door of the BIA, they took over the building for six days.

## The Wounded Knee occupation

In April 1973 Anna Mae and Nogeeshik learned that their AIM friends had taken over the village of Wounded Knee, on the Pine Ridge Reservation in South Dakota, and decided to join them. (Wounded Knee was the site of the 1890 massacre of over 150—some estimates place the number as high as 370—Indian men, women, and children by U.S. military forces.) The Wounded Knee occupation had been initiated in protest of the corrupt practices of tribal chairman Richard Wilson, and the brutality of his police force, the Guardians of the Oglala Nation (commonly referred to as the "GOON squad"). The occupation lasted ten weeks and drew the participation of two thousand Indians and their supporters.

The occupation also attracted large numbers of armed FBI agents, U.S. marshals, and members of tribal and local police forces. The law enforcement officials surrounded the encampment, equipped with firearms, armored personnel carriers, grenade launchers, 600 cases of tear gas, helicopters, and Phantom jets.

Anna Mae and Nogeeshik helped out by sneaking food and medical supplies into Wounded Knee at night. Anna Mae also helped build bunkers and took her turn on night patrols. On April 12, at Wounded Knee, Aquash and Nogeeshik were married in a traditional Sioux ceremony.

## Continues work for AIM

When the Wounded Knee standoff came to an end, the Aquashes returned to Boston. Anna Mae continued to work on behalf of AIM and in 1974 moved to St. Paul, Minnesota, to work in the AIM national headquarters. Her job was to form AIM support groups around the country and to personally deliver sensitive AIM communiques. She was also working on a history of North American Indians, as told to her by Indian elders of the day. In 1974 Aquash established the West Coast office of AIM in Los Angeles.

The operatives of the FBI's COINTELPRO took notice of Aquash's ascendancy within AIM and placed her under constant observation. COINTELPRO, which stands for Counter-Intelligence Program, was a secret FBI operation in the 1960s and 1970s. FBI agents, ostensibly combating domestic terrorism, gathered information on and attempted to destroy the anti-Vietnam War movement, the civil rights movement, and militant organizations of people of color.

## Trouble on the Pine Ridge Reservation

In the summer of 1975 Aquash and AIM security chief Leonard Peltier (1944– ; see entry) responded to requests by Pine Ridge traditionalists to protect them from Dick Wilson's

# Daughter of the Earth: Song for Anna Mae Aquash

Folksong writer Ellen Klaver wrote the following piece as a tribute to Anna Mae Aquash:

*She came down from the North Country, from Canada*
*Where the northern lights shine shimmering above the fir*
*The strength of the continent was deep inside her heart*
*Strength that was needed in these times*

*She came to help the people as they struggled to be free*
*From the ones who sought to kill the land for money*
*They said they owned our Mother Earth and called it USA*
*Born of broken treaties and murder*

*Oh Anna Mae, oh Anna Mae*
*I feel your spirit and sometimes I can hear it*
*Saying keep on strong, keep on going on*
*Daughter of the Earth*

*The FBI had told her they would kill her if they could*
*Like so many others before her*
*But she was not afraid of them, her path was clear and true*
*"I am a woman working for my people"*

*So they shot her down and left the body lying in a field*
*Believing in the power of the metal gun*
*But the power lies within the land, it can't be owned or sold*
*And gives us what survives beyond our lives*

*Oh Anna Mae, oh Anna Mae*
*I feel your spirit and sometimes I can hear it*
*Saying keep on strong, keep on going on*
*Daughter of the Earth*

*Whenever I am frightened I just think of her*
*Her courage in confronting the death machine*
*To live for what sustains us all, to work to keep it whole*
*To die because some want to see it broken*

*Oh Anna Mae, oh Anna Mae*
*They stole your life away but they can't steal what you had to say*
*To keep on strong, keep on going on*
*Daughter of the Earth*

*Oh Anna Mae, oh Anna Mae*
*I feel your spirit and sometimes I can hear it*
*Saying keep on strong, keep on going on*
*Daughter of the Earth*

GOON Squads. Since the siege of Wounded Knee, many AIM members and traditionalists had been shot by the GOON squads or had died under mysterious circumstances. With twenty-three killings in 1974, Pine Ridge had the nation's highest per-capita number of murders.

It was amidst this atmosphere of tension that two FBI agents came to the Pine Ridge Reservation on June 26, 1975, in search of an Oglala Sioux Indian teenager named Jimmy Eagle.

Eagle was wanted for armed robbery, for allegedly brandishing a pocket knife while stealing a white man's cowboy boots. A gunfight broke out, leaving the two agents and a twenty-four-year-old Indian man dead.

AIM members quickly left the reservation, fearing, correctly, that the FBI's response would be swift and brutal. Aquash, who had not been at the reservation on the day of the shoot-out, spent the next few weeks counseling residents about their rights. When Aquash learned the FBI was looking for her, she joined several other AIM members who were camping out on the nearby Rosebud Reservation.

## Running from the law

Aquash was arrested by the FBI during a raid on Rosebud Reservation in September 1975 and charged with harboring explosives in her tent. She was told by FBI agent David Price, however, that the real reason for the raid was to get information about the shoot-out. When Aquash claimed she knew nothing about the killings of the FBI agents, she was warned by Price that she would be "dead within a year."

**Edgar Bear Runner, coordinator of the twenty-fifth anniversary of the Wounded Knee takeover, pays his respects at Anna Mae Aquash's grave in Oglala, South Dakota.**
*Photograph by Jill Kokesh. Reproduced by permission of AP/Wide World Photos.*

When Aquash was released on bail a few days later, she fled to Washington state. In November, as Aquash drove away from Washington's Port Madison Reservation, federal agents followed her. They pulled her over in Oregon, a few miles from the Idaho border. The agents found firearms and explosives in Aquash's car and arrested her. While in jail in Vale, Oregon, Aquash told a reporter from the *Idaho Statesman*, "If they take me back to South Dakota I'll be murdered."

## Returned to South Dakota

Soon thereafter Aquash was extradited (taken back) to South Dakota, where she was charged with possession of firearms and explosives in the latest incident, as well as in the

Rosebud raid. Government officials offered to reduce the charges against her in exchange for her testimony against Leonard Peltier who, along with two others, had been charged with the murder of the FBI agents.

Aquash refused, offering the following statement: "You [the government] are continuing to control my life with your violent, materialistic needs. I do realize your need to survive and be a part of this creation. But you do not understand mine and therefore I refuse to issue a plea of guilty.... I have a right to continue my cycle in this universe undisturbed." In an unexpected twist, the judge released Aquash on her own recognizance. She left the courthouse and once again went underground (into hiding from the law).

## Targeted for death

On February 24, 1976, Aquash's body was found by Lakota cattle rancher Roger Amiott as he prepared to install a fence around the perimeter of his property. The corpse, wrapped in a blanket, was partially deteriorated, indicating that it had been there for quite some time. The body was taken to the Pine Ridge Public Health Service for an autopsy. Exposure was determined to be the cause of death. To identify the corpse, the hands were cut off and sent to an FBI lab in Washington, D.C. Meanwhile, the body was buried as an anonymous "Jane Doe" in a Catholic cemetery.

About one week later, the body was identified as Anna Mae Aquash. When Aquash's family was notified, they demanded a second autopsy. It did not make sense that Anna Mae, who had an entire lifetime of experience at survival in northern winters, would have died of exposure. With the help of AIM, Aquash's sisters located an independent coroner. The body was exhumed, and the coroner discovered a bullet hole at the base of Aquash's skull. The true cause of her death had been a gunshot at point-blank range.

## Laid to rest

Aquash's comrades in AIM reburied her with traditional rites. Her body was laid to rest next to that of Joe Stunts, the Indian who was killed in the FBI shoot-out. Both graves were marked with four colorful flags, symbolizing each of the four winds, as well as an upside-down American flag—the symbol of AIM.

Despite calls from two U.S. Congressmen and several Canadian lawmakers for a full investigation, no serious attempt was made to find Aquash's killer or killers. The murder remains unsolved.

## Sources

### Books

Brand, Johanna. *The Life and Death of Anna Mae Aquash.* Toronto: James Lorimer and Company Publishers, 1993.

Churchill, Ward, and Jim Vander Wall. *Agents of Repression: The FBI's Secret Wars against the Black Panther Party and the American Indian Movement.* Boston: South End Press, 1988.

Malinowski, Sharon, and Simon Glickman, eds. *Native North American Biography,* Vol. 1. Detroit: U•X•L, 1996, pp. 13–18.

Matthiessen, Peter. *In the Spirit of Crazy Horse.* New York: Viking Press, 1980.

Smith, Paul Chaat, and Robert Allen Warrior. *Like a Hurricane: The Indian Movement from Alcatraz to Wounded Knee.* New York: The New Press, 1996.

### Periodicals

Weir, David, and Lowell Bergman. "The Killing of Anna Mae Aquash." *Rolling Stone.* April 7, 1977: 51–55.

# Ella Jo Baker

**Born December 13, 1903**
**Norfolk, Virginia**
**Died December 13, 1986**
**New York, New York**

**African American organizer for the NAACP and the SCLC and advisor to the SNCC**

Ella Jo Baker was a brilliant "behind the scenes" organizer, considered by many to be the "godmother" of the civil rights movement. Baker championed the ideal of grassroots (local level) empowerment and member-controlled leadership in civil rights organizations. She was a living example of her philosophy that the best leaders empowered others to lead.

In an activist career spanning fifty years, Baker accomplished a tremendous amount. She established numerous chapters of the National Association for the Advancement of Colored People (NAACP) and sparked the formation of both the Southern Christian Leadership Conference (SCLC) and the Student Nonviolent Coordinating Committee (SNCC). And by taking an active role in political affairs at a time when women were expected to be submissive and quietly mind the business of the home, Baker served as a role model for a generation of young female activists.

An unsung heroine of the civil rights movement, Ella Jo Baker was instrumental in the creation of several important civil rights organizations, including the Southern Christian Leadership Conference.

## Early years

Baker was born in 1903 in Norfolk, Virginia. Her father was a waiter, and her mother was a schoolteacher. At the age

Portrait: Reproduced by permission of AP/Wide World Photos.

31

of eight, Baker moved to Littleton, North Carolina. For the next seven years Baker lived on land where her grandparents had once lived and worked as slaves, but later purchased. Baker attended high school in Raleigh, North Carolina, then stayed in Raleigh to attend the predominantly black Shaw University. She graduated from Shaw in 1927, at the top of her class.

Later that year Baker moved to Harlem in New York City. She spent the next two years working in a factory and waitressing. In 1929 Baker accepted a position on the editorial staff of the *American West Indian News*.

## Becomes social activist

Baker began her career as a social activist in 1932, in the middle of the Great Depression (the worst economic crisis ever to hit the United States, lasting from 1929 to 1939). Her first position was as director of the Young Negroes Cooperative League. During that time, Baker also worked as a labor and consumer educator for the Works Progress Administration (WPA)—one of the many social programs initiated by President Franklin Delano Roosevelt (1882–1945) to provide jobs and pull the nation out of the Depression.

In the mid-1930s Baker was also active with a women's rights organization called the Women's Day Workers and Industrial League. She wrote a book in 1935 entitled *Crisis* that exposed the miserable working conditions of domestic servants.

## Works with NAACP

Baker joined the NAACP in 1938 and in 1940 was named national director of branches (a position also known as field secretary). Her main responsibility was to recruit members throughout the South. She also promoted job training programs for black workers. Baker resigned from the national NAACP in 1946, citing differences with the organization's top-down leadership style. She felt that the organization would be stronger if the grassroots constituency was empowered to make its own decisions, rather than taking its directions from national leaders.

In the late 1940s and early 1950s Baker worked as a freelance consultant to numerous civil rights groups, including the National Urban League (an African American community service organization active primarily in cities) and In Friendship (a New York-based organization that raised funds for civil rights activists in the South). Baker quickly earned a reputation as an effective organizer.

In 1954 Baker became president of the New York City NAACP branch. Through the mid-1950s she organized parents to fight for racial integration of public schools. (Although the 1954 *Brown v. Board of Education of Topeka, Kansas* Supreme Court ruling outlawed segregation in public schools, it was several more years before most school districts allowed integration to proceed.)

## Formation of the Southern Christian Leadership Conference

In December 1956 Baker approached Martin Luther King Jr. (1929–1968; see entry) with the idea of forming an organization of black ministers to coordinate civil rights activities in the South. At the time, King was president of the Montgomery Improvement Association, the organization that had just finished coordinating the successful 382-day-long Montgomery bus boycott. Baker, who had been one of the boycott's strongest supporters in the North, had been impressed by the ability of King and other ministers to rally large numbers of participants. Baker felt that the momentum of the boycott should be preserved.

After some debate, King agreed with Baker's idea of forming a permanent organization. The Southern Christian Leadership Conference (SCLC) was founded in January 1957 by sixty-five black ministers from eleven southern states. The group set up headquarters in Atlanta, Georgia, and selected King as president. The ministers hired Baker as acting executive director and office manager.

Baker's role in the SCLC's success has been greatly overlooked in history books. As an experienced activist, Baker navigated the group through the murky political waters of the period. During her two and a half years with the SCLC, Baker was the organization's senior strategist, producer and distributor of literature, and public relations director. She also coordinated the group's voter registration program, called Crusade for Citizenship.

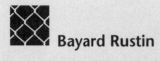

## Bayard Rustin

One of Ella Baker's colleagues in the northern effort to support the Montgomery bus boycott was Bayard Rustin (1912–1987). Rustin and Baker were similar in that both worked behind the scenes of the civil rights movement. Rustin served as an advisor to Martin Luther King Jr. (1929–1968; see entry), and to African American labor leader A. Philip Randolph (1889–1979). Rustin's crowning achievement was the coordination of the 1963 March on Washington for Peace, Jobs, and Justice.

Rustin was born in West Chester, Pennsylvania, on March 17, 1912, to a family of pacifists and Quakers. (A pacifist is a person who opposes war or violence as a means of settling disputes. Quakers, also called the Society of Friends, are Christians who oppose war, oathtaking, and religious rituals.) His involvement in social causes began at an early age, with his membership in the Young Communist League in Harlem in New York City.

In 1941 Rustin parted ways with the communists and began working as an aide to A. Philip Randolph. In that capacity he helped Randolph plan a national march to protest discrimination against African Americans in the defense industry. The threat of the march pressured president Franklin D. Roosevelt (1882–1945) to sign an executive order barring discrimination in defense hiring. The march was therefore called off.

A lifelong pacifist, Rustin refused induction into the army during World War II (1939–45). As a result, he spent two years in prison. There he met other radical pacifists, some of whom later founded the Congress on Racial Equality (CORE). After his release from prison in 1945, Rustin worked with the pacifist, antiracist group Fellowship of Reconciliation to organize the Journey of Reconciliation (JOR). The JOR was a bus ride through the segregated South by integrated groups of people (it

"The kind of role that I tried to play [at the SCLC]," Baker said in the 1980 book about women activists entitled *Moving the Mountain,* "was to pick up pieces or put together pieces out of which I hoped organization might come. My theory is, strong people don't need strong leaders."

## The birth of the SNCC

In April 1960 Baker organized a conference at Shaw University for members of the student sit-in movement. (Sit-ins

**Bayard Rustin.** *Reproduced by permission of AP/Wide World Photos.*

studied the philosophy of nonviolent protest. (Nonviolent protest—often called passive resistance—is the quiet but firm refusal to comply with unjust laws.) In 1957, near the start of the Montgomery bus boycott, Rustin mentored Martin Luther King Jr. in the tenets of Gandhian nonviolence.

King, like many other leaders in the civil rights movement, publicly distanced himself from Rustin. Rustin was kept on the outside not only because of his prior affiliation with communism, but also because he was gay. In his early years Rustin tried to conceal his homosexuality. In the late 1960s and early 1970s, however, he acknowledged his homosexuality and spoke out in favor of gay rights.

was the late 1940s precursor to the 1961 Freedom Rides).

Rustin traveled to Africa and India in the early 1950s, where he met with the sons of slain Indian independence leader Mohandas Gandhi (1869–1948) and

From 1964 until his death in 1987, Rustin served as director of the New York City-based civil rights organization, the A. Philip Randolph Institute.

were a form of civil rights protest in which black students, sometimes joined by white students, would request service at segregated lunch counters; the students refused to leave when denied service.) Baker felt that students, with their boundless energy and optimism, had a great potential to bring about social change. She urged them to form an organization through which they could coordinate their actions.

The three largest civil rights organizations—the SCLC, the NAACP, and CORE—sent representatives to the conference to try to convince the students to form a wing of their respective organizations. Baker, however, steered the students away from associating with any of the established civil rights organizations. She advised them to form an independent organization that would reflect and respond to the needs and experiences of the students. The new student organization, she argued, should be energetic and militant, not cautious and conservative like the established groups.

Baker also sought to foster the students' natural tendency toward participatory democracy—what she called "group-centeredness." The established civil rights organizations were all led by strong directors who made the decisions and handed down instructions to the members. In her years with the NAACP and the SCLC, Baker had become disillusioned with the "top-down" leadership style. According to Baker, the sign of a healthy organization was "the development of people who are interested not in being leaders as much as in developing leadership among other people."

The end result of the Shaw University conference was the birth of the Student Nonviolent Coordinating Committee, better known by the initials SNCC (pronounced "snick"). Baker stayed with the SNCC through the early 1960s as an informal counselor. She gave strategy advice, helped resolve conflicts between members, and introduced the students to older activists she had met while recruiting for the NAACP throughout the South. The SNCC quickly rose to the fore of the civil rights movement. Its activists were recognized as hard-working, fearless, and committed warriors in the fight for racial equality.

## Helps found the Mississippi Freedom Democratic Party

In 1964 Baker assisted Mississippi civil rights activists in founding a new political party, the Mississippi Freedom Democratic Party (MFDP). The MFDP was organized as an alternative to the regular Democratic Party, which excluded blacks. Baker gave the keynote address at the MFDP convention in Jackson, Mississippi, and set up the MFDP's Washington, D.C., office.

On August 6, 1964, delegates from the MFDP headed for Atlantic City, New Jersey, where they challenged the regular Democratic Party for representation of the people of

Mississippi at the national Democratic presidential convention. Baker was instrumental in drumming up support in the capital for the MFDP's challenge. Although the MFDP was unable to unseat the regular Democratic Party, it forced a change in rules to favor integrated state party delegations at future conventions and dramatized the plight of black Mississippians before a national television audience.

## Active in later years

Baker remained active in the fight for civil rights and human rights even as a senior citizen. She stood up not only for the rights of racial minorities but for the rights of women and workers of all races. Baker served as advisor to numerous social justice organizations and was a national board member of the Puerto Rican Solidarity Committee. She was in constant demand as a speaker at conferences and demonstrations throughout the nation.

**Members of the Mississippi Freedom Democratic Party try to attend the second session of the 1964 Democratic Party national convention in Atlantic City, New Jersey.**
*Reproduced by permission of AP/Wide World Photos.*

Baker died in Harlem in 1986. The pallbearers at her funeral included many former SNCC activists who had been inspired by Baker, including Julian Bond (1940– ), Charles McDew, Charles Sherrod, Kwame Toure (1941–1998; formerly Stokely Carmichael), Robert Zellner (1939– ), Reginald Robinson, and Jamil Abdullah Al-Amin (formerly H. Rap Brown; 1943– ).

## Sources

### Books

Cantarow, Ellen. *Moving the Mountain: Women Working for Social Change.* Old Westbury, NY: The Feminist Press, 1980.

Carson, Clayborne. *In Struggle: SNCC and the Black Awakening of the 1960s.* Cambridge: Harvard University Press, 1981.

Crawford, Vicki L., Jacqueline Anne Rouse, and Barbara Woods, eds. *Women in the Civil Rights Movement: Trailblazers and Torchbearers, 1941–1965.* Brooklyn, NY: Carlson Publishing, Inc., 1990.

Dallard, Shyrlee. *Ella Baker: A Leader Behind the Scenes.* Englewood Cliffs, NJ: Silver Burdett Press, Inc., 1990.

Giddings, Paula. *When and Where I Enter: The Impact of Black Women on Race and Sex in America.* New York: Bantam Books, 1984.

Grant, Joanne. *Ella Baker: Freedom Bound.* New York: John Wiley and Sons, Inc., 1998.

Levy, Peter B. *The Civil Rights Movement.* Westwood, CT: Greenwood Press, 1998.

Robinson, Jo Ann Gibson. *The Montgomery Bus Boycott and the Women Who Started It.* Knoxville: University of Tennessee Press, 1987.

Robnett, Belinda. *How Long? How Long? African-American Women in the Struggle for Civil Rights.* New York: Oxford University Press, 1997.

Salmond, John A. *My Mind Set on Freedom: A History of the Civil Rights Movement, 1954–1968.* Chicago: Ivan R. Dee, 1997.

# César Chávez

**Born March 31, 1927**
**Yuma, Arizona**
**Died April 23, 1993**
**San Luis, Arizona**

**Mexican American labor leader**
**and civil rights leader**

César Chávez is widely considered to have been the greatest Mexican American civil rights leader in history. Chávez brought the terrible plight of migrant farm workers—most of whom were of Mexican descent—to the attention of the American public. He was a charismatic leader who turned the farm workers' strike into a national movement for social justice.

In the 1960s Chávez founded the United Farm Workers (UFW) union, an organization that continues to work on behalf of agricultural workers throughout the United States. While the war against injustice in the fields is far from over, Chávez's efforts have made conditions for many farm workers better today than they would have been thirty years ago.

## The plight of migrant farm workers

In California's San Joaquín Valley, where the UFW originated, workers migrated from one grape harvest to the next. The workers performed back-breaking labor for long hours and were constantly exposed to dangerous pesticides. (In fact, the average life expectancy of a farm worker in 1965

"It is my deepest belief that only by giving our lives do we truly find life. I am convinced that the truest act of courage, the strongest act of manliness ... is to sacrifice ourselves for others."

Portrait: Reproduced by permission of AP/Wide World Photos.

was forty-nine years; the average life expectancy of a white U.S. citizen, in comparison, was seventy years.)

Farm workers typically lived in rundown one-room shacks with no heat or running water. Those who could not afford to pay for housing slept under their cars. Farm workers had little time for schooling, so most were illiterate. Many growers promised farm workers one wage and paid them significantly less. The typical farm worker did not speak English and thus was powerless to assert his or her rights. In the 1960s most farm workers earned less than $2,000 per year—barely enough to survive on.

## Early years as a farm worker

Chávez learned about the plight of farm workers first-hand as a child. Chávez was born into a poor farming family in 1927, in Yuma, Arizona, just before the onset of the Great Depression (the worst economic crisis ever to hit the United States, lasting from 1929 to 1939). The Chávez family struggled to hold on to its farm through the Depression, only to be wiped out by a drought in 1937.

When Chávez was ten years old, his family began following the harvests through Arizona and California. Like other migrant children, Chávez found it difficult to attend school. He had to switch schools every time his family moved on to the next job. Chávez attended more than thirty-seven schools in all and only completed the eighth grade.

One subject young Chávez learned a lot about—both in school and out of school—was discrimination against Mexican Americans. Chávez was told in at least one school that none of the teachers wanted Mexicans in their classrooms. Most restaurants in the 1930s and 1940s refused to serve Mexican Americans or other people of color, and movie theaters had segregated seating. Mexican Americans lived in fear of brutality at the hands of police. Even while serving in the navy during World War II (1939–45), Chávez faced discrimination because of his race.

## Starts family, joins Community Service Organization

In 1948 Chávez married his sweetheart of six years, Helena Fabela, and the couple settled down in a one-room shack in Delano, California. Over the next several years, César and Helena had eight children. Chávez worked picking cotton and grapes, hitchhiking to work and back since he had no car.

One day in 1948 the workers at Chávez's job site walked out of the fields in protest over low pay and unsafe working conditions. Most of the workers were not U.S. citizens and feared being deported (expelled from the country). Thus they ended their strike after three days, having made no gains.

Chávez was inspired by that strike—his first example of farm workers banding together to assert their rights. To overcome the fear of deportation, Chávez began teaching the workers English so they could start the process of becoming U.S. citizens.

In 1952 Chávez met Fred Ross, founder of the Community Service Organization (CSO). The CSO, Ross explained to Chávez, was working to advance the civil rights of farm workers. Ross convinced Chávez to join the organization. Chávez began spending several hours after work each day going door-to-door, teaching people how to become U.S. citizens and how to register to vote, as well as helping them solve any number of other problems. In 1958 Chávez was promoted to the position of CSO director in California and Arizona.

## The farm workers union and the grape strike

In 1962 Chávez resigned from the CSO so he could devote his energies to organizing farm workers. Chávez took the money he had saved while working for the CSO and, along with two other organizers—Dolores Huerta (1930–; see entry) and Gilberto Padillo—established the National Farm Workers Association (NFWA). The leaders of the NFWA put in long hours, talking to workers in the fields about their conditions and urging them to join the NFWA. By 1965 the NFWA boasted 1,700 members.

In September 1965 the NFWA was suddenly forced to decide whether or not to go on strike. The 600 Filipino workers of the Agricultural Workers Organizing Committee (AWOC) had gone on strike, and the growers had responded by firing the strikers and throwing them out of their homes. The Filipino workers looked to the NFWA for support. By continuing to work, the Mexican workers would hurt the

Filipinos' cause. By joining the strike, they would be standing up for the rights of all farm workers.

Chávez felt that joining the strike was a risky move. His young union had no strike fund, and NFWA members faced the possibility of losing their jobs and being deported. Nonetheless, on Mexican Independence Day—September 16, 1965—the NFWA voted to go on strike. Workers walked out of the vineyards surrounding Delano, demanding a living wage, decent housing, and humane working conditions. Chávez threw himself into the strike effort.

## Initiates grape boycott and march

Soon after the strike began, Chávez and other union leaders initiated a grape boycott. They asked the American public not to buy grapes until conditions improved for migrant workers. Students, religious leaders, labor unions, and civil rights organizations supported the farm workers. They promoted the boycott in their communities and sent the strikers food and money. Many people came to Delano to join picket lines.

To further raise the stakes, in February 1966 Chávez led the strikers on a 250-mile-long march from Delano to the state capital of Sacramento. Twenty-one days into the march, Chávez received word that one of the largest grape growers, the Schenley Corporation, had given in to the strikers' demands. The settlement with Schenley was the first major farm labor contract in the history of the United States.

After the settlement, NFWA merged with AWOC to form the United Farm Workers. The UFW chose to affiliate with the nation's largest labor conglomerate, the American Federation of Labor-Congress of Industrial Organizations (AFL-CIO). The UFW continued working to force the more than two dozen remaining growers to the table.

The marchers reached Sacramento on Easter Sunday, April 11, 1966. Chávez gave a triumphant speech on the steps of the state capitol building and read from the Plan de Delano, the document that explained the reasons behind the march.

"Now we will suffer for the purpose of ending the poverty, the misery, and the injustice," Chávez read. "This Pil-

## Luis Valdez and Teatro Campesino

Playwright and filmmaker Luis Valdez (1940– ) introduced a cultural dimension to the grape workers' strike. His traveling theater group, called Teatro Campesino (Spanish for "Farm Workers Theater"), provided workers with a creative outlet and a humorous diversion during the long, difficult strike years.

Valdez had grown up in a family of migrant workers. He managed to finish high school—a rare achievement for a migrant child—and went on to San Jose State University. He graduated with a bachelor of arts degree in English in 1964. For the next year Valdez worked with the foremost street theater organization of the 1960s, the San Francisco Mime Troupe.

Two months into the grape pickers' strike Valdez came to César Chávez with the idea of starting Teatro Campesino. Valdez recruited strikers and their supporters and began putting on shows on picket lines, at fundraisers, and along the march route from Delano to Sacramento. The characters were identified by cardboard signs reading "huelgista" (striker), "patroncito" (boss), and "esquiról" (scab). Farm workers enjoyed

**Luis Valdez.** *Reproduced by permission of Arte Público Press.*

the opportunity to ridicule the growers by putting on "patroncito" signs and acting like buffoons. They also acted out their life stories and pieces of Mexican folklore.

Valdez went on to write and direct numerous plays and movies about the Mexican American experience. His most famous production was the 1987 movie *La Bamba,* which chronicled the short life of popular Mexican American rock and roll singer Ritchie Valens.

grimage is witness to the suffering we have seen for generations…. Across the San Joaquín Valley, across California, across the entire Southwest of the United States, wherever there are Mexican people, wherever there are farm workers, our movement is spreading like flames across a dry plain. Our Pilgrim-

Senator Robert Kennedy, an outspoken supporter of civil rights, was with César Chávez when he broke his protest fast on March 10, 1968.
*Reproduced by permission of Archive Photos.*

age is the match that will light our cause for all farm workers to see what is happening here, so that they may do as we have done."

## Fasts for twenty-five days

By February 1968 the strike had been dragging on for two and a half years, and thousands of farm workers were still out of work. Some of the strikers began discussing committing acts of sabotage against crops and equipment. Chávez, an adherent of Indian nationalist leader Mohandas Gandhi (1869–1948) and Martin Luther King Jr. (1929–1968; see entry), claimed that the only lasting victories came by nonviolent means. To demonstrate the power of nonviolence, he began a fast on February 14.

Chávez's fast lasted twenty-five days. During that time thousands of supporters visited the room where Chávez was fasting, to speak with him, to play music for him, or just to look at him. When Chávez had lost thirty-five pounds and became too weak to walk, his doctor convinced him to break his fast.

On March 10, 1968, Chávez broke bread with Senator Robert F. Kennedy (1925–1968)—brother of assassinated president John F. Kennedy (1917–1963) and an outspoken supporter of civil rights—by his side. "The world must know," said Kennedy, "that the migrant farm worker, the Mexican American, is coming into his own right."

Chávez addressed his supporters at a mass after breaking his fast. "When we are really honest with ourselves, we must admit that our lives are all that really belong to us," said Chávez. "So it is how we use our lives that determines what kind of men we are. It is my deepest belief that only by giving our lives do we truly find life. I am convinced that the truest act of courage, the strongest act of manliness ... is to sacrifice ourselves for others."

## Grape strike ends in victory

In July 1970, almost five years after the strike had begun, the remaining 26 nonunion Delano grape growers finally met the workers' demands. The owners' resolve had been weakened by the boycott's economic impact. The growers signed contracts granting farm workers $1.80 per hour plus 20 cents per box of grapes picked; protection against pesticides; seniority for striking workers; and a union hiring hall. The contracts covered 40,000 grape workers.

After the grape strike, Chávez and the UFW turned their attention to the plight of lettuce pickers. Here the UFW had to confront not only the growers, but another union—the Teamsters. The Teamsters had emerged as a rival to the UFW in organizing farm workers. On behalf of lettuce pickers, the Teamsters had signed contracts with a number of growers that, according to UFW leaders, were not beneficial to the workers.

## The Agricultural Labor Relations Act

The battle over representation of lettuce pickers came to a head in 1975 when the California state legislature enacted the Agricultural Labor Relations Act. That legislation gave agricultural workers the right to organize and the right to determine which union would represent them. In elections held in August 1975, the workers overwhelmingly sided with the UFW.

The UFW was never again as effective as it had been during the mid-1960s grape strike. The UFW's decline in effectiveness was due to many factors: competition with other unions for farm workers' membership; an inability to garner widespread support; and tighter immigration laws that resulted in a greater proportion of undocumented farm workers (the UFW only organizes workers who are in the United States legally). Union membership declined in the 1970s and 1980s. In the 1990s the UFW claimed about 10,000 members and held about 100 contracts with agricultural employers.

## Conducts fast to protest pesticide use

In the 1980s Chávez began a crusade against the use of dangerous pesticides in the vineyards. (Pesticides are poisonous chemicals sprayed on crops to kill insect pests or weeds. Many pesticides are hazardous to the health of humans and wildlife.) Chávez pointed out that not only did pesticides sicken farm workers, but they were dangerous to grape consumers. He called upon the public to boycott grapes until the pesticides were discontinued. That boycott, however, failed to garner the widespread support enjoyed by the original boycott.

In 1988 Chávez went on another fast to protest continued pesticide use. "And the fast will endure," wrote Chávez, "until the fields are safe for farm workers, the environment is preserved for future generations, and our food is once again a source of nourishment and life."

Chávez announced an end to his fast thirty-six days after he had begun. At his side were Ethel Kennedy (Robert Kennedy's widow), his wife Helena, his mother Juana, and civil rights leader Jesse Jackson (1941– ).

Chávez died in April 1993 while conducting UFW business in Arizona. His funeral drew more than 30,000 mourners, who formed a three-mile-long procession to his gravesite.

## Sources

### Books

Cedeño, Maria E. *César Chávez: Labor Leader.* Brookfield, CT: The Millbrook Press, 1993.

Ferriss, Susan, and Ricardo Sandoval. *The Fight in the Fields: César Chávez and the Farmworkers Movement.* New York: Harcourt Brace and Company, 1997.

Griswold del Castillo, Richard, and Richard A. Garcia. *César Chávez: A Triumph of Spirit.* Norman, Oklahoma: University of Oklahoma Press, 1995.

Levy, Jacques. *César Chávez: Autobiography of La Causa.* New York: W. W. Norton and Company, 1975.

Matthiessen, Peter. *Sal Si Puedes: César Chávez and the New American Revolution.* New York: Random House, 1969.

Nagel, Rob, and Sharon Rose, eds. *Hispanic American Biography,* Vol. 1. Detroit: U•X•L, 1995, pp. 41–45; Vol. 2, pp. 223–25.

Rosales, F. Arturo. *Chicano! The History of the Mexican American Civil Rights Movement.* Houston, TX: Arte Público Press, 1997.

Sigler, Jay A., ed. *Civil Rights in America: 1500 to the Present.* Detroit: Gale, 1998.

### Other

*Chicano! The History of the Mexican American Civil Rights Movement* (four episodes; videocassette). Los Angeles: NLCC Educational Media, 1996.

# Septima P. Clark

**Born May 3, 1898**
**Charleston, South Carolina**
**Died December 15, 1987**
**Charleston, South Carolina**

**African American educator**
**and civil rights organizer**

Septima P. Clark dedicated her life to the pursuit of political, economic, and social rights for African Americans. She was a key player in the civil rights movement, organizing quietly behind the scenes and using education to create social change. Perhaps Clark's greatest strength was her ability to empower others to stand up for their rights.

Clark is best remembered for her role as coordinator of the "citizenship school" program, first of the Highlander Folk School and later of the Southern Christian Leadership Conference (SCLC). Clark set up schools throughout the South, at which African Americans learned how to read and write and fill out voter registration forms. According to Andrew Young (1921– )— civil rights activist, and later, United States representative to the United Nations and mayor of Atlanta—the citizenship schools laid the foundation for the entire civil rights movement.

## Early years

Clark was born in Charleston, South Carolina, in 1898. Before the Civil War (1861–65), Clark's father, Peter Poinsette,

According to Martin Luther King Jr., civil rights organizer Septima Clark was the "Mother of the Movement."

47

had been a slave on a farm owned by Joel Poinsette. Her mother, Victoria Warren Anderson Poinsette, had been born in Charleston and raised from a young age in Haiti. After the Civil War, Peter worked as a caterer and Victoria cleaned laundry for a living.

Clark described her father as "gentle" and her mother as "haughty" (due to having had English schoolmasters in Haiti). Clark claimed that the combination of her parents' attributes helped her as a civil rights worker. "When I went to Mississippi and Texas and places like that," Clark once stated, "I had a feeling that his [Peter's] nonviolence helped me to work with the people there and her [Victoria's] haughtiness helped me to stay."

Early in life Clark decided she wanted to be a teacher, one of the few careers open to women at that time. After finishing primary school she attended the Avery Normal Institute, a private school that trained blacks to be teachers. In 1916 Clark received her teaching certificate and accepted a position on John's Island, off the coast of South Carolina.

## Teaches in segregated school

Clark was one of two teachers in a black creosote (sticky tar) schoolhouse into which 132 African American pupils were crowded. Across the road, Clark recalled, was a sparkling white schoolhouse in which three white pupils took instruction from one teacher. Clark and her coworker together made $60 a month, while the white teacher alone made $85 a month. Clark taught on Johns Island for three years, during which time she was an outspoken advocate for pay equity among teachers, regardless of race.

In 1919 Clark returned to Charleston and began teaching at the Avery Normal Institute. She could not get a teaching position in the public schools because, at that time, blacks were barred from those positions. (There were separate public schools for black children and white children, and white teachers staffed both.)

## Becomes active in civil rights movement

Soon thereafter, Clark began attending meetings of the National Association for the Advancement of Colored People

(NAACP). She became active in the NAACP's campaign to allow black teachers to teach in Charleston public schools. Clark and others in the NAACP collected thousands of signatures in a door-to-door petition drive and delivered them to the South Carolina state legislature.

By the end of 1919 the law had been changed to allow black public-school teachers; by 1920 there were African American principals in Charleston public schools. Clark's commitment to civil rights work was bolstered by this initial victory.

## Marries and starts a family

In 1920 Clark married a seaman named Nerie Clark. The couple had two children: a daughter who died one month after birth and a son, Nerie Clark Jr. In 1925 Clark's husband died of kidney disease at the age of thirty-five, leaving Septima to raise the couple's son alone. For the next four years Clark made ends meet by living with her husband's relatives in Dayton, Ohio, and Hickory, North Carolina.

In 1929 Clark and her son moved to Columbia, South Carolina. Clark worked as a teacher in the Columbia public schools and continued her own education. Through it all, Clark found it very difficult to support her son. Six years after moving to Columbia, Clark sent him to live with his grandparents in Hickory.

Clark then resumed her college education, taking classes at night and in the summers. She earned a bachelor of arts degree from Benedict College in 1942 and a master of arts degree from Hampton Institute in 1947.

## The salary equalization campaign

In the mid-1930s Clark continued her campaign for teacher pay equity. She worked alongside NAACP lawyer Thurgood Marshall (1908–1993), Booker T. Washington High School principal J. Andrew Simmons, and others, in a decade-long campaign to "force the equalization of white and Negro teachers' salaries on the basis of certification."

The group filed a class action lawsuit in federal district court. Hearings on the matter were held in the South Carolina House of Representatives where, due to segregation laws, Clark and her African American colleagues were denied seating on the main floor (they had to watch the proceedings from the balcony). In 1945 the suit was decided in favor of the African American teachers. As a result, Clark saw her own pay as a schoolteacher triple.

## Gets fired for civil rights involvement

In 1947, at the age of forty-nine, Clark moved back to Charleston and secured a teaching position in the public schools. She also continued her civil rights activism. Clark was vice president and membership director of the Charleston NAACP and attended desegregation workshops at the Highlander Folk School near Monteagle, Tennessee. (The Highlander Folk School, founded in 1932, was a racially integrated, social-justice and civil rights organization. For more information on Highlander, see Myles Horton entry.)

The South Carolina legislature passed a law in 1956 prohibiting any state or city employee from associating with civil rights organizations. Clark immediately organized a petition drive in opposition to the new law. When Clark, along with five of her colleagues, confronted the school superintendent on the matter, she was fired. After having taught for forty years in the South Carolina public schools, Clark lost her retirement benefits. It was not until 1981 that the South Carolina legislature admitted that Clark had been wrongfully terminated. The legislature gave her back pay and restored her pension.

## Becomes director at Highlander Folk School

After Clark's dismissal from her teaching job, Highlander Folk School director and co-founder Myles Horton (1905–1990; see entry) recruited Clark to be director of Highlander's citizenship school program. Highlander had started out as a training center for union activists and an educational center for poor people in the 1930s. In the 1950s it had shifted its emphasis to civil rights and race relations—in particular the desegregation of public schools in the South.

"Highlander workshops were planned and conducted to emphasize a cooperative rather than a competitive use of learning," wrote Clark in her 1962 memoir *Echo in My Soul.*

"They hoped through the teaching of leaders to advance a community…. People came to Highlander to seek enlightenment on issues whose proper solution, followed by adequate social action, would promote the advancement of all. Highlander Folk School's workshops included persons of all races and levels of economic and education success."

One of the Highlander School's most famous graduates was civil rights pioneer Rosa Parks (1913–; see box in Myles Horton entry). Seven weeks after returning from Highlander, Parks refused to give up her seat on a bus and sparked the Montgomery bus boycott. Fannie Lou Hamer (1917–1977; see entry), the fiery spokesperson for the Mississippi Freedom Democratic Party, also took her training at Highlander. And Esau Jenkins, a farmer, bus driver, and father of seven, initiated a school desegregation campaign on Johns Island, South Carolina, after attending a Highlander workshop.

## Sets up Highlander Folk School "citizenship schools"

In 1953 Highlander began sponsoring "citizenship schools." The purpose of the schools was to prepare adult students to more fully participate as citizens in American society. The citizenship schools taught reading, writing, and math, as well as community organizing strategies. Students gained basic skills, such as how to fill out voter registration applications and drivers' license applications and how to write checks and money orders.

After completing her training at Highlander, Clark traveled through the South setting up citizenship schools wherever she could—in private homes, country stores, beauty parlors, and even outdoors. She recruited teachers and students for the schools. To be a teacher, one only had to be a resident of the local community, a high-school graduate, and at least twenty-one years of age.

Between 1954 and 1961 Clark and another staffer, Bernice Robinson, established thirty-seven citizenship schools throughout the deep South. Many graduates of the citizenship schools successfully registered to vote—an activity that was dangerous and difficult for African Americans prior to the Voting Rights Act of 1965. Some graduates went on to lead their own voter registration drives. "The Citizenship School Program became the basis for the civil rights movement," Robinson explained in an interview published in *Women in the Civil Rights Movement: Trailblazers and Torchbearers, 1941–1965,* "because it was through these classes that people learned about their rights and *why* they should vote."

Clark also conducted workshops at the Highlander School with veteran civil rights organizer Ella Baker (1903–1986; see entry) in 1960. In those workshops the women taught young activists the leadership skills necessary to coordinate school desegregation and voter registration drives.

## Joins forces with Martin Luther King Jr.

In 1961, fearing a cut-off in funding for his organization, Myles Horton transferred stewardship of the citizenship schools program to the Southern Christian Leadership Conference (SCLC; a civil rights organization of black ministers led by Martin Luther King Jr. [1929–1968; see entry]). Clark also made the switch to the SCLC at that time. At the age of sixty-three, Clark became the SCLC's director of education and teaching and the first woman to sit on the SCLC's executive board.

Under the sponsorship of the SCLC, the citizenship schools provided instruction in literacy, constitutional rights, tactics for creating social change, and voter registration. Participants learned how to rally their communities to demand improvements in schools, roads, and neighborhoods.

By the end of 1963 the citizenship schools program had begun to falter. "Many states are losing their citizenship schools because there is no one to do follow-up work," Clark wrote in a letter to King. "I'm the only paid staff worker doing field visitation.... Direct action is so glamorous and packed with emotion that most young people prefer demonstrations over genuine education."

Clark stayed with the SCLC through June 1970. After the passage of the Voting Rights Act of 1965, which removed the remaining obstacles to voter registration by African Americans, Clark conducted crash courses in voter registration. In a twenty-minute session she could teach people how to sign their names on registration forms. Waiting cars would then take participants to the courthouse. From May through August

1965, Clark and her staff helped more than 7,000 African Americans in Alabama become registered voters.

## Continues the struggle for civil rights

After Clark left the SCLC, she joined the staff of the American Field Service (AFS), a service organization that raised scholarship funds for underprivileged youths and established daycare centers. In 1976 Clark was elected to the school board in Charleston, South Carolina—the district from which she had been fired two decades earlier. At the age of seventy-eight, Clark became the first black woman ever to sit on the Charleston School Board.

In her later years Clark was the recipient of numerous honors and awards. In 1976 she won the Race Relations Award from the National Education Association. She was awarded an honorary doctorate degree from the College of Charleston in 1978. The following year President Jimmy Carter (1924– ) presented Clark with a "Living the Legacy" Award.

"If I were young again, starting all over, I'd do the same things over and over again," wrote Clark in her autobiography *Ready from Within*. "I don't think my ideas would change.... I have been oppressed, and so I am always going to have a vote for the oppressed, regardless of whether that oppressed is black or white or yellow or the people of the Middle East ... I feel that I have grown old with dreams that I want to come true, and that I have grown old believing there is always a beautiful lining to that cloud that overshadows things."

## Sources
### Books

Branch, Taylor. *Parting the Waters: America in the King Years 1954–63.* New York: Touchstone, 1988.

Clark, Septima Poinsette, and Cynthia Stokes Brown. *Ready from Within: Septima Clark and the Civil Rights Movement.* Navarro, CA: Wild Trees Press, 1986.

Clark, Septima Poinsette, and LeGette Blythe. *Echo in My Soul.* New York: E. P. Dutton and Co., Inc., 1962.

McFadden, Grace Jordan. "Septima P. Clark and the Struggle for Human Rights," in *Women in the Civil Rights Movement: Trailblazers and Torchbearers, 1941–1965,* edited by Vicki L. Crawford, Jacqueline

Anne Rouse, and Barbara Woods. Brooklyn, NY: Carlson Publishing, Inc., 1990.

Levy, Peter B. *The Civil Rights Movement.* Westwood, CT: Greenwood Press, 1998.

Olendorf, Sandra B. "The South Carolina Sea Island Citizenship Schools, 1957–1961," in *Women in the Civil Rights Movement: Trailblazers and Torchbearers, 1941–1956,* edited by Vicki L. Crawford, Jacqueline Anne Rouse, and Barbara Woods. Brooklyn, NY: Carlson Publishing Inc., 1990, p. 180.

Payne, Charles. *I've Got the Light of Freedom: The Organizing Tradition and the Mississippi Freedom Struggle.* Berkeley: University of California Press, 1995.

Salmond, John A. *My Mind Set on Freedom: A History of the Civil Rights Movement, 1954–1968.* Chicago: Ivan R. Dee, 1997.

# Rodolfo "Corky" Gonzales

**Born June 18, 1929**
**Denver, Colorado**

**Chicano rights activist, poet, and playwright**

Rodolfo "Corky" Gonzales founded the Crusade for Justice and cofounded the La Raza Unida political party.

Rodolfo "Corky" Gonzales was a leader of the Chicano rights movement in the 1960s and 1970s. ("Chicano" is a name that American youth of Mexican heritage created for themselves. The term is loosely based on an Aztec [ancient tribe of Mexican Indians] word, "Meshicano." For young Mexican Americans, the name "Chicano" represented their pride in their cultural heritage.)

Gonzales first worked to assist Chicano youth in his hometown of Denver, Colorado, through government-sponsored social programs. In 1965 he founded Crusade for Justice, a Chicano-rights organization that protested police brutality and discrimination in public schools. In the early 1970s Gonzales participated in the formation of La Raza Unida, a national political party for Mexican Americans. Gonzales is also famous for writing the epic poem *I am Joaquín*, which is considered the anthem of the Chicano rights movement.

## Migrant worker to famous boxer

Gonzales was born in a barrio (Hispanic neighborhood) of Denver in 1929, to a family of migrant farm workers.

In the fall and winter Gonzales attended public school in Denver, and in the spring and summer he worked alongside his family in the sugar beet fields of Colorado.

While in high school, Gonzales discovered that he had a talent for boxing. He earned money in prizefights, which was his way out of working in the fields. As a teenager Gonzales captured the Golden Gloves title, and at the age of eighteen he became a professional boxer. After winning sixty-five of his seventy-five matches, Gonzales retired from boxing in 1955. He later became an owner-operator of a neighborhood bar and a bail bondsman.

## Rises in Democratic Party ranks

In the late 1950s Gonzales became involved in local Democratic Party politics. He rose quickly within the ranks of the Democratic Party. In 1957 he was elected the precinct captain of the Denver Democratic Party, becoming the first Mexican American ever to hold that position. In 1960 Gonzales directed John F. Kennedy's (1917–1963) successful presidential campaign in Colorado.

## Directs "War on Poverty" youth programs

From 1964 until 1966 Gonzales served as director of Denver's War on Poverty youth programs. (The War on Poverty was a set of social programs intended to provide economic opportunities to the nation's poorest citizens, initiated by Democratic president Lyndon B. Johnson [1908–1973].) While working for the War on Poverty, Gonzales witnessed the corruption of government officials, the discrimination against Mexican Americans in government programs, and the under-representation of Hispanics in government agencies.

In 1966, thoroughly disillusioned, Gonzales left his job and withdrew his membership from the Democratic Party. "I became disenchanted with the electoral system and disenchanted with the two political parties," stated Gonzales in a 1984 interview. "And I recognized in my character that I could not compromise."

## Founds Crusade for Justice

Gonzales's next project was founding the Crusade for Justice—an independent, grassroots organization that pro-

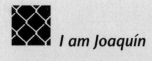

## I am Joaquín

In 1967 Gonzales wrote the epic poem entitled *I am Joaquín,* which is widely regarded as the anthem of the Chicano rights movement. Joaquín, a common Mexican name, was routinely used by police officers to refer to Chicanos whose real names they did not know. In the poem, Joaquín—who is representative of every Mexican American—traces the history of the ancient Aztecs, Mexicans, and Mexican Americans.

"Writing *I am Joaquín* was a journey back through history," wrote Gonzales in his introduction to the poem, "a painful self-evaluation, a wandering search for my peoples and, most of all, for my own identity. The totality of all social inequities and injustice had to come to the surface.... *I am Joaquín* was written as a revelation of myself and of all Chicanos who are Joaquín."

"I am Joaquín," reads the poem, "Lost in a world of confusion, caught up in a whirl of a gringo society. Confused by the rules, scorned by attitudes, suppressed by manipulations, and destroyed by a modern society ... I am Joaquín. The odds are great but my spirit is strong, my faith unbreakable. ... I SHALL ENDURE! I WILL ENDURE!"

*I am Joaquín* was published in both Spanish and English. It was recited at demonstrations, performed by theater troupes, and even made into a film. *I am Joaquín* embraced the essence of Chicano nationalism and inspired a spiritual and cultural awakening within a generation of Mexican Americans.

vided Chicanos with social services, leadership education, and cultural programs. The Crusade also sought to protect Chicanos from police abuses and opposed anti-Chicano discrimination in Denver's schools, jails, and welfare system. Through the Crusade, Gonzales attempted to instill in Chicanos a sense of political and economic self-determination, as well as ethnic pride.

In the latter half of the 1960s Gonzales published the *El Gallo: La Voz de la Justicia* (pronounced el GUY-yo: la vose day la hoo-stee-see-a; translated as "the rooster: the voice of justice"), a Spanish-language newspaper. He also wrote two plays: *The Revolutionist* and *A Cross for Maclovio.*

## Builds school

In 1968 Gonzales purchased a school and church building, which he converted into the Crusade's headquarters. Gonzales partitioned the space into a school, a theater, a gymnasium, a nursery, a bookstore, and a cultural center. The school, which included kindergarten through twelfth grade, was called Tlatelolco after the ancient Aztec city near present-day Mexico City. The Tlatelolco School offered courses in Mexican history and culture in addition to the standard academic subjects.

## Sponsors National Chicano Youth Liberation Conference

In March 1969 the Crusade for Justice sponsored a five-day gathering entitled the National Chicano Youth Liberation Conference. Just a few days before the conference, hundreds of Denver high school students had walked out of their classes. This was one of a series of uprisings by Chicano students throughout the Southwest. The student protests were in response to discrimination against Mexican Americans in public schools.

Among the students' complaints were that the schools forbade Spanish-speaking and did not teach Mexican history. School counselors directed Chicano students into vocational classes, while they advised white students to take college preparatory classes. (In March 1968 Denver students had staged a three-day walkout in response to one teacher's racist remarks; Gonzales was among the twenty-five people arrested in demonstrations.)

More than 1,500 young Chicanos from all over the United States gathered for the conference. They attended workshops on civil rights issues and cultural topics, such as Mexican poetry, literature, song, dance, and theater. They also tried to define what it meant to be Chicano within the larger context of American society. The conference attendees concluded that although the dominant society treated them as foreigners, the United States was their home. The Crusade for Justice sponsored a subsequent National Chicano Youth Liberation Conference in 1970.

## The Poor People's March on Washington

Shortly before his death, Martin Luther King Jr. (1929–1968; see entry) had begun organizing a Poor People's March to be held in the spring of 1968. King hoped to draw thousands of poor people of all races to the nation's capital, where they would set up a tent city and lobby legislators for programs that would expand economic opportunity. After King's assassination, the march continued under the leadership of his aides Reverend Ralph Abernathy (1926–1990) and Reverend Jesse Jackson (1941– ).

King had invited Gonzales to co-chair the Mexican American contingent of the march along with New Mexico land reclamation activist Reies López Tijerina (pronounced RAY-ayes LO-pez Tee-hay-REE-nah; 1926– ). "Where are we going?" asked Gonzales at the start of the march. "We're going to try and fulfill Dr. Martin Luther King's dream, and if we Mexican Americans march to Washington, it is to tell this country that poverty is not a Negro problem. Poverty is a Mexican American problem; poverty is an American Indian problem; poverty is a Puerto Rican problem; poverty is an Appalachian problem."

In Washington, D.C., Gonzales unveiled his "Plan of the Barrio." This document called for greater educational, employment, and housing opportunities for Mexican Americans, as well as the return of stolen lands in the Southwest to their rightful Mexican American owners.

## Cofounds La Raza Unida

In late 1969 Chicano activists in Crystal City, Texas, founded the La Raza Unida (pronounced la RAHssa oonEEda; translated as "The People United") political party, which was comprised of and devoted to Mexican Americans. In early 1970 Gonzales established a chapter of La Raza Unida in Colorado. Like other Chicano activists, he had come to the conclusion that neither the Democratic Party nor the Republican Party could be counted on to act in the interest of Hispanics. "The two-party system," commented Gonzales, "is one animal with two heads eating out of the same trough."

The primary mission of the La Raza Unida Party was to bring relief to working-class Mexican Americans. La Raza's platform called for bilingual education, the regulation of public utilities (to prevent gas and electricity companies from sticking consumers with sharp price increases), farm subsidies, and a tax structure that favored low-income people. Party activists registered large numbers of Mexican Americans to vote.

Gonzales organized a national convention of the La Raza Unida Party in El Paso, Texas, in September 1972 (a presidential election year). More than 3,000 delegates attended from the sixteen states with party chapters. La Raza established itself as an independent party, choosing not to endorse presidential candidates from either of the two major parties. Gonzales vied for the position of national chair of La Raza with Crystal City organizer José Angel Gutiérrez, and lost.

In the two years following the national convention, La Raza Unida went into decline. By 1974 the only location in which La Raza Unida candidates held office was Crystal City. Many people who had begun their political careers in La Raza Unida went on to become active in the Democratic or Republican Party.

## Continues to work with Chicano youth

After the La Raza convention, Gonzales recommitted his energies to working with Denver's Chicano youth. He also became an active supporter of the United Farm Workers union (for more information, see César Chávez, Dolores Huerta, and Philip Vera Cruz entries).

In the late 1970s—while continuing as head of Crusade for Justice—Gonzales returned to his old passion, boxing. He assisted in the training of amateur and professional boxers. In 1987 Gonzales was severely injured in an automobile crash. Since that time, he has been forced to slow the pace of his civil rights activities. Gonzales continues to reside in Denver.

## Sources

### Books

Gonzales, Rodolfo. *I Am Joaquín/Yo Soy Joaquín.* New York: Bantam Books, 1972.

Martinez, Elizabeth Sutherland, and Enriqueta Longeaux y Vásquez. *Viva la Raza!: The Struggle of the Mexican-American People.* Garden City, NY: Doubleday and Company, Inc., 1974.

Nagel, Rob, and Sharon Rose, eds. *Hispanic American Biography,* Vol. 1. Detroit: U•X•L, 1995, pp. 94–97.

Rosales, F. Arturo. *Chicano! The History of the Mexican American Civil Rights Movement.* Houston, TX: Arte Público Press, 1997.

Sigler, Jay A., ed. *Civil Rights in America: 1500 to the Present.* Detroit: Gale Research Inc., 1998.

Steiner, Stan. *La Raza: The Mexican-Americans.* New York: Harper & Row, 1969.

## Web Sites

Biographies: Rodolfo Gonzales. Chicano! [Online] Available http://www.pbs.orb/chicano/bios/gonzales.html (last accessed on February 7, 1999).

Partido Nacional de La Raza Unida. "A Brief History of La Raza Unida." [Online] Available http://members.tripod.com/~larazaunida/hist.htm (last accessed February 7, 1999).

## Other

*Chicano! The History of the Mexican American Civil Rights Movement* (four episodes; videocassette). Los Angeles: NLCC Educational Media, 1996.

# Fannie Lou Hamer

**Born October 6, 1917**
**Montgomery County, Mississippi**
**Died March 14, 1977**
**Ruleville, Mississippi**

**African American voter registration worker with the Student Nonviolent Coordinating Committee and cofounder of the Mississippi Freedom Democratic Party**

"I'm sick and tired of being sick and tired."

Fannie Lou Hamer was a heroine in the struggle for civil rights in Mississippi. To engage in any type of civil rights activity in Mississippi took tremendous courage. Prior to and during the civil rights movement, Mississippi was nicknamed the "closed society" because it was undeniably the most segregated state in the union.

For most of her life Hamer toiled in the cotton fields of Sunflower County. When Hamer was forty-four years old, she came in contact with student civil rights activists at a voter registration meeting. Hamer, who had previously been unaware she was legally entitled to vote, went to the courthouse the very next day and attempted to register. Although she lost her home and job because of that gesture, Hamer refused to be intimidated. She entered the voter registration campaign with enthusiasm. After a lifetime of hardship, disempowerment, and resentment, Hamer felt she had little to lose.

Virtually overnight, Hamer became one of the civil rights movement's most tenacious warriors. She attained legendary status for her courage, her commitment to the rights of African Americans and poor people of all colors, and her booming voice with which she belted out inspirational hymns, freedom songs, and emphatic speeches. Hamer eventually became known as the "angriest woman in Mississippi." Her oft-repeated statement—"I'm sick and tired of being sick and tired"—reflected southern blacks' frustration with the lack of racial justice in America.

## A childhood of work and poverty

Hamer was born Fannie Lou Townsend in hilly Montgomery County, Mississippi, the youngest of twenty children born to sharecropper parents. (Sharecropping is a system of farming in which a landless farmer works a plot of land and in return gives the landowner a share of the crop.) After the family paid the plantation owner for housing, supplies, and any food they could not grow themselves (such as flour and sugar), they had very little money left over.

At age two, Hamer moved with her family to a plantation in the flat Delta lands of Sunflower County, Mississippi. Shortly thereafter Hamer contracted polio (a crippling viral disease, often affecting children, that can lead to permanent partial paralysis and physical deformities). Her parents could not afford medical care. The disease affected Hamer's leg and, as a result, she walked with a limp the rest of her life.

Hamer had little time to attend school. From the time she was six years old, Hamer worked alongside her parents and siblings in the fields. At the age of thirteen she could pick 300 to 400 pounds of cotton per day. Hamer watched her mother work herself to exhaustion day in and day out, with little to show for it, and came to the conclusion that something was wrong in Mississippi.

Hamer's parents were continually trying to better their condition. Once they saved enough money to buy three mules with which they hoped to start their own farm. A spiteful white neighbor ruined their dream by poisoning the animals; that action plunged the family back into poverty.

## Marries a sharecropper

In 1944 Hamer married a sharecropper and tractor driver named Perry "Pap" Hamer. For the next eighteen years the couple worked on a plantation outside of Ruleville, in Sunflower County. Fannie Lou Hamer was eventually promoted from sharecropper to "time-keeper," a job that entailed keeping track of other workers' hours and informing them when it was starting time, break time, and quitting time.

Hamer had plenty of grievances during that period: her home had no working bathroom; a white doctor had sterilized her (conducted surgery that would prevent her from having children) without her consent; the children of black workers had little opportunity for schooling; and there were few economic opportunities for blacks in Mississippi. Hamer discussed these concerns with her fellow workers, but she did not know how to bring about changes.

## Introduced to civil rights activism

The powerlessness Hamer had felt all her life evaporated on August 30, 1962, when she attended a voter registration meeting of the Student Nonviolent Coordinating Committee (SNCC; pronounced "snick"). The SNCC was an organization of student civil rights activists that emerged out of the early 1960s lunch counter sit-in movement. (In the lunch counter sit-in movement, black students—sometimes joined by white students—would request service at segregated lunch counters. When the students were denied service, they would refuse to leave.) Hamer learned that although blacks had a legal right to vote, only 155 out of the 13,524 blacks living in Sunflower County were actually registered to vote. Inspired by the seriousness and commitment of the young people, Hamer, then forty-four years old, decided to join their effort.

"When they asked for those to raise their hands who'd go down to the courthouse the next day, I raised mine," Hamer recalled. "The only thing they could do to me was kill me, and it seemed like they'd been trying to do that a little bit at a time ever since I could remember."

The day after the meeting, Hamer and seventeen other African Americans rented an old school bus and traveled to the county seat in Indianola to try to register. The entire group failed the literacy test and all were denied registration. (The literacy test had been instituted by the Mississippi legislature in 1890 as a means of keeping blacks from voting. Given only to black applicants, the test required would-be voters to read and/or interpret a section of the state constitution to the satisfaction of the registrar.) On the way back to Ruleville, police pulled the bus over and arrested the driver for the ridiculous charge of operating a bus that was "too yellow" and could be confused with a school bus. The group chipped in to pay the $35 fine so they could continue to Ruleville.

## Suffers retribution, strengthens commitment

In retribution for simply trying to register to vote, Hamer's landlord ordered her to leave her home of eighteen years. Hamer moved into the home of a friend in Ruleville. Ten days later, sixteen shots were fired into the friend's windows in an attempt on Hamer's life.

Hamer was soon hired by the SNCC as a field worker in the voter registration drive. As a result, Hamer's husband lost his house and his job. To "get even" for his wife's activism, the employers in the area refused to hire "Pap" Hamer. The couple moved into a tiny house in Ruleville and were forced to survive on the $10 per week Hamer was paid by the SNCC.

As the SNCC's Sunflower County supervisor, Hamer addressed groups of African Americans about the need to exercise their political power. She helped volunteers prepare to take the literacy test so they could register to vote. Hamer herself took the literacy test two more times before she finally passed and became a registered voter in January 1963. Even then, however, she could not vote because she did not have the money to pay the poll tax (a tax that blacks were required to pay in order to vote. Before casting their votes, black voters had to provide proof that they had paid the tax).

## Beaten in Winona

In 1963, during her return home from a voter registration training workshop in South Carolina, Hamer's bus pulled into a bus station in Winona, Mississippi. While Hamer waited on the bus, five of her companions entered the "whites only" waiting room. Hamer then saw her companions being arrested. When she stepped off the bus to check out the situation, she was also arrested.

The group was taken to the jail, where each member was severely beaten. Hamer was placed in a cell with two black male prisoners who were told by police that they had to give her a beating that would make her "wish she was dead" or face the consequences themselves. The men beat Hamer so badly with a blackjack (a metal ball swung on a chain) that she could not walk and her hands turned blue from the blows they received while protecting her head. That beating left Hamer with permanent kidney damage and vision problems. The beaten civil rights workers were only released when James Bevel and Andrew Young, ministers with the Southern Christian Leadership Conference (SCLC), personally came to the jail demanding to see them.

In a subsequent lawsuit brought by SNCC lawyers against the Winona police, an all-white jury decided that the defendants were not guilty. "We're tired of all this beating," Hamer later said in reference to her Winona experience. "It's been a hundred years [since the end of slavery] and we're still being beaten and shot at, crosses are still being burned, because we want to vote. But I'm going to stay in Mississippi, and if they shoot me down, I'll be buried here."

## The Mississippi Freedom Democratic Party

In the summer of 1964 Hamer cofounded a new political party, called the Mississippi Freedom Democratic Party (MFDP). The MFDP was organized as an official party, according to state law. It functioned as an alternative to the regular Democratic Party, which excluded blacks. MFDP organizers signed up 80,000 members in time for the party's August 6 statewide convention. At the convention, members elected a slate of sixty-eight delegates (four of them whites). Hamer was elected the party's vice-chair. MFDP leaders, claiming their party was much more representative of the people of Mississippi than was the regular Democratic Party, made plans to challenge the Democrats at the national Democratic Party convention later that month.

On August 24 the MFDP delegates arrived at the Democratic Party national convention in Atlantic City, New Jersey. The MFDP declared that it was the legitimate claimant to Mississippi's seats on the convention floor. The MFDP also argued that it, unlike the Democrats, stood behind the national

Democratic Party candidates and platform. (During the years when segregation prevailed, the Democratic Party was the only party with any power in the South. Southern Democrats typically sided with northern Republicans in Congress.)

The convention's credentials committee was authorized to decide which Mississippi delegation to recognize. Numerous MFDP delegates testified before this committee, describing the exclusion of blacks from the political process in Mississippi, as well as the terrible conditions in which blacks were forced to live.

## Offers compelling testimony

Hamer gave the MFDP's most compelling speech. Her address was recorded by the national media and aired later that evening. It would have aired live, but President Lyndon Johnson (1909–1973; served in office from 1963 to 1969) purposely prevented it by calling an impromptu press conference.

Hamer described the hardships of growing up poor and black in Mississippi, her attempts to register to vote, and her beating in Winona. "They beat me and they beat me with the long, flat blackjack," Hamer testified. "I screamed to God in pain. My dress worked itself up. I tried to pull it down. They beat my arms 'til I had no feeling in them."

"If the Freedom Party is not seated now," concluded Hamer, "I question America. Is this America, the land of the free and the home of the brave, where we have to sleep with our telephones off the hooks because our lives be threatened daily, because we want to live as decent human beings in America?"

The credentials committee offered a compromise: the Democrats would be seated; the MFDP would get two "at-large" seats in the convention (they would not represent the state of Mississippi); and the Democrats would have to swear loyalty to the party's presidential nominee as a condition of being seated. The committee ruled that in the future, only delegations not tainted by segregationist practices would be seated at national conventions. The vast majority of the MFDP delegates rejected the compromise. "We didn't come all this way for no two seats when all of us is tired," explained Fannie Lou Hamer.

## Challenges the seating of Mississippi congressmen

In 1964 Hamer ran for Congress in Mississippi's Second congressional District, on the MFDP ticket. Although she received more votes than her white opponent, Congressman Jamie Whitten, the state did not recognize Hamer as the victor. Nor did the state Democratic Party recognize the victories of the other four congressional candidates representing the MFDP.

Hamer and other MFDP members traveled to Washington, D.C., to file an official protest against the exclusionary Mississippi Democratic Party and its all-white congressional delegation. Congress conducted an investigation into the matter but, as expected, ruled in favor of the Democrats. At a demonstration in front of the Capitol building, Hamer said, "We'll come back year after year until we are allowed our rights as citizens."

## Works for educational and economic development

Hamer not only worked for the political enfranchisement of African Americans but also worked to bolster their educational and economic status. Hamer was instrumental in bringing Head Start, an early childhood learning program, to Ruleville. Hamer also helped establish day-care centers and supported an organization that constructed low-income housing.

In 1969 Hamer founded the Freedom Farm Corporation—a 40-acre cooperative farm on which needy families of any race could raise their own food and livestock. In its first year of operation, the Freedom Farm provided food for 1,500 people.

In the late 1960s Hamer fulfilled a long-time ambition and taught a course in contemporary black history at Shaw University in Raleigh, North Carolina. Her classes were packed not only with students but with the students' parents and professors.

**Fannie Lou Hamer (with microphone) speaks to MFDP sympathizers outside the Capitol in Washington, D.C., shortly after Congress refused to recognize several MFDP political victories.**
*Reproduced by permission of AP/Wide World Photos.*

Hamer, who had little formal education, was awarded honorary doctoral degrees from several colleges and universities, including Shaw University, Howard University, Morehouse College in Atlanta, Tougaloo College in Mississippi, and Columbia College in Chicago. In 1965 *Mississippi* magazine named Hamer one of the state's six "women of influence" and in the early 1970s the city of Ruleville began commemorating a Fannie Lou Hamer Day.

Hamer continued working for black people's economic and political rights until her death of breast cancer in 1977. Reflecting on Hamer's life, Washington, D.C., congressional representative and activist Eleanor Holmes Norton stated that Hamer "had a singular capacity to impart courage and to chase timidity. She was a mixture of strength, humor, love, and determined honesty. She did not know the meaning of self-pity."

## Sources

### Books

*African American Biography.* Vol. 2. Detroit: U•X•L, 1994, pp. 307–09.

Altman, Susan. *The Encyclopedia of African-American Heritage.* New York: Facts on File, Inc., 1997, pp. 107–8.

Crawford, Vicki L., Jacqueline Anne Rouse, and Barbara Woods, eds. *Women in the Civil Rights Movement: Trailblazers and Torchbearers, 1941–1965.* Brooklyn, NY: Carlson Publishing, Inc., 1990.

Giddings, Paula. *When and Where I Enter: The Impact of Black Women on Race and Sex in America.* New York: Bantam Books, 1984.

Kling, Susan. *Fannie Lou Hamer: A Biography.* Chicago: Women for Racial and Economic Equality, 1979.

Mills, Kay. *This Little Light of Mine: The Life of Fannie Lou Hamer.* New York: Dutton, 1993.

Smallwood, David, et al. *Profiles of Great African Americans.* Lincolnwood, IL: Publications International, Ltd., 1996, pp. 86–87.

Smith, Sande, ed. *Who's Who in African-American History.* New York: Smithmark, 1994.

# Harry Hay

**April 7, 1912**
**Worthing, Sussex, England**

**English-born American gay rights activist**

Harry Hay began working for gay rights two decades before the Stonewall Rebellion—the 1969 event that most people consider the start of the gay liberation movement in America. An organizer, writer, actor, and philosopher, Hay has forged a radical path in defiance of reactionary forces (people and institutions that work to forestall social change). He stood up for the rights of gay people during the McCarthy era in the 1950s; counseled gay draft resisters during the Vietnam War in the 1960s; and argued for creativity and radicalism within the mainstream gay rights movement in the 1990s. Now approaching ninety years of age, Hay still plays an active role the gay liberation movement and in other campaigns for social change.

Harry Hay founded the first organization of the modern gay liberation movement.

## Childhood years

Hay was born in 1912 in the seaside town of Worthing in Sussex, England. His parents were American citizens living abroad. In 1914 the family moved to Chile, where Hay's father (Harry Hay Sr.) was working as a manager at the Anaconda Copper Mine. The family returned to Orange County, Califor-

Portrait: Reproduced by permission of Daniel Nicoletta.

nia, in 1916, following an accident in which Harry Sr., was badly injured. The family moved to Los Angeles in 1919.

Hay's main childhood interests were music and horse-back riding. He had developed a love of music in Chile, where he listened to villagers singing hymns to the Sun, and later studied classical music in Los Angeles. From age eleven to thirteen Hay learned to ride horses with an organization called the Woodcraft Rangers Boys' Group. Hay spent the summers of his teenage years working in the agricultural fields of Nevada.

Hay attended Los Angeles High School and graduated with honors in 1929. He then went to work as an apprentice for a local lawyer. It was during this period that Hay admitted to himself his homosexual leanings (sexual attraction to members of one's own gender). He did not share those feelings with anyone at that time, out of a fear of being ostracized (excluded or banished).

"Ostracism means you don't exist at all," Hay stated in a 1998 interview with Anne-Marie Cusac of *The Progressive*. "And that's a very difficult situation to live with. As gay people, we had been chasing ostracism at that point for probably 300 years. You just knew that you should have dropped into your black hole."

## Supports workers' rights during Depression

Hay enrolled in Stanford University's independent study program in 1930, concentrating on poetry and drama. He also sang in the university glee club. In 1931 Hay "came out" to his friends, announcing he was gay. While many people distanced themselves from Hay after his announcement, a core group of friends stayed with him. Hay left school in 1932 after his studies were disrupted by a severe sinus infection.

In 1933, at the height of the Great Depression, Hay started using his acting talents to promote workers' rights. (Lasting from 1929 to 1939, the Great Depression was the worst economic crisis in the history of the United States; unemployment during that time was extremely high.) He joined a street theater troupe and performed on picket lines and at labor demonstrations in support of fair treatment and reasonable wages for workers. Hay's experiences during that time set him on a lifelong course of social activism.

## Works with the Communist Party

Hay's labor-rights work brought him into contact with the Communist Party, one of the leading organizations promoting unionism, cultural expression, and civil rights in the 1930s. (Communism is a system of government in which a single authoritarian political party has control. Under this system, there is no private property and the state controls manufacturing and industry.) Hay worked with the Communist Party from 1933 to 1948, directing plays with pro-union themes at the party's New Theater League in New York City and teaching a course entitled "The Historical Development of Folk Music" at the Southern California Labor School and at the People's Educational Center in Hollywood, California. Hay became something of an expert in folk music—an important element of the labor movement in the 1930s and 1940s—counting among his friends such legendary folksingers as Woody Guthrie and Pete Seeger.

Hay kept his homosexuality secret during his years with the Communist Party because of the party's antigay stance. He even adopted a heterosexual (sexual attraction to members of the opposite gender) lifestyle by marrying another party member, Anita Platky, and raising two adopted daughters with her. The couple's marriage lasted thirteen years.

## Founds the Mattachine Society

In 1948 Hay realized that he could no longer ignore his homosexuality. One night, while drinking beer with several gay friends at the University of Southern California, he engaged the group in a discussion about the need to form a gay rights organization. The group would both support the presidency of Progressive Party candidate Henry Wallace and fight back against the rising tide of antihomosexual action during the McCarthy era. (Senator Joseph McCarthy [1909–1957] spearheaded a series of investigations—later commonly referred to as "witch-hunts"—from 1950 to 1954 to rid government, educational institutions, and entertainment industries, as well as prohibit immigration, of anyone considered "subversive" [generally meaning communist or homosexual]. Hay was called to testify before McCarthy's House Un-American Activities Committee [HUAC] in 1955.)

The morning after the gathering, Hay found that he was the only one of his friends who was serious about forming such a group. It took him two years to convince anyone to join him in his effort. In 1950 Hay and four friends formed an organization to advocate for the civil liberties and human rights of gay people called the International Bachelors Fraternal Order for Peace and Social Dignity. It was a secret organization because members feared that if they were found out they would lose their jobs.

In 1951 the organization's name was changed to the Mattachine Society. The name "Mattachine" was taken from a medieval fraternity of French monks who performed prohibited fertility songs and dances. By some accounts, the Mattachines also expressed unpopular ideas while wearing masks. "The Mattachine troupes conveyed vital information to the oppressed in the countryside of thirteenth-to-fifteenth century France," stated Hay in *Outstanding Lives*. "I hoped that such a society of modern homosexual men, living in disguise in twentieth century America, could do similarly for us oppressed Queers." ("Queer" is a name used by some homosexuals to describe themselves.)

The Mattachine Society was founded two decades before the Stonewall Rebellion, the June 1969 event typically considered the start of the gay rights movement. (The Stonewall Rebellion was a two-day-long riot in Greenwich Village, New York City, by thousands of lesbians and gay men in response to a police raid on a gay bar. The rebellion helped lay the groundwork for the gay liberation movement of 1970s.)

## Mattachine Society achieves victory

The Mattachine Society achieved its first victory in February 1952 by securing the acquittal of a founding member, Dale Jennings, on charges of "lewd and dissolute behavior." (During that time, undercover police officers commonly tricked men they suspected of being gay into committing illegal sexual acts, then arrested them, as a form of harassment.) The Jennings case was the first time that a gay man had fought those charges—all the others had paid fines to avoid publicity. Mattachine lawyers caught the arresting police officer in a lie and uncovered a case of jury tampering. Once it became known that the Mattachine Society could defend its members

from false charges, membership in the society grew from a few hundred to a few thousand within a single year.

As a leader of the Mattachine Society (and even after his affiliation with the society ended), Hay wrote and spoke extensively on gay rights; organized protests, conferences, and workshops; and established society chapters around the country.

## Explores roots of gay identity

In the 1950s Hay researched the historical roots of gay identity and consciousness. He also helped found the Mattachine Society's *ONE Institute Quarterly of Homophile Studies*, the first gay/lesbian scholarly journal in the United States. In 1958 Hay published "The Moral Climate of Canaan in the Time of Judges" in the *ONE Institute Quarterly*. His article was an exploration of gay consciousness as exhibited by the mother-goddess religious beliefs of Canaanites (pronounced KAY-nan-ites; the ancient inhabitants of the Middle East).

**The actions of activists such as Harry Hay have led to the formation of numerous gay rights organizations. Here Anne Maguire (center) speaks at a rally for the Irish Lesbian and Gay Organization.**
*Photo by Marty Lederhandler. Reproduced by permission of AP/Wide World Photos.*

## Draft resistance, Native American rights, and gay consciousness

In 1963 Hay met his life partner, John Burnside, inventor of the teleidoscope (a tool that projects patterns of light, like those made by a kaleidoscope, onto a wall or other surface). Hay and Burnside established the Circle of Loving Campanions in 1965, a support group and consciousness-raising society for gay men and lesbians. Also in the mid-1960s, during the height of the Vietnam War (1954–75), Hay and a colleague named Don Slater set up draft resistance counseling centers for gay men throughout California.

Hay moved to New Mexico with Burnside in 1970 to establish a teleidoscope factory in a small Tewa Indian town. At the same time, Hay founded a chapter of Circle of Loving Companions at the University of New Mexico.

Hay's activism expanded beyond gay-rights concerns during the 1970s. He worked with the Committee for Traditional Indian Land and Life to protect Native American rights. Hay also participated in the successful mission of the Nationwide Friends of the Rio Grande to prevent developers from putting up structures, thereby reducing the water available to farmers for irrigation.

## Founds Radical Faeries

In 1979 Hay and Burnside moved to Los Angeles and sponsored a "Spiritual Conference for Radical Faeries." More than 200 gay men attended the Labor Day weekend gathering, at which they discussed "breakthroughs in gay consciousness." The establishment of the Radical Faeries signaled a new stage in the evolution of the gay liberation movement. It was the first organization in which gay men fully embraced and celebrated their sexuality and explored the spiritual significance of homosexuality.

## Continues activism

In 1995, at the age of eighty-three, Hay attended the twenty-fifth anniversary of the Stonewall Rebellion in New York City. Dismayed by the "mainstream" tendencies dominating the modern gay rights movement (especially the emphases on professionalism, fundraising, and middle-class values), Hay led a splinter group of about 70,000 people from the Radical Faeries, ACT-UP (AIDS Coalition to Unleash Power; a militant organization that support the rights of people with AIDS and demands increased funding to combat the disease), the American Civil Liberties Union (ACLU), and others, on a march to Central Park.

In 1996 Hay published a collection of essays and political speeches entitled *Radically Gay: Gay Liberation in the Words of Its Founder*. In his book Hay made the argument that gays are a cultural minority, with a shared history and common values. He also stressed the importance of self-acceptance for gay men and lesbians and attacked the growing antigay sentiment in the United States.

Hay continues to speak out, especially regarding the dangers posed to the liberties of gay people by conservative lawmakers and evangelists. "If [a gay person] is very visible, the Christian fundamentalists find you full of sin, don't they?" Hay asked in his 1998 interview with *The Progressive*. "And they will brand you full of sin. If anything goes wrong in the country, it's your fault. It's God's will. And don't forget that God is tremendously important in this picture. It's been used before ... it was used in Germany. It's what the Nazis did.... Give yourself permission to enjoy being gay.... Give yourself permission to be free."

## Sources

### Books

Adam, Barry D. *The Rise of a Gay and Lesbian Movement.* Boston: Twayne Publishers, 1987.

Brelin, Christa, and Michael J. Tyrkus, eds. *Outstanding Lives: Profiles of Lesbians and Gay Men.* Detroit: Visible Ink Press, 1997, pp. 172–78.

Hay, Harry. *Radically Gay: Gay Liberation in the Words of Its Founder.* Boston: Beacon Press, 1996.

Katz, Jonathan. *Gay American History: Lesbians and Gay Men in the U.S.A.* New York: Harper and Row Publishers, 1976.

Newton, David E. *Gay and Lesbian Rights: A Reference Handbook.* Santa Barbara, CA: ABC-CLIO, 1994.

### Periodicals

Cusac, Anne-Marie. "Harry Hay" (interview). *The Progressive.* September 1998: 19+.

Cusac, Anne-Marie. "Radically Gay" (book review). *The Progressive*. January 1997: 34+.

"Radically Gay: Gay Liberation in the Words of Its Founder" (book review). *Publishers Weekly*. May 13, 1996: 66.

Rothschild, Matthew. "A Hero of Ours." *The Progressive*. September 1998: 4.

# Myles Horton

**Born July 5, 1905**
**Savannah, Tennessee**
**Died January 19, 1990**
**New Market, Tennessee**

**African American educator, civil**
**rights activist, and labor activist**

**M**yles Horton believed that all individuals possessed the power to improve their condition and make the world a better place for all. He also believed that experiential, student-led learning was the key to unlocking an individuals' true potential. Horton put his beliefs into practice at the Highlander Folk School (later renamed the Highlander Research and Education Center), which he founded and directed for nearly sixty years.

Highlander, nestled in the mountains of Tennessee, was racially integrated from its inception, making the facility a one-of-a-kind institution in the pre-civil rights era. Highlander first served as a training institute for union activists and an educational and community center for the impoverished residents of the Appalachian Mountains. In the early 1950s, when the rumblings of discontent over racial injustice were beginning to intensify, Highlander shifted its emphasis to school desegregation and voting rights.

Under Horton's direction, the Highlander school helped thousands of people develop the skills and confidence needed to challenge segregation laws. Many of the people

"I think that people aren't fully free until they're in a struggle for justice. And that means for everyone. It's a struggle of such importance that they are willing, if necessary, to die for it."

trained at Highlander, including Martin Luther King Jr. (1929–1968; see entry), Rosa Parks (1913– ; see box in this entry), Fannie Lou Hamer (1917–1977; see entry), and John Lewis (1940– ; see entry), went on to play key roles in the civil rights movement.

## Childhood and education

Horton was born in Savannah, Tennessee, in 1905. Both of his parents worked as teachers, and his father also worked at a variety of jobs such as sharecropping and selling insurance. (Sharecropping is a system of farming in which a landless farmer works a plot of land and in return gives the landowner a share of the crop.) Horton's father was also a prolific storyteller—a trait that he passed on to Myles. Myles's mother instilled in her son one of his most important lifelong values: "Love your neighbor, that's all it's all about."

After high school Horton enrolled in Cumberland College in Lebanon, Tennessee. As a freshman Horton led a student protest against fraternity members' tradition of hazing first-year students. In the summer of 1927, following his junior year, Horton taught Bible school for the Presbyterian Church in the impoverished mountain community of Ozone, Tennessee. That experience was critical in Horton's development, setting him on his lifelong path of adult education. During his senior year, Horton joined the student Young Men's Christian Association (Y.M.C.A.) and attempted to open the segregated organization to people of all races.

## Heads North to continue education

After graduating from Cumberland in 1928, Horton went on to the Union Theological Seminary in New York City, at the time a hotbed of radicalism. There Horton was exposed to the philosophy of nonviolence taught by Indian independence leader Mohandas Gandhi (1869–1948). He also learned about the roots of economic inequality from the writings of German economist and philosopher Karl Marx (1818–1883). During this time Horton joined the Fellowship of Reconciliation, an organization rooted in pacifism (the rejection of all forms of violence) and antiracism.

Horton left the Union Theological Seminary in 1930, then spent a year studying at the University of Chicago. At the university he met Jane Addams (1860–1935), a women's rights advocate and founder of Hull House, a settlement house and community center for poor immigrant workers located in the slums of Chicago. At Addams's urging, Horton traveled to Denmark to study the folk school movement. The Danish folk schools highlighted the influence of common people on world history and culture. Horton then returned to Tennessee, intent on founding a folk school in his home state.

## Founds the Highlander Folk School

In 1932 Horton established the Highlander Folk School in the Appalachian Mountains near Monteagle, Tennessee. Dr. Lillian Johnson, a leader in the movement for women's voting rights and a member of a wealthy Memphis banking family, donated the school building and the land on which it sat. A group of Horton's former professors provided the school's start-up money. The word "Highlander" was a nickname by which residents of the Appalachian Mountains were known.

One of Highlander's original missions was to provide leadership training for union activists and oppressed workers from Appalachia, particularly coal miners, timber cutters, and textile workers. The school offered workshops, cosponsored by the Congress of Industrial Organization (CIO; a federation of labor organizations that later merged with the American Federation of Labor), on labor history, economics, workers' rights, race relations, and organizing strategies. The sessions were informal and directed by the students. This type of education—what Horton termed "experiential learning"—was intended to give students the practical skills they needed to deal with real-life situations.

Highlander also served as a school for adults from the surrounding impoverished region and a community center. Four nights a week there were classes on psychology, current events, geography, and political science. Highlander offered an extensive lending library, square dances, free music lessons for children, a nursery school, a community cannery, and a quilting cooperative.

In 1935 Horton married Zilphia Johnson (thereafter known as Zilphia Horton), a musician from Arkansas who had joined the Highlander staff. Zilphia served as the school community relations director. She was also in charge of the school's music and drama programs and helped coordinate worker support and education. Zilphia, together with folk musicians Pete Seeger, Frank Hamilton, and Guy Carawan, is credited with adapting an old Negro spiritual into "We Shall Overcome"—the song that became the anthem of the civil rights movement.

## Highlander shifts focus to desegregation

In the 1950s Highlander switched its focus from labor education to civil rights and race relations—in particular, the desegregation of southern public schools. "The next great problem is not the problem of conquering poverty, but conquering meanness, prejudice, and tradition," wrote members of the Highlander board at its April 1953 meeting. "Highlander could become the place in which this is studied, a place where one could learn the art of practice and methods of brotherhood. The new emphasis at Highlander should be on the desegregation of the public schools in the South."

Horton explained the timing of Highlander's shift to civil rights in his autobiography, *The Long Haul*. "You try to anticipate a social movement," wrote Horton, "and if it turns out that you've guessed right, then you'll be on the inside of a movement helping with the mobilization and strategies, instead of on the outside jumping on the bandwagon and never being an important part of it.... You do things in advance to prepare the groundwork for a larger movement."

Horton approached the task before him from two angles: leadership training and adult education. To accomplish the former, he sponsored workshops for racially mixed groups of students and veteran activists on the philosophy and practice of nonviolence. To reach and recruit adults to the movement, Horton developed an educational model called the "citizenship school."

## Citizenship schools

Citizenship schools were classes for adults that covered such basic skills as reading, writing, and math. Students were also taught how to fill out voter registration applications and drivers' license applications and how to write checks and money orders. The schools were intended not only to boost the voter registration of African Americans but to prepare students to more fully participate in the mainstream of American life. (Blacks were kept from voting throughout the South until 1965 by a variety of legal means, as well as the threat of physical violence. If prospective black voters could not read and write, they had no chance of passing the "literacy test" that was required for voting.)

"We weren't thinking of it primarily as a literacy program," Horton wrote regarding the citizenship schools in his autobiography, "because teaching people to read and write was only one step toward their becoming citizens and social activists. The immediate goal was getting the right to vote. Becoming literate was only a part of a larger process.... Our objective was to help them understand that they could both play a role at home and help change the world."

Highlander not only sponsored citizenship schools at its Monteagle location but in numerous locations throughout the South. Horton hired Septima Clark (1898–1987; see entry), a schoolteacher from Charleston, South Carolina, who had been fired because of her involvement in the National Association for the Advancement of Colored People (NAACP), to direct Highlander's citizenship school program. Clark set up scores of citizenship schools, with local people serving as teachers. Thousands of poor blacks learned to read and write in citizenship school classes held in private homes, country stores, beauty parlors, and even outdoors.

Many citizenship school graduates went on to become civil rights organizers. Rosa Parks, for example, made her stand on a Montgomery bus just seven weeks after returning from Highlander. Fannie Lou Hamer, spokesperson for the Mississippi Freedom Democratic Party, also went through a Highlander citizenship school. And Esau Jenkins, a farmer, bus driver, and father of seven from Johns Island, South Carolina, undertook a school desegregation campaign following his attendance at a citizenship school.

The citizenship schools were widely hailed as the nation's most successful mass-literacy program. Andrew Young (1921– )—civil rights activist and, later, U.S. representative to

## Rosa Parks

Rosa Parks (1913– ) made her legendary refusal to give up her seat on a Montgomery, Alabama, city bus on December 1, 1955. Just seven weeks earlier, Parks, the secretary of the Montgomery branch of the National Association for the Advancement of Colored People (NAACP), had attended a training session at the Highlander Folk School.

"I found out for the first time in my adult life," Parks stated about her experience at Highlander in the video documentary *Eyes on the Prize*, "that this could be a unified society, that there was such a thing as people of differing races and backgrounds meeting together in workshops and living together in peace and harmony. It was a place I was very reluctant to leave."

Park's courageous stand on the bus, and her subsequent arrest, sparked a 382-day bus boycott that led to the desegregation of Montgomery buses and inspired African Americans in many other southern cities to challenge segregation on their buses.

Parks was born in Tuskegee, Alabama, in 1913. When she was two years old her parents separated, and she moved to Montgomery with her mother and brother. Parks was schooled at home until the age of eleven, after which she attended the all-black Montgomery Industrial School for Girls. Parks then studied for a brief time at Alabama State University.

Park's 1955 bus protest was not her first instance of civil rights activism. In the 1930s she had worked to free the Scottsboro Boys, nine young black men falsely accused of raping two white women. And in 1944 Parks had refused to move to the back of a city bus, which resulted in her being forced off the bus. In

the United Nations and mayor of Atlanta—remarked that the citizenship schools had laid the foundation for the entire civil rights movement.

## Highlander comes under attack

Because Highlander was an integrated institution, in defiance of Jim Crow laws, it constantly came under fire from racist groups and conservative lawmakers. (The Jim Crow laws were a network of legislation and customs that dictated the separation of the races on every level of society.) The Ku Klux

**Rosa Parks.** *Photograph by George Dabrowski. Reproduced by permission of Archive Photos.*

In 1957 Parks and her husband Raymond moved to Detroit, Michigan, to escape publicity and find employment. Parks still resides in Detroit, where she is active in community and youth programs.

In 1999 Parks was awarded the Congressional Gold Medal through a bill widely supported by both houses of Congress. Senator Spencer Abraham of Michigan, lead sponsor of the Senate bill, praised Parks for "proving that one woman can make a difference in the lives of many." After receiving the Gold Medal, Parks was invited to speak before a joint session of the Alabama Legislature. In issuing the invitation, Alabama state representative Alvin Holmes acknowledged that "The state of Alabama [where Parks made her courageous 1955 stand] has never given any kind of recognition to Rosa Parks."

1955, when Park's bus protest captured national attention, she was working as a seamstress at Fair Department Store. The publicity around her arrest, however, cost Parks her job.

Klan (KKK) paid many visits to the small school, vandalizing the property, threatening the staff, and spray painting "KKK was here."

In 1957 Senator James O. Eastland, the notorious segregationist from Mississippi and chair of the Senate Internal Security subcommittee, together with Arkansas attorney general Bruce Bennett, embarked on a mission to shut down Highlander. Eastland and Bennett accused Horton of being a communist (Horton admitted to welcoming communists as he did all interested parties, but denied embracing communism himself), and charged that Highlander was operating in violation of segregation laws. In 1957 the Internal Revenue Service acted on those charges by withdrawing Highlander's tax-exempt status.

Shortly thereafter prosecutors from Tennessee, at Eastland's urging, fabricated charges that Highlander was selling alcohol without a license. In 1960 the Tennessee courts ordered that Highlander close its doors. Horton left Monteagle and soon reopened the school in Knoxville, Tennessee, naming it the Highlander Research and Education Center.

## Highlander moves to new location

In 1972 Highlander moved to a new location, a 100-acre farm outside of New Market, Tennessee, overlooking the Great Smoky Mountains National Park. In the 1970s Highlander shifted its focus to environmental concerns (such as nuclear waste and strip mining) and issues of economic justice.

Highlander continues to operate as an educational center for individuals and grassroots organizations. "The center's social concerns," states the Highlander Center World Wide Web page, "include civil rights, community empowerment, cultural diversity, economic democracy, environmental justice, global education, labor rights, leadership training of youth and adults, sexual discrimination and women's rights."

Horton remained a central figure at the Highlander center until his death in January 1990. Throughout his life Horton remained true to the principle he expressed in his autobiography: "I think that people aren't fully free until they're in a struggle for justice," he wrote. "And that means for everyone. It's a struggle of such importance that they are willing, if necessary, to die for it. I think that's what you have to do before you're really free. Then you've got something to live for."

## Sources

### Books

*African American Biography.* Vol. 3. Detroit: U•X•L, 1994, pp. 578–80.

Bledsoe, Thomas. *Or We'll All Hang Separately: The Highlander Idea.* Boston: Beacon Press, 1969.

Egerton, John. *Speak Now against the Day: The Generation before the Civil Rights Movement in the South.* New York: Alfred A. Knopf, 1994.

Horton, Myles, with Judith Kohl and Herbert Kohl. *The Long Haul: An Autobiography*. New York: Doubleday, 1990.

Langston, Donna. "The Women of Highlander," in *Women in the Civil Rights Movement: Trailblazers and Torchbearers, 1941–1965,* edited by Vicki L. Crawford, Jacqueline Anne Rouse, and Barbara Woods. Brooklyn, NY: Carlson Publishing, Inc., 1990, pp. 145–65.

Levy, Peter B. *The Civil Rights Movement*. Westwood, CT: Greenwood Press, 1998.

Williams, Juan. *Eyes on the Prize: America's Civil Rights Years, 1954–1965.* New York: Penguin Books, 1987.

## Periodicals

Isserman, Maurice. "The Long Haul: An Autobiography" (book review). *The Nation*. November 12, 1990: 566+.

Karamargin, C. J. "Senate Oks Top Honor for Parks." *Detroit Free Press*. April 20, 1999: 4B.

"Myles Horton" (obituary). *The Nation*. February 19, 1990: 224.

"Parks Gets Invitation to Alabama." *Detroit Free Press*. April 29, 1999: A1.

## Web Sites

Highlander Center. [Online] Available http://www.beacham.com/carawan/highlander/html (last accessed April 26, 1999).

## Other

*The Adventures of a Radical Hillbilly* (videocassette). New York: WNET/13TV, 1981.

# Dolores Huerta

**Born April 10, 1930**
**Dawson, New Mexico**

**Mexican American labor leader and community organizer**

Dolores Huerta cofounded the United Farm Workers and is currently the union's secretary-treasurer.

**W**hile Dolores Huerta has been involved in many facets of the civil rights movement, she is best known for her role in the United Farm Workers (UFW) union. Since co-founding the UFW with César Chávez (1927–1993; see entry) in 1965, Huerta has acted as the union's chief negotiator, director of the national grape boycott, political strategist, and lobbyist. Even while raising her eleven children, Huerta put in consistently long hours in the fight for farm workers' rights. Undeterred by old age, she continues to serve as secretary-treasurer of the UFW.

## Childhood during the Depression

Huerta was born in 1930 in the small mining town of Dawson, New Mexico. Her parents divorced when she was five years old, and Huerta moved, with her mother and two brothers, to Stockton, California (an agricultural community in the Central San Joaquín Valley).

It was not easy for Huerta's mother to make ends meet, raising three children during the Great Depression (the worst economic crisis ever to hit the United States, lasting from 1929 to 1939). Huerta's mother was forced to work two jobs, at a cannery during the day and at a restaurant at night. Huerta and her siblings were often left in the care of their maternal grandfather, with whom Huerta developed a special bond.

In the 1940s Huerta's mother remarried, and the family bought a restaurant and a hotel. The whole family worked at those establishments and they often offered free food and lodging to farm worker families. Huerta got involved in many youth activities. She joined the Girl Scouts, sang in the church choir, and took violin, piano, and dance lessons.

## Faces discrimination in school

Huerta was an excellent student, but she often faced discrimination because of her Mexican heritage. "When I was in high school I got straight A's in all of my compositions," Huerta stated in a 1974 interview. "I used to be able to write really nice, poetry and everything. But the teacher told me at the end of the year that she couldn't give me an A because she knew that somebody was writing my papers for me. That really discouraged me, because I used to stay up all night and think and try to make every paper different."

Huerta also kept in touch with her father, Juan Fernández. Fernández was a coal miner, migrant worker, and union activist. He earned a college degree while Huerta was a young child, and in 1938 was elected to the state House of Representatives in New Mexico. As an assemblyman he fought for the passage of stronger labor laws. Huerta was inspired by the successes of her father.

## Becomes a community organizer

After completing high school in Stockton, Huerta took an unusual step for a Mexican American woman in those days: she went to college. Huerta graduated with a teaching degree from the University of Pacific's Delta Community College and found a job as an elementary school teacher. Many of Huerta's students, the children of farm workers, came to school hungry and without shoes. After a few months of teaching Huerta left her job to become a community organizer. "I thought I could do more by organizing farm workers," said Huerta, "than by trying to teach their hungry children."

Huerta got involved with the Community Service Organization (CSO), a civil rights organization founded by activist Fred Ross in Los Angeles in 1952. The CSO sponsored voter registration drives, supported the rights of farm workers, and worked to dismantle segregation and end police brutality.

"This [the CSO] was, of course, something I had been looking for all my life," Huerta remarked in a 1997 chronicle of the farm worker movement called *The Fight in the Fields*. "When Fred showed us pictures of people in Los Angeles that had come together, that had organized, that had fought the police and won, that had built health clinics, that had gotten people elected to office, I just felt like I had found a pot of gold!"

## Organizes CSO chapter

In 1955 Huerta cofounded the Stockton chapter of the CSO. She lobbied the local government to make improvements in the barrios (Hispanic neighborhoods), conducted citizenship classes for farm workers (most of whom were Mexican citizens), and registered people to vote.

In 1957 Huerta assisted organizers of the mostly Filipino Agricultural Workers Organizing Committee (AWOC). Working with AWOC convinced her of the need for, and the possibility of organizing, effective farm worker unions.

## Becomes lobbyist

Huerta also served as the CSO's lobbyist in the state capital, Sacramento. (A lobbyist is someone who, representing a certain constituency, attempts to influence lawmakers' decisions.) Huerta's greatest victory as a lobbyist was convincing the legislature to drop citizenship as a requirement for public assistance programs. While working for the CSO, Huerta met fellow CSO organizer César Chávez (1927–1993; see entry).

## Cofounds farm workers' union

In the early 1960s Chávez had tried to convince the CSO to sponsor a union for farm workers. When the CSO refused, Chávez resigned and asked Huerta to join him in organizing their own farm worker union. Huerta, by then a single mother with seven children (she was twice married and divorced), accepted. In 1962 Huerta moved her family to Delano, California. There she and Chávez formed the National Farm Workers Association (NFWA), the predecessor to the United Farm Workers union.

## Concerned with workers' plight

Like Chávez, Huerta had long been concerned with the plight of migrant farm workers. This population of poor, mainly Mexican, workers traveled up and down the San Joaquín Valley, harvesting crops for wealthy growers. The workers toiled long hours under the hot sun. Equipped with only short-handled hoes (six- to twenty-four-inch-long instruments—called *el cortitos* by farm workers—that have since been outlawed), they had to constantly stoop over or kneel.

César Chávez (far left, looking at documents) and Dolores Huerta formed the National Farm Workers Association, the predecessor to the United Farm Workers union. *Reproduced by permission of AP/Wide World Photos.*

In addition to the physical hazards of back-breaking labor, farm workers were exposed to a host of dangerous pesticides. The average life expectancy of a farm worker was forty-nine years in 1965; in comparison, the average life expectancy of a white U.S. citizen was seventy years.

Most farm workers lived in one-room shacks with no heat or running water. In the 1960s farm workers typically earned less than $2,000 per year—barely enough to survive on. Growers often paid the workers less than the promised wage; since most farm workers did not speak English and lived in constant fear of deportation, they were at the growers' mercy.

## Negotiates contracts for grape workers

In 1965 the 1,700 members of the NFWA joined the 600 mostly Filipino workers of the Agricultural Workers Organizing Committee (AWOC) in a strike against the Delano-area grape growers. Within weeks there were 5,000 grape pickers on strike throughout the San Joaquín Valley. The striking workers demanded a living wage, decent housing, and humane working conditions. No one could have predicted that the strike would last five and a half years and ultimately end in victory.

Shortly after the strike began, union organizers initiated a grape boycott, asking the American public not to buy grapes until conditions improved for migrant workers. In the late 1960s Huerta promoted the boycott on the East Coast.

Huerta helped establish UFW chapters in numerous urban areas and recruited local volunteers to promote the grape boycott. People in many cities picketed stores that sold boycotted grapes and pressured supermarkets to stop carrying the products. The boycott won the endorsement of mayors, religious leaders, and labor leaders. Even dock workers in Sweden, England, and France refused to unload California grapes.

By July 1970 growers could no longer deny that the grape boycott was causing them serious economic harm and agreed to come to the bargaining table. As the UFW's chief negotiator, Huerta hammered out contracts with nearly thirty different grape growers. (The NFWA and the AWOC merged to form the UFW in 1966.) More than 40,000 grape workers were covered by contracts guaranteeing $1.80 per hour plus 20 cents for each box of grapes picked; health benefits for workers; the disuse of the toxic pesticides DDT and parathion; seniority for workers who had been on strike; and a hiring hall at which the union could hire new workers.

"I think we brought to the world, the United States anyway, the whole idea of boycotting as a nonviolent tactic," Huerta stated in *Notable Hispanic American Women*. "I think we showed the world that nonviolence can work to make social change."

## A long career with the UFW

Huerta remained Chavez's second-in-command in the UFW for nearly thirty years, until Chavez's death in 1993. Huerta first served as the union's vice president and was later made the secretary-treasurer. She has solicited support for the farm workers' cause from women's groups, religious groups,

## Jesse De La Cruz

Jesse De La Cruz was born to a migrant worker family in Bakersfield, California, in 1919. She grew up moving from one work camp to the next, switching schools every couple of months. Like most migrant children, she lived in poverty and only completed school up to the sixth grade. From the age of ten, when her mother died, De La Cruz and her siblings were raised by their grandmother.

My grandmother would get us together," De La Cruz stated in *The Fight in the Fields,* "and she'd cry with us, because there was nothing to eat. It's a very sad childhood to look back to."

Although De La Cruz had long been angered at the injustices suffered by herself and other farm workers, she could not see any way to make things better. Her life changed one day in 1962 when César Chávez, organizer of the fledgling National Farm Workers Association (NFWA; later became the United Farm Workers), came to her home and asked her to join the union.

At the age of forty-two, after having raised her six children and her adopted niece, De La Cruz became an organizer with the NFWA. She spoke with workers in the fields, convincing them of the need to unionize. When the famous Delano grape strike erupted in 1965, De La Cruz cajoled people not to cross the picket line. "You want to be a slave all your life?" she shouted at strike-breakers. "What has the grower ever done for you?"

**Jesse De La Cruz.** *Reproduced by permission of AP/Wide World Photos.*

De La Cruz was active in the fight to ban the short-handled hoe in 1975. The short-handled hoe, called *el cortito* by farm workers, made people work stooped over or on their knees. Many farm workers experienced chronic excessive back pain as a result of their daily use of *el cortito.*

De La Cruz—who worked ten hours a day for seventeen years with an eight inch hoe—testified at Senate hearings. She invited senators to experience what it felt like to use a short-handled hoe. "Just stand up and hold the tips of your shoes," she told them, "and walk up and down this room and see how many times you can do it."

Hispanic associations, student groups, and peace and justice organizations. Huerta has engaged in fundraising, negotiating, coordinating picket lines, and strategizing for the union.

Together with Chávez, Huerta established the National Farm Workers Service Center, Inc., an institution that provides affordable housing and operates five Spanish-language radio stations. She also helped set up pension and medical plans for UFW members.

Huerta has organized farm workers in support of several political candidates sympathetic to the farm workers' cause. Shortly before his assassination in 1968, presidential candidate Robert Kennedy (1925–1968) acknowledged Huerta's role in his win of the California Democratic primary.

Huerta has testified before numerous state and national panels on the dangers of pesticides. She has also worked for the passage of major pieces of legislation that support poor people, farm workers, and immigrants, such as Aid to Families with Dependent Children and disability and unemployment insurance for farm workers. From 1988 to 1993 Huerta served on the federal government's Commission on Agricultural Workers.

## Victimized by police brutality

Huerta's political activities have landed her in jail more than twenty times, mostly for disregarding injunctions against picketing. In 1988, while protesting the antilabor policies of presidential candidate George Bush (1924– ) in San Francisco, Huerta was beaten by police. She was attempting to comply with police orders to move back when an officer swung his baton at Huerta's abdomen. She sustained several cracked ribs and a ruptured spleen, and had to undergo emergency surgery for the removal of her spleen.

The incident generated national headlines and caused a huge public outcry. Chávez pushed for a full investigation. Footage captured by television cameras clearly showed the police officer assaulting Huerta. Huerta was awarded $825,000 by the city in an out-of-court settlement, and the San Francisco police department was forced to revise its crowd-control tactics. After receiving the money, Huerta joked that she would finally have to open a bank account.

# Honors and appointments

Huerta was inducted into the Women's Hall of Fame in 1993. That same year she received a Medal of Liberty from the American Civil Liberties Union and an Outstanding American Award from the Eugene V. Debs Foundation. She serves as vice president of the California AFL-CIO (American Federation of Labor-Congress of Industrial Organizations) and vice president of the Coalition for Labor Union Women. She is on the board of directors of numerous organizations, including Democratic Socialists of America, Latinas for Choice, Fairness and Accuracy in Reporting (FAIR), and the Center for Voting and Democracy.

# Sources

## Books

Cantarow, Ellen. *Moving the Mountain: Women Working for Social Change.* Old Westbury, NY: The Feminist Press, 1980, pp. 94–151.

Ferriss, Susan, and Ricardo Sandoval. *The Fight in the Fields: César Chávez and the Farmworkers Movement.* New York: Harcourt Brace and Company, 1997.

Griswold del Castillo, Richard, and Arnoldo De León. *North to Aztlán: A History of Mexican Americans in the United States.* New York: Twayne Publishers, 1996.

Griswold del Castillo, Richard, and Richard A. Garcia. *César Chávez: A Triumph of Spirit.* Norman, Oklahoma: University of Oklahoma Press, 1995.

Mirandé, Alfredo, and Evangelina Enríquez. *La Chicana.* Chicago: University of Chicago Press, 1979.

Nagel, Rob, and Sharon Rose, eds. *Hispanic American Biography,* Vol. 1. Detroit: U•X•L, 1995, pp. 106–9.

Rosales, F. Arturo. *Chicano! The History of the Mexican American Civil Rights Movement.* Houston, TX: Arte Público Press, 1997.

## Web Sites

United Farm Workers. Dolores Huerta Biography. [Online] Available http://www.ufw.org (last accessed February 5, 1999).

## Other

*Chicano! The History of the Mexican American Civil Rights Movement* (four episodes; videocassette). Los Angeles: NLCC Educational Media, 1996.

# Elaine H. Kim

**Born February 26, 1942**
**New York, New York**

**Korean American professor, author, activist**

Elaine H. Kim was influential in the creation of Asian American Studies programs in colleges and universities and she continues to be an advocate for the rights of Asian Americans, women, and all people of color in the United States.

Elaine H. Kim is a widely published author, a leading Korean American activist, and a professor of Asian American studies at the University of California, Berkeley. Kim was instrumental in establishing Berkeley's Asian American studies program in the 1970s. She has published numerous books, articles, and essays on Asian Americans, race relations, and Asian American women's issues. In the 1990s—through a video documentary and several articles—Kim attempted to explain the significance of the 1992 Los Angeles riots for the Korean American community.

The recipient of a Fulbright Fellowship in 1987, Kim advocates that all people of color in the United States work collectively to overcome racism. "The African American-led civil rights movement of the 1960s made it possible to imagine that a person like me could be an American," wrote Kim in *East to America: Korean American Life Stories,* "and I have been committed to equality and the creation of self-determined identities and futures for Americans of color ever since."

## Early experiences

Kim was raised in suburban Washington, D.C., in Takoma Park and Silver Spring, Maryland. Kim's father came to the United States from Korea in 1926 on a student visa. He later worked as a waiter, a peddler of Japanese novelties, a staff member at the South Korean embassy, and as a small-businessman. Kim's mother came to Hawaii from Korea as an infant in 1903. She grew up as a migrant worker in the agricultural fields of Hawaii and California.

Kim learned about racism firsthand at an early age. Kim's white classmates considered her, as a Korean American, superior to African Americans but inferior to whites. "It was clear that racism against African Americans was as American as apple pie," Kim stated in a 1994 speech at the University of Maryland, "and that as an Asian American I was viewed as occupying a space higher than black and lower than white, for which I was supposed to be grateful. Sometimes students would say to me, 'Well, at least you're not black.'"

Kim recalled that in her second-grade textbook there was a picture of the globe, with a Caucasian child standing on top and an Asian child, upside-down, on the bottom. The Asian child was stereotypically depicted, with slitted eyes, buck teeth, orange skin, and a pigtail. While in elementary and junior high school, Kim's brother was regularly beaten up by a group of white schoolboys. These same boys would yell racial slurs at Kim as she walked by.

"When I was growing up in Maryland in the 1950s," wrote Kim in *East to America,* "most people I met asked me 'what I was' and didn't know that Korea was not a province or state in China. Our American 'world' history classes began with Greece and Rome and ended in the U.S."

Kim graduated high school in 1959 and then entered the program in English and American literature at the University of Pennsylvania. She completed her bachelor's degree in 1963, then went to Columbia University in New York City. Two years later, Kim earned a master's degree in English and comparative literature.

## From Columbia to Korea to Berkeley

In 1966 Kim traveled to Seoul, South Korea, to learn more about her heritage. She spent one year living with her half-sister and teaching English at Ewha University. During her visit Kim was dismayed to discover the blatant sexism existent in Korean society. In a 1992 keynote speech presented to the Women's Organization Reaching Koreans, Kim claimed that she "returned feeling neither 'Korean' nor 'American.'"

"I was changed forever when I visited Korea at the age of twenty and saw my relatives for the first time," wrote Kim in *East to America*. "Finding myself among so many people similar to me in shape and color made me feel as though I came from *somewhere*.... But like other U.S.-born Korean Americans, I came to understand that there is no ready-made community, no unquestioned belonging, even in Korea, for as soon as people heard me speak or saw me grin like a fool for no reason, ... as soon as they noticed me looking brazenly into people's eyes when they talked, they let me know that I could not possibly be 'Korean.'"

In 1968 Kim returned to the United States and entered a Ph.D. program in English at the University of California, Berkeley (UCB). Finding little support for her desire to study non-Western literature, Kim transferred to Berkeley's education department.

## Participates in Third-World strikes

In 1968 and 1969 Kim participated in a series of student demonstrations known as the "Third World Strikes." A coalition (or group) of students of color called the Third World Liberation Front led demonstrations that disrupted classes at UCB and San Francisco State College for several weeks. Striking students called for the creation of Ethnic Studies programs that would teach the history and accomplishments of non-Europeans in the United States. Because of the students' actions, Ethnic Studies programs were instituted at the two campuses. Today, Ethnic Studies programs (which have since been divided into Asian American studies, African American studies, Hispanic American studies, and Native American studies) are common at colleges and universities throughout the United States.

In the early 1970s Kim played a key role in developing the Asian American studies program within the Ethnic Studies program at Berkeley. She designed the curricula for courses in English as a second language, as well as literature courses that

highlighted the writings of Asian Americans, African Americans, American Indians, and Hispanic Americans.

Kim's dissertation, entitled *Asian American Literature: An Introduction to the Writings and Their Social Context,* was published by Temple University Press in 1982. The book, a compilation of writings by Asian Americans, was the first academic survey of Asian American literature and is still regarded as a classic in the field.

## Explores the impact of L.A. riots

In late April 1992 South-Central Los Angeles erupted in the worst riots in America's history. The rioting was sparked by the brutal beating of black motorist Rodney King by four white Los Angeles police officers and the subsequent acquittal of those officers by an all-white jury. In four days of rioting, 52 people were killed; 2,383 were injured; 8,801 were arrested, and about 3,700 buildings burned to the ground. The riots

A National Guardsman on patrol during the Los Angeles riots of April 1992. In the aftermath of the riots, Elaine Kim emerged as a leading authority on the tensions between African Americans and Korean Americans.
*Reproduced by permission of Corbis-Bettmann.*

resulted in the almost total destruction of Koreatown. Television cameras filmed gun-wielding Korean American store owners trying to fend off African American looters. In the media the conflict between Los Angeles's African Americans and Korean Americans overshadowed the primary issue: the brutality of white police officers toward an African American.

Kim emerged as a leading authority on the significance of the tensions between blacks and Koreans. She explored this theme in numerous articles and a video documentary entitled *Sa-I-Gu: From Korean Women's Perspective* ("Sa-I-Gu" is Korean for "April 29").

"Without an understanding of our histories," Kim wrote in a *Newsweek* article entitled "They Armed in Self-Defense," "Korean Americans and African Americans, it seems, are ready to engage in a zero-sum game over the crumbs of a broken society, a war in which the advancement of one group means deterioration for the other.... When the Los Angeles Police Department and the state government failed to respond to the initial outbreak of violence in South-Central, I suspected that Korean Americans were being used as human shields to protect the real source of rage.... The shopkeepers who trusted the government to protect them lost everything."

## Professional activities and publications

In the 1980s and 1990s Kim was involved with a number of organizations supporting the rights of Asian Americans and women. Her affiliations included the Association for Asian American Studies; Asian Immigrant Women Advocates; Asian Women United of California; National Organization for Women (NOW) Legal Defense Fund; Center for Women's Policy Studies; U.S. Korea Foundation; Japan Pacific Resource Network; Northern California Korean Coalition; and Korean Community Center of the East Bay.

Since the publication of her dissertation in 1982, Kim has written or edited numerous books and articles. The year 1983 saw the publication of Kim's book *With Silk Wings: Asian American Women at Work*. Kim served on the editorial board of the 1989 book *Making Waves: An Anthology of Writings by and about Asian American Women*. In 1994 Kim and coauthor L. H. Lang wrote *Writing Self, Writing Nation*; and in 1996 Kim coedited, with Eui-Young Yu, *East to America: Korean American Life Stories*. Kim served on the editorial board of the 1997 anthology *Making More Waves: New Writing by Asian American Women* and in 1998 coedited, with Chungmoo Choi, *Dangerous Women: Gender and Korean Nationalism*. Kim's articles have been published in many newspapers and magazines, including the *Philadelphia Inquirer, Newsweek, San Francisco Bay Guardian, A. Magazine, Amerasia Journal,* and *Korean Journal.*

Kim is currently chair of the Department of Ethnic Studies at the University of California, Berkeley, and president of the Association for Asian American Studies. She also serves on the board of directors of the Korean Community Center of the East Bay, in Oakland, California, and is a founder of Asian Immigrant Women Advocates and Asian Women United of California.

## Sources

### Books

Aguilar-San Juan, Karin. *The State of Asian America: Activism and Resistance in the 1990s*. Boston: South End Press, 1994.

Kim, Elaine H., and Eui-Young Yu, eds. *East to America: Korean American Life Stories*. New York: The New Press, 1996.

Kim, Elaine H. "War Story," in *Making Waves: An Anthology of Writings by and about Asian American Women,* edited by Asian Women United of California. Boston: Beacon Press, 1989.

Kim, Elaine H. "Meditations on the Year 2000: Policy for Women," in *The State of Asian Pacific America: Policy Issues to the Year 2020*. Los Angeles: LWAP Asian Pacific American Public Policy Institute and UCLA Asian American Studies Center, 1993.

Zia, Helen, and Susan B. Gall, eds. *Asian American Biography,* Vol. 1. Detroit: U•X•L, 1995, pp. 118-21.

### Periodicals

Kim, Elaine H. "They Armed in Self-Defense." *Newsweek*. May 18, 1992: 10.

### Other

*Sa-I-Gu: From Korean Women's Perspective* (videocassette). San Francisco: CrossCurrent Media; National Asian American Telecommunications Association, 1993.

# Martin Luther King Jr.

**Born January 15, 1929**
**Atlanta, Georgia**
**Died April 4, 1968**
**Memphis, Tennessee**

**African American civil rights leader and minister**

"Oppressed people cannot remain oppressed forever. The urge for freedom will eventually come."

*Reverend King in his "Letter from a Birmingham Jail"*

Martin Luther King Jr. spent the final decade of his life in relentless pursuit of racial equality and social justice. As president of the Southern Christian Leadership Conference (SCLC), King led a peaceful movement for racial equality and justice in the southern United States. With his gift for impassioned and inspirational speech, King convinced ordinary people to take courageous actions they would have never before imagined possible. In a span of ten years, King and his fellow civil rights activists transformed the South from a bastion of white supremacy into a region where African Americans had the right to vote, the right to attend integrated schools, and the right to take any seat on a public bus.

King promoted the philosophy of and practice of nonviolence—the rejection of all forms of violence. (The foundation of nonviolence is that violence cannot be overcome by more violence.) King argued that people of conscience could best demonstrate the righteousness of their cause by acting in a nonviolent manner. Tragically, the man who preached nonviolence to the United States, and who was granted the Nobel

Peace Prize for his efforts, had his own life cut short by an assassin's bullet.

## Religious upbringing and education

King was born in 1929 in Atlanta, Georgia, into a religious family. King's father, Martin Luther King Sr., was the pastor of Atlanta's Ebenezer Baptist Church. King's mother, Alberta (Williams) King, was a schoolteacher and a minister's daughter.

Although King had a religious upbringing and religious education, he originally intended to pursue a career in either law or medicine. After graduating from Booker T. Washington High School at the age of fifteen, King continued his studies at Morehouse College in Atlanta. During the course of his studies, King decided to become a minister. After graduating from Morehouse with a bachelor of arts degree in 1948, he enrolled in Crozer Theological Seminary in Chester, Pennsylvania. King, one of just six African American students in a class with 100 whites, was elected president of the student body. He graduated at the top of his class with a bachelor of divinity degree from Crozer in 1951, then went to Boston University to pursue his doctorate.

## Discovers Gandhi's teachings

While in Boston, King discovered the teachings of Mohandas (also called Mahatma) Gandhi (1869–1948), the leader of India's independence movement against Great Britain. Gandhi advocated nonviolence—the use of moral persuasion, not weapons, to defeat one's enemies. King later took Gandhi's philosophy of nonviolence and applied it to the civil rights movement in America.

While he was at Boston University, King met a music student named Coretta Scott (1927– ). The two were married by King's father in 1953. The newlywed Kings then moved to Montgomery, Alabama, where Martin had been offered the ministry of the Dexter Avenue Baptist Church.

## The Montgomery bus boycott

King's first experience with social justice movements came in 1955, during the Montgomery bus boycott. The boy-

Civil rights pioneer Rosa Parks is fingerprinted after being arrested for refusing to move to the back of a city bus in Montgomery, Alabama.
*Reproduced by permission of AP/Wide World Photos*

cott had been sparked by Rosa Parks's (1913– ; see box in Myles Horton entry) refusal to move to the back of a city bus, and her subsequent arrest, on December 1, 1955. Two local organizations, the National Association for the Advancement of Colored People (NAACP) and the Women's Political Council (WPC), proposed that African Americans boycott city buses to protest racist policies and Parks's arrest.

Then twenty-six years old, King was selected by a group of black ministers and community members to be president of the Montgomery Improvement Association (MIA)—the organization that had been created to coordinate the boycott.

At the conclusion of the first day, King stood in the pulpit of his overflowing church and made the case for continuing the boycott. "There comes a time that people get tired," proclaimed King. "We are here this evening to say to those who have mistreated us for so long that we are tired—tired of being ... kicked about by the brutal feet of oppression.

When the history books are written in future generations the historians will pause and say, 'There lived a great people—a black people—who injected new meaning and dignity into the veins of civilization.' That is our challenge and our overwhelming responsibility."

The decision was made to continue the boycott until black riders would no longer be forced to give up their seats to whites. The boycotters also demanded more respectful treatment of blacks by bus drivers and the hiring of black drivers. The boycott lasted 382 days and was ultimately successful. On December 20, 1956, the Montgomery City Lines bus company was served with a court order to abandon its policy of racial segregation.

## The founding of the SCLC

As the bus boycott came to a close, King was approached by Ella Baker (1903–1986; see entry), a fifty-two-year-old civil rights activist from New York, with the idea of forming a permanent organization of black ministers to coordinate civil rights activities in the South. After some debate, King agreed. On January 10 and 11, 1957, sixty-five black ministers from eleven southern states came to King's father's church, the Ebenezer Baptist Church in Atlanta, Georgia, to found the Southern Christian Leadership Conference (SCLC). The group selected King as the SCLC's first president. The SCLC quickly rose to prominence as the South's most respected civil rights organization.

King then traveled throughout the South, supporting local civil rights struggles and giving speeches. In 1958 King accepted an invitation to celebrate the independence of the African country of Ghana. The following year King visited India to reaffirm his belief in Gandhian nonviolence. He moved to Atlanta in 1960 to devote more time to the SCLC and to serve alongside his father as pastor of the Ebenezer Baptist Church.

## King's arrest and Kennedy's intervention

In October 1960 King went to Atlanta, Georgia, to support a student-led civil rights campaign. The students boycotted and demonstrated at eight stores with racially segregated lunch counters. On October 19, 1960, King and thirty-six students were arrested at Rich's department store.

Atlanta officials released the students but held King. They claimed that King had violated his probation (the probation stemmed from an earlier incident in which he had been arrested for driving without a Georgia driver's license). King was sentenced to four months of hard labor at the notorious Reidsville State Prison.

King's sentence came to the attention of Democratic presidential candidate John F. Kennedy (1917–1963). (The election was less than one month away at the time of King's arrest.) At the urging of his aides, Kennedy decided to step in to help King. Kennedy had his brother and campaign manager (and later attorney general) Robert Kennedy (1925–1968) pressure the sentencing judge to commute (legally end) King's sentence. That action resulted in King's release. Many people believe that John F. Kennedy's support for King was instrumental in Kennedy's narrow victory over Richard Nixon (1969–1974) in the presidential election in November 1960.

## The Birmingham protest campaign

In 1963 King and the SCLC sought to desegregate Birmingham, Alabama, which, according to King, was "probably the most thoroughly segregated city in the United States." The SCLC decided on a course of action that included boycotts of selected downtown department stores (those that had segregated lunch counters or otherwise discriminated against blacks), marches, and demonstrations.

On Wednesday, April 3, 1963, King and the other SCLC leaders presented Birmingham city officials with a petition demanding the desegregation of downtown lunch counters and stores and an end to discrimination in employment. As organizers had anticipated, city officials disregarded the petition.

On Palm Sunday the Reverend A. D. King, King's younger brother, led a prayer procession through downtown Birmingham. The demonstrators were assaulted by baton-wielding police and their attack dogs. Four days later, on April 10, a circuit court judge barred further demonstrations.

On April 12—in defiance of the court order—King and SCLC vice president Ralph Abernathy (1926–1990) led a march to city hall. The protesters, singing hymns, were halted by police and arrested. King spent a week in jail, during which time he wrote his famous "Letter from a Birmingham Jail" (see box).

On April 20 King and Abernathy were freed on bond. The following week, 2,000 children marched in the streets for civil rights. On the second day of the demonstration, Birmingham police turned their assaultive forces on the youths. As the children fled, police clubbed them, set dogs upon them, and blasted them with firehoses. Outraged by the attack on the youngsters, thousands of people demonstrated in Birmingham, and more than 2,000 were arrested.

The disturbances finally brought Birmingham merchants and lawmakers to the table. On May 10, 1963, an accord was reached that promised an end to segregation of downtown stores (including lunch counters, rest rooms, fitting rooms, and drinking fountains) and the hiring of blacks in clerical and sales positions. King declared the accord to be "the most magnificent victory for justice we've seen in the Deep South."

## "Letter from a Birmingham Jail"

While sitting in isolation in a Birmingham jail in April 1963 for his activities in the Birmingham desegregation campaign, King read a statement by a group of white religious leaders in the local newspaper. The clergymen called the Birmingham demonstrations "unwise and untimely," stating that they did "not believe that these days of new hope are days when extreme measures are needed in Birmingham." (The "new hope" referred to a newly elected mayor and city council.)

King wrote a response—his famous "Letter from a Birmingham Jail"—on the margins of newspaper and sheets of toilet paper. He then had the letter smuggled out of jail. King's letter was originally published in the form of a pamphlet distributed by a Quaker organization called the American Friends Service Committee. It was reprinted in dozens of newspapers and magazines around the country. In all, there were over one million copies of King's letter eventually put into circulation.

## The March on Washington

In June 1963 President Kennedy proposed a sweeping civil rights bill that would outlaw segregation of all public accommodations, speed up school desegregation, and make it easier for blacks to register to vote. King and other civil rights leaders began organizing a march on Washington to show support for the proposed legislation.

On the morning of Wednesday, August 28, 1963, 250,000 people descended upon Washington, D.C., in the

Martin Luther King Jr. (third from right) and other civil rights leaders meet to discuss the March on Washington. The other men are (from left): John Lewis of the SNCC, Whitney Young of the National Urban League, A. Philip Randolph of the American Labor Council, James Farmer of CORE, and Roy Wilkins of the NAACP.

*Reproduced by permission of AP/Wide World Photos.*

largest protest march to that date. The marchers carried signs reading, "Voting Rights Now," "Integrated Schools Now," "Equal Rights Now," and "Jobs for All Now." Several civil rights leaders delivered speeches at the Lincoln Memorial.

The speech that moved the audience more than any other that day was the final one, delivered by King. His address, entitled "I Have a Dream," eventually became one of the most recognized and reprinted speeches in modern U.S. history.

After his appearance at the march, King became the undisputed leader of the civil rights movement in America. That same year, King was chosen as "Man of the Year" by *Time* magazine. And in 1964 King received an even higher honor—the Nobel Peace Prize.

## The crusade for voting rights

Even after the passage of the 1964 Civil Rights Act, it was very difficult for African Americans to register to vote in the South. King and other civil rights leaders believed that stronger federal legislation was needed to outlaw the variety of practices used by racist officials to keep blacks from voting.

To draw attention to their cause, civil rights leaders organized a major voting rights campaign in Selma, Alabama. Selma provided a glaring example of blacks being denied the right to vote. While the majority of the citizens of Selma were black, less than 3 percent of black adults were registered to vote.

King arrived in Selma on January 2, 1965, and declared, "We are not asking, we are demanding the ballot." Throughout the month of January, more than 2,000 people marched to the courthouse and unsuccessfully attempted to register to vote. When the protesters refused to leave, they were arrested. In the first three days of February, King was among the more than 1,500 people arrested at the court-house. While detained, King wrote a letter that was published in *The New York Times*. In his letter, King asked why it was so difficult for blacks to vote, noting that "This is Selma, Alabama. There are more Negroes in jail with me than there are on the voting rolls."

## The Selma to Montgomery march

In early March the SCLC planned a fifty-four-mile-long protest march from Selma to the state capital of Montgomery. In Montgomery the marchers would present a list of griev-ances to the governor. The march began three times before marchers were finally allowed to proceed to Montgomery. On the first attempt, known as "Bloody Sunday" (March 7), the marchers were attacked by police and state troopers on the Edmund Pettus Bridge at the edge of Selma. On the second attempt, marchers encountered troops and turned around on the bridge without incident.

On March 25, 3,200 participants gathered for their third and final attempt. A federal judge had finally ruled that the march could proceed. When the procession reached Mont-gomery four days later, the number of marchers had reached 25,000. King gave a triumphant speech on the steps of the state capitol before a crowd of 50,000 people.

## Johnson introduces bill

The events in Selma convinced President Lyndon B. Johnson (1908–1973) to introduce a voting rights bill in Congress. The 1965 Voting Rights Act passed on August 6, 1965. This landmark legislation outlawed all practices used to deny blacks the right to vote and empowered federal registrars to register black voters.

## King visits riot-torn Watts

King visited the Watts section of Los Angeles in August 1965, shortly after six days of rioting had reduced the forty-five-square-mile area to ruins. Watts was one of many black inner-city ghettoes in the northern and western United States that exploded in anger between the years 1964 and 1968.

King learned that while southern blacks had been victimized by legally sanctioned racial segregation, northern and western blacks suffered from oppressive poverty, overcrowding, and discrimination in housing and employment. The civil rights legislation that King had worked so hard to pass had little effect on the lives of nonsouthern blacks. King's Watts visit led him to the conclusion that racial justice could only be achieved by a drastic change in the nation's economic structure.

## The SCLC's "Campaign to End Slums"

After visiting Watts, King convinced the SCLC of the need to begin organizing slumdwellers around issues of poverty. Thus, in January 1966, King and his staff launched the "Campaign to End Slums" in Chicago, Illinois. The group chose Chicago, the nation's second-largest city, because the majority of its black residents faced relentless poverty and discrimination. Through a variety of segregation practices, blacks in Chicago were confined to the ghetto.

King and his aides were optimistic at the start of the campaign. Nevertheless, after nine months the campaign ended in failure. King found that he did not have as great a following among northern blacks as he did among southern blacks and that his Chicago constituency was not devoted to nonviolence. King was also deterred by the extreme racial hatred exhibited by white Chicagoans and the tactics of Mayor Richard Daley.

Daley, whose political machine controlled all city services from trash removal to public housing to welfare, denied essential services to residents who participated in the campaign.

King, anxious to end the campaign, announced on August 26 that a settlement had been reached. City officials and real estate agents pledged an end to housing discrimination, and King agreed to end the demonstrations. King and his aides then left Chicago. The pledges of city officials and real estate agents, however, went unfulfilled.

## Continues to support poor people

After his experience in Chicago, King became even more convinced that the only way to eliminate racism was to eliminate the income gap between rich and poor in America. King made his priority the rights of poor people of all races.

At the same time, King became an outspoken opponent of the Vietnam War (1954–1975). He not only opposed

**After Martin Luther King Jr.'s death, SCLC vice president Ralph Abernathy (at podium) assumed leadership of the Poor People's March on Washington.**
*Reproduced by permission of AP/Wide World Photos.*

**Martin Luther King's funeral procession. King was assassinated on April 4, 1968, at the Lorraine Hotel in Memphis, Tennessee.**
*Reproduced by permission of AP/Wide World Photos.*

the war because of his pacifist views but because African Americans were dying in disproportionate numbers and spending for the war had detracted from federal antipoverty programs.

## The "Poor People's March"

In the fall of 1967 King began organizing a Poor People's March on Washington, to be held the following spring. King conceived of a march in which thousands of poor people of all races would come to the nation's capital, set up a tent city, and lobby legislators for programs that would expand economic opportunity. "We will place the problems of the poor at the seat of the government of the wealthiest nation in the history of mankind," proclaimed King at the project's inauguration.

King was prevented from leading the Poor People's March by an assassin's bullet. After his death, SCLC vice president Ralph Abernathy took over the project reins. In May 1968 the Poor People's March arrived in Washington, D.C., and set up a tent city, called Resurrection City. The whole affair received scant mention in the press. By late June, when ceaseless rains had turned the tent city into a muddy swamp, organizers ended their campaign.

## King's final days

On March 28, 1968, King arrived in Memphis, Tennessee, to aid striking black sanitation workers. King led a protest march to city hall, in support of the workers' demands for better wages and working conditions. Along the march route, a riot broke out that left sixty people injured and a sixteen-year-old boy dead. Despite having received several death threats, King vowed to stay in Memphis until he could lead a nonviolent demonstration.

On April 3, King addressed a gathering at the Mason Temple Church. The next morning, April 4, 1968, while standing on the balcony of the Lorraine Hotel, King was assassinated. He was carried to his final resting place, near the Ebenezer Baptist Church in Atlanta, on a mule-drawn cart. Eighteen years after King's death, a national holiday was established in his honor.

## Sources

### Books

*African American Biography.* Vol. 3. Detroit: U•X•L, 1994. pp. 456–59.

*African Americans: Voices of Triumph: Perseverance.* Alexandria, VA: Time-Life Books, 1993.

Carson, Clayborne, and Peter Holloran, eds. *A Knock at Midnight: Inspiration from the Great Sermons of Reverend Martin Luther King, Jr.* New York: Warner Books, Inc., 1998.

Garrow, David J. *Protest at Selma: Martin Luther King, Jr., and the Voting Rights Act of 1965.* New Haven, CT: Yale University Press, 1978.

King, Martin Luther, Jr. *A Testament of Hope: The Essential Writings of Martin Luther King, Jr.* San Francisco: Harper and Row Publishers, 1986.

Levine, Michael L. *African Americans and Civil Rights from 1619 to the Present.* Phoenix, AZ: Oryx Press, 1996.

Patterson, Lillie. *Martin Luther King, Jr., and the Freedom Movement.* New York: Facts on File, 1989.

Salmond, John A. *My Mind Set on Freedom: A History of the Civil Rights Movement, 1954–1968.* Chicago: Ivan R. Dee, 1997.

Weisbrot, Robert. *Marching Toward Freedom, 1957–1965.* New York: Chelsea House Publishers, 1994.

Williams, Juan. *Eyes on the Prize: America's Civil Rights Years, 1954–1965.* New York: Penguin Books, 1987.

# Yuri Kochiyama

**Born c. 1921**
**San Pedro, California**

**Asian American civil rights
and human rights activist**

**Y**uri Kochiyama's tireless quest for civil rights has spanned four decades. Kochiyama, who is of Japanese ancestry, champions justice and equality for all people of color. Overcoming racial and cultural barriers, Kochiyama has supported with the Black Panther Party, the Young Lords Party (a militant Puerto Rican rights group), the Asian American rights movement, the anti-Vietnam War movement, Puerto Rican independence groups, the movement to support political prisoners, and the campaign for reparations (compensation) for Japanese American internment camp survivors.

Kochiyama's priority has been, and continues to be, to unite all people of color in opposition to social and economic injustice. "There are so many issues that all people of color should come together on," stated Kochiyama in a 1993 documentary about her life entitled *Yuri Kochiyama: Passion for Justice.* "Unless we know ourselves and our history and other people and their history, there is no way that we really can have positive ... interactions where there is real understanding.... Knowledge of history can be used as a weapon to divide us further or to seek truth and learn from past errors.... Our ultimate

"Unless we know ourselves and our history and other people and their history, there is no way that we really can have positive ... interactions where there is real understanding."

**Yuri and Bill Kochiyama.**
*Reproduced by permission of Yuri Kochiyama*

objective in learning about anything is to try to create and develop a more just society than we have seen."

## Early years

Kochiyama was born Mary Nakahara (Kochiyama is her married surname; she assumed the name Yuri in the 1960s) in San Pedro, California. Her parents were Japanese immigrants, and her father worked as a fisherman. Kochiyama attended school in San Pedro and completed an associate's degree at Compton Junior College in Los Angeles. Kochiyama describes her youthful years as free from political concerns.

Kochiyama's life was turned upside down in 1941, when Japanese forces bombed Pearl Harbor in Hawaii. As a result of the bombing, the U.S. government began rounding up Japanese immigrants for questioning. On December 7—the day of the attack—737 Japanese Americans were arrested on suspicion of sabotage and treason. Four days after the attack, the Federal Bureau of Investigation (FBI) arrested another 1,370 Japanese Americans considered to be "dangerous enemy aliens." Despite the lack of any evidence that Japanese Americans were involved in or had any knowledge of Japan's sneak attack on Pearl Harbor (no such evidence ever surfaced), Japanese Americans were treated with suspicion.

## Father is arrested

Kochiyama's father, Seiichi Nakahara, was among those people arrested by the FBI. On December 7, 1941, while Nakahara lay in bed recovering from surgery the previous day, three FBI agents ordered him to put on his bathrobe and slippers and took him to the federal penitentiary at Terminal Island. On January 21, 1942, Nakahara was returned to his home. He was in terrible condition, unable to speak. He died that morning. The FBI sent the family a memo stating that anyone attending Nakahara's funeral would be subject to federal surveillance. Her twin brother Peter volunteered immediately in the U.S. Army

## Family sent to camp

Soon thereafter, Kochiyama, her brother, and her mother were sent to an internment camp in Jerome, Arkansas.

The family was among the 120,000 persons of Japanese descent to be incarcerated in camps in the United States during World War II (1939–45). Kochiyama attributes her understanding of racism in American to her experience in the prison camp.

## Meets future husband

While imprisoned in Arkansas, Yuri met Bill Kochiyama—the man who would become her husband. Bill escaped the camp by joining the segregated (separated by race) Japanese American combat unit, the 442nd Regiment Combat Team. (The 442nd eventually became the most highly decorated military unit in United States history.)

At the war's end, the couple got married and moved to New York City. The Kochiyamas lived in a housing project called the Amsterdam Houses, behind Lincoln Center. Surrounded by African American and Puerto Rican neighbors, Kochiyama began to learn about the civil rights movement. She started clipping articles, listening to speakers, and attending rallies. Gradually, she became involved in civil rights activities.

## Becomes community activist

In 1960 the Kochiyama family—which by then included six children—needed a larger home. They moved into an apartment in a twenty-story housing project on 126th Street in Harlem. (Yuri Kochiyama still occupies this apartment.) As the Kochiyamas would soon learn, Harlem in the 1960s was a hotbed of political and social change.

Many of the Kochiyamas' neighbors belonged to the Harlem Parents Committee (HPC), a group working for improvements in the public school system. The HPC operated the Harlem Freedom School, which supplemented children's education with courses in African American and African history. Kochiyama and her three oldest children took advantage of the educational opportunity and enrolled in the Freedom School.

## Joins strikes and picket lines

When the HPC called a one-day school strike on February 3, 1964, Kochiyama decided it was time to get involved. She helped the HPC in its efforts to close down every public school in New York City. The group's demands included an end to racial discrimination and the inclusion of African and African American history in the schools' curricula.

In the summer of 1963 Kochiyama took her children to Brooklyn to join the picket line at the Downstate Medical Center construction site. The protests, sponsored by the Congress on Racial Equality (CORE), were an attempt to force contractors to hire black and Puerto Rican construction workers. (CORE was famous for organizing Freedom Rides through the segregated South in 1961. Freedom Riders tested the Supreme Court's ban on segregated interstate [across state lines] buses and stations.) Kochiyama, along with other picketers, used their bodies to block delivery trucks approaching the site—acts of civil disobedience for which they were arrested.

## Friendship with Malcolm X

Kochiyama first met Malcolm X (1925–1965; see entry) in the summer of 1963 in a Brooklyn courthouse, following the arrest of Kochiyama and several other Downstate Medical Center picketers. Kochiyama was familiar with the separatist teachings of Malcolm X, as well as the appeals for integration by other civil rights leaders. When Kochiyama shook Malcolm X's hand that day in the courtroom, she told him she admired his leadership but disagreed with his opposition to integration. Malcolm X invited Kochiyama to discuss the matter with him further.

"Malcolm gave me a totally different perspective of the black struggle in America," stated Kochiyama in *Yuri Kochiyama: Passion for Justice*. "I am speaking of the 1960s at which time most of the civil rights leaders were talking about integration—that blacks should try to integrate into the mainstream. Malcolm did not believe there could be integration in such a racist society. And worse than integration, he felt, was assimilation: to be like those in power."

Prior to meeting Malcolm X, Kochiyama had believed that it was sufficient to fight for people's basic needs—education, housing, health care, and jobs. Malcolm X taught her that oppressed people must learn about their history in order to effect social change and achieve equality. Kochiyama became an adherent of Malcolm X and was active in his Organization of Afro-American Unity.

It did not take long for Malcolm X and Kochiyama to develop a deep mutual respect and a close friendship. While on a spiritual pilgrimage through the Middle East in 1964, Malcolm X sent the Kochiyamas eleven postcards from nine countries. Shortly thereafter, Malcolm X came to the Kochiyamas's home to speak to a delegation of antinuclear activists and journalists from Japan.

## Present at final speech

Kochiyama was present at Malcolm X's final speech, given in February 1965 at Harlem's Audubon Ballroom. Kochiyama heard gunshots and saw Malcolm X fall. "I just went straight to Malcolm and I put his head on my lap," Kochiyama told Norimitsu Onishi of *The New York Times* in 1996. "He just lay there. He had difficulty breathing and he didn't utter a word." Every year on May 19—Malcolm X's birthday—Kochiyama joins other people in a pilgrimage to his

Malcolm X (far right, at podium) at a rally in Harlem. Yuri Kochiyama became a follower of Malcolm X's teachings, especially his belief that oppressed people must learn about their history in order to effect social change and achieve equality.
*Reproduced by permission of AP/Wide World Photos.*

## "A Praise Song for Yuri"

The following is a tribute to Kochiyama written by New York civil rights activist Jamal Joseph:

*Constellations of beauty appear in our world because you are in our life.*

*And we recognize that it's not possible to put every feeling into words or every definition into a sentence.*

*But this needs to be a tribute to your life, Yuri.*

*A praise song, a freedom chant, based on action.*

*Like Harriet, like Sojourner, like Angela, like Assata, like you, Yuri.*

(The references in the last line of the song are to Underground Railroad conductor Harriet Tubman [1821?–1913; see box in Sojourner Truth entry], abolitionist Sojourner Truth [1797–1883; see entry], and Black Panther Party members Angela Davis and Assata Shakur.

gravesite in upstate New York. "Malcolm X was the one person who changed my life more than anyone else," said Kochiyama in *Yuri Kochiyama: Passion for Justice*, "because he gave me a different perspective of the struggle in America."

## Active in Asian American movement

In the late 1960s Kochiyama became active in the Asian American movement. That movement, which began in 1968 and continued through the early 1970s, had as its objectives an end to the Vietnam War (1954–75), an end to discrimination against Asian Americans, the inclusion of Asian American studies programs in colleges and universities, and the granting of reparations to Japanese American survivors of internment camps.

In New York City Kochiyama worked with Asian Americans for Action (AAA). AAA sponsored numerous anti-Vietnam War marches, with slogans such as "Stop Vietnamization: Asians Killing Asians" and "Stop Killing our Yellow Brothers." AAA was also active in Chinatown, where it founded a free health clinic with other groups and opposed discrimination in jobs, housing, and health care. In 1973 AAA activists engaged in a campaign similar to the job fight at the Downstate Medical Center a decade earlier. The city of New York was constructing Confucius Plaza in Chinatown, yet it refused to hire Chinese construction workers. Asian American activists, including Kochiyama, forced the city to change that policy.

## World War II reparations

Yuri and Bill Kochiyama worked with other people in the Asian American movement to pressure Congress to compensate Japanese Americans who had been interned during World War II. In 1981 Congress established the Commission on Wartime Relocation and Internment of Civilians, a panel charged with assessing the harm suffered by Japanese Americans during World War II and making recommendations for compensation. Bill Kochiyama was among the camp survivors who testified before the commission. In its final report, entitled *Personal Justice Denied,* the commission urged Congress to issue apologies to the 60,000 Japanese American prison camp survivors and offer them reparations in the amount of $20,000 each. Congress adopted those recommendations in the Civil Liberties Act of 1988.

## Still part of the struggle

In 1993 Kochiyama lost her husband of forty-eight years—and her partner in the movement for civil rights—Bill Kochiyama. Shortly before Bill's death, the Kochiyamas were presented with the Outstanding Service Award by the Asian American Studies Association. In 1996 the Japanese American Citizens League presented Yuri Kochiyama with its highest civic honor.

Now in her late seventies, Kochiyama is finally showing signs of slowing down. "My mother is such an active person," her daughter Audee Kochiyama Holman said in a 1992 interview. "Her level of energy at age seventy, her level of commitment, is still the same as it was twenty years ago." In the spring of 1995 Kochiyama helped students at Columbia University in New York win concessions from the administration to increase the number of Asian American and Hispanic courses and more racial minorities on the faculty. Kochiyama regularly speaks at schools throughout the United States and continues to work on behalf of political prisoners (most notably former Black Panther and radio journalist Mumia Abu-Jamal, who sits on death row for a murder of which he was convicted in what many people believe was an unfair trial).

The Kochiyama apartment, once described as the "Grand Central Station for the movement," still serves as headquarters for numerous organizations. While Kochiyama now lives there alone (two of her children died in auto accidents and the other four moved to the West Coast), she has a constant stream of visitors. Kochiyama is one of the few tenants in the housing project who is not African American or Puerto Rican. Asked why she stays, Kochiyama responded in a 1996 *New York Times* report, "Living in the projects, we've met so many wonderful, wonderful people.... They've been like a university to me."

## Sources

### Books

Aguilar-San Juan, Karin, ed. *The State of Asian America: Activism and Resistance in the 1990s*. Boston: South End Press, 1994.

### Periodicals

"Obituary: William Kochiyama, Japanese Advocate, 72." *New York Times*. October 28, 1993: D27.

Onishi, Norimitsu. "Harlem's Japanese Sister." *New York Times*. September 22, 1996: 41, 47.

### Web Sites

Cha, Ariana E. "U-M to Honor Crusader, Malcolm X Pal." *Detroit Free Press*. February 3, 1997. [Online] Available http://www.freep.com/blackhistory/qyuri3.htm (last accessed January 7, 1999).

Kao, Malcolm. "Center Acquires Yuri Kochiyama Collection." [Online] Available http://www.sscnet.ucla.edu/aasc/ccx/kochiyama.html (last accessed April 15, 1999).

Kochiyama, Bill, and Yuri Kochiyama. "My America." [Online] Available http://www.pbs.org/myamerica/honk/location/miss.html (last accessed January 7, 1999).

"Yuri Kochiyama." *Detroit Free Press*. February 3, 1997. [Online] Available http://vh1380.infi.net/blackhistory/qubox3.htm (last accessed January 7, 1999).

### Other

*Yuri Kochiyama: Passion for Justice* (videocassette). YK Project, 1993.

# John Robert Lewis

**Born February 21, 1940**
**Troy, Alabama**

**African American civil rights
leader and congressman**

J ohn Robert Lewis came of age at a time when African Americans in large numbers were beginning to challenge the laws
and social customs that relegated blacks to the status of second-class citizens. Lewis helped initiate the Nashville student
sit-in movement, was a founding member of the Student Nonviolent Coordinating Committee (SNCC), and was a pioneering Freedom Rider. In 1963, as chairman of the SNCC, Lewis
delivered the most angry and forceful of all the political
speeches at the March on Washington. And in 1965 Lewis was
nearly killed by state troopers' blows during the famous
"Bloody Sunday" civil rights march in Selma, Alabama.

Lewis was elected to represent the district that includes
Atlanta, Georgia, in the U.S. House of Representatives in 1986.
Today he is an influential member of Congress and one of a
handful of black elder statesmen. Lewis has been arrested more
than forty times and has been beaten so savagely that his head
still bears scars. Yet he continues to work for the creation of
what he calls a "beloved community"—a society that is truly
integrated, nonviolent, and economically just. Former SNCC
member and current head of the National Association for the

John R. Lewis was at the
center of the civil rights
movement, from the
Freedom Rides to the
March on Washington to
the Selma-to-
Montgomery march.

Portrait: Reproduced by
permission of John R. Lewis.

Advancement of Colored People (NAACP) Julian Bond (1940– ) said about Lewis: "In the middle of a bunch of courageous young people, he was the most courageous." And according to Andrew Young (1932– ), former aide to Martin Luther King Jr. (1939–1968; see entry), "John Lewis always knew what he was about: He was out to redeem the soul of America."

## A boyhood of hard work and religion

Lewis was born in Pike County, Alabama, in 1940, the third of ten children of sharecropper parents. (Sharecropping is a system of farming in which a landless farmer works a plot of land and in return gives the landowner a share of the crop.) In the rural area that Lewis called home, all of his neighbors—most of whom were relatives—worked land owned by the same white man.

Lewis hated picking cotton as a child, both because it was back-breaking work and, in his words, "a dead-end way of life." "Imagine how much cotton must be picked to total a hundred pounds," wrote Lewis in his 1998 memoir *Walking with the Wind*. "Imagine a man picking a little over two hundred pounds in a day, and his wife, working right beside him, picking almost that much. Imagine that their payment at the end of that day is 35 cents per hundred pounds, or a total of one $1.40 for 400 pounds of cotton.... Those numbers are precisely what my mother and father were picking and earning at the time I was born."

Lewis developed an early interest in religion and, by the age of seven, was giving sermons to the only captive audience around—the family's flock of chickens. When Lewis was fifteen years old, he began preaching in local churches and earned the nickname "the boy preacher from Troy." One night, on his family's vintage, battery-powered radio (his house had no electricity), Lewis tuned in to a sermon by the Reverend Martin Luther King Jr. Lewis was mesmerized by King's homily, which combined appeals for integration with scripture. From that time on, Lewis addressed racial justice themes in his own sermons.

## Organizes sit-ins in Nashville

Unable to afford tuition at King's alma mater, Morehouse College in Atlanta, Lewis enrolled in the American Bap-

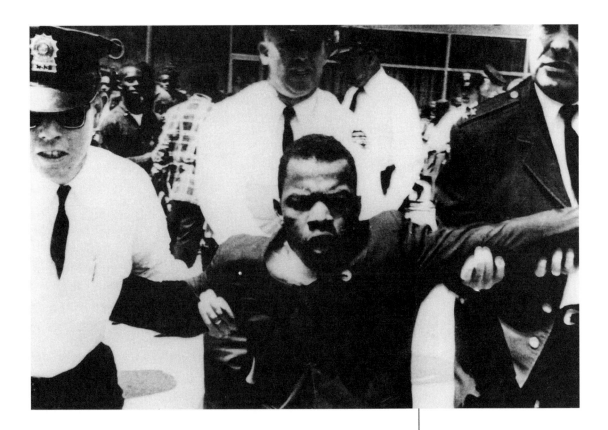

tist Seminary in Nashville, Tennessee, in 1957. He then decided that he would rather attend Troy College, the all-white institution in his hometown. Lewis enlisted the help of King and prepared for a legal battle. Lewis's parents, however, feared retribution by whites and convinced Lewis to return to Nashville.

Lewis began studying the teachings of Indian independence leader Mohandas Gandhi (1869–1948) and attending workshops on nonviolence. (The foundation of nonviolence is that violence cannot be overcome by more violence.) He also joined an emerging civil rights group, the Nashville Student Movement. In February 1960 the Nashville Student Movement thrust itself into the sit-in movement that had begun in Greensboro, North Carolina, and was taking hold throughout the South. (Sit-ins were a form of civil rights protest in which black students, sometimes joined by white students, would request service at segregated lunch counters, then refuse to leave when denied service.)

**John R. Lewis is arrested in Nashville, Tennessee, following a sit-in.**
*Reproduced by permission of AP/Wide World Photos.*

John R. Lewis in 1963, shortly after he became chairman of the Student Nonviolent Coordinating Committee. *Reproduced by permission of AP/Wide World Photos.*

Lewis and his fellow protesters were harassed daily by whites. Opponents of the sit-ins beat, kicked, and cursed at student activists. Lewis and his friends were pelted with gum and french fries and had cigarettes burned into their backs. Lewis was arrested four times during six weeks of sit-ins. The Nashville Student Movement was ultimately successful in its goal of integrating the city's business district.

## The founding of the SNCC

While several members of the Nashville Student Movement attended an historic student conference from April 16 to 18, 1960, Lewis was not among them—he volunteered to stay behind to coordinate protest activities in Nashville. At the conference, held at Shaw University in Raleigh, North Carolina, and coordinated by veteran organizer Ella Baker (1903–1986; see entry) more than 300 student activists from fifty-six southern colleges and high schools, as well as nineteen northern colleges, founded the Student Nonviolent Coordinating Committee (SNCC; pronounced "snick"). The students defined the SNCC as an independent organization based on the principles of nonviolence, integration, and racial equality. The SNCC's goal was to achieve racial equality at all levels of society.

The SNCC quickly rose to the fore of the civil rights movement, gaining a reputation as an organization of fearless and dedicated fighters. Lewis became one of the SNCC's most respected leaders and served as chair of the organization from 1963 to 1966.

## Embarks on Freedom Rides

In 1961 Lewis headed for Washington, D.C., to participate in the Freedom Rides. The purpose of the Freedom Rides was to test the enforcement of a pair of Supreme Court rulings striking down the constitutionality of segregated seating on interstate (crossing state lines) buses and trains, as well as segregation in terminal waiting rooms, rest rooms, and restaurants. The Freedom Rides were the idea of James Farmer (1920– ), founder of the Congress on Racial Equality (CORE)— a civil rights organization that practiced nonviolent direct action.

On May 4, following three days of training in the practice of nonviolent action, the interracial group of thirteen riders divided into two groups. One group boarded a Greyhound bus and the other a Trailways bus in Washington, D.C. The riders' destination was New Orleans, Louisiana. Their first confrontation came in Rock Hill, South Carolina. Lewis and another rider were beaten by a group of whites as they attempted to enter the terminal's "whites-only" restroom.

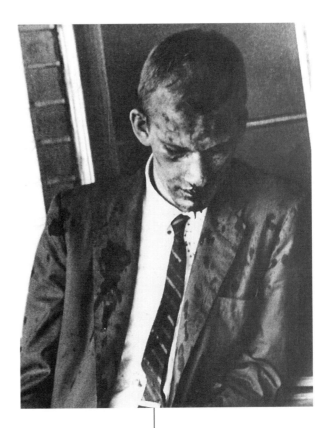

Freedom Rider Jim Zwerg sustained severe spinal injuries after being beaten in Montgomery, Alabama. *Reproduced by permission of AP/Wide World Photos.*

## Riders faced with brutality

After many of the riders were brutally beaten in Anniston and Birmingham, Alabama, Lewis and other SNCC members recruited new volunteers and resumed the rides. At their next destination, Montgomery, the riders encountered the most hostile crowd yet. As the freedom riders disembarked at the bus station, they were charged by a mob of about 1,000 people. Lewis was knocked unconscious; his bloodied face was pictured in major daily newspapers around the world. A white rider, Jim Zwerg, was beaten so mercilessly that he sustained severe spinal injuries and lost several teeth.

"There were screaming, spitting, men swinging fists and weapons," stated Lewis in a 1998 interview with *People Weekly,* "women swinging heavy purses, little children clawing with their fingernails at the faces of anyone they could reach."

Lewis and a handful of the other riders decided to continue on as far as Jackson, Mississippi. When the group

**The March on Washington**

On August 28, 1963, Lewis was catapulted into the national spotlight as he delivered an angry speech before 250,000 people at the Lincoln Memorial in Washington, D.C. The March on Washington had been organized by Martin Luther King Jr., labor leader A. Philip Randolph (1889–1979), and other leaders of major civil rights groups to show support for a sweeping civil rights bill proposed by President John F. Kennedy (1917–1963).

While most of the political speeches that day were optimistic and conciliatory, Lewis's address was markedly agitated. His original text was so inflammatory that other civil rights leaders forced him to tone it down the night before the march.

Lewis's words reflected the sentiments of SNCC workers in the trenches of the Deep South, who had endured beatings and jailings and witnessed the deaths of their friends. Lewis told the crowd to remember that there were people too poor to attend the march, people who were "receiving starvation wages ... or no wages at all." He talked about sharecroppers in the Mississippi Delta earning "less than $3.00 a day for twelve hours of work." He told the crowd about several SNCC activists who were "in jail on trumped-up charges," including three in Americus, Georgia, who had been charged with inciting insurrection and faced the death penalty.

Lewis gave his support to Kennedy's civil rights bill only "with great reservations," asserting that the legislation would not "protect young children and old women from police dogs and fire hoses." "[We] do not want to be free gradually," stated Lewis. "We want our freedom and we want it now.... By the force of our demands, our determination and our numbers, we shall splinter the segregated South into a thousand pieces, and put them back together in the image of God and democracy." He called upon civil rights supporters to "stay in the streets of every city, every village and every hamlet of this nation ... until the unfinished revolution of 1776 is complete."

reached Jackson they took seats in the bus terminal's "whites-only" waiting room. They were immediately handcuffed, charged with disturbing the peace and trespassing, and were jailed. Although they were grateful to have escaped another beating, the group faced thirty days in the Parchman Prison Farm. There they were subjected to the guards' electric cattle prods and firehoses. "I thought of the concentration camps in Germany," commented Lewis, "but this was 1961 in America."

That fall the Interstate Commerce Commission strengthened rules against segregation in interstate transportation. The commission mandated that signs be posted in all buses, trains, and terminals stating that seating was "without regard to race, color, creed and national origin."

## Conducts voter registration drives

After the Freedom Rides, Lewis spent three years conducting voter registration drives with the SNCC all throughout the South. "We were the guerrillas, going into areas where other groups would not," Lewis remarked in his *People Weekly* interview. "Home was wherever you found a bed and a blanket. You traveled constantly, and you traveled light." In 1964 Lewis assisted Robert Moses (1935; see entry), the SNCC's leading organizer in Mississippi, with the massive voter registration project known as Freedom Summer.

## Struggles to redefine goals

As 1964 drew to a close, SNCC veterans were reassessing their commitment to nonviolence. Many of them, physically and psychologically exhausted from the beatings and intimidation they had endured, had come to the conclusion that practicing nonviolence in the South was useless. Several SNCC workers began to carry weapons. There was a growing trend toward separatism (the rejection of white culture and institutions in favor of separate African American culture and institutions) in the movement.

Like his comrades, Lewis was struggling to redefine his beliefs and his goals. Remarkably, it was a two-day-long conversation with Malcolm X (1925–1965; see entry) that helped Lewis focus his thoughts. In the fall of 1964, while participating in an SNCC delegation to Africa, Lewis ran into Malcolm X in Kenya. Malcolm X was on his way home from a pilgrimage to the Muslim holy land of Mecca, where he had lived and prayed with Muslims of all races. That experience had convinced Malcolm to rethink his own separatist stance. Lewis listened carefully to what Malcolm X had to say.

When Lewis returned to the United States, he announced his vision of the SNCC: an organization committed to nonviolence and open to participation by sincere white supporters, but "black-controlled, dominated, and led."

## Tensions grow between the SNCC and the SCLC

Tensions between Lewis and other SNCC members, and between the SNCC and the more conservative Southern Christian Leadership Conference (SCLC), surfaced in Selma, Alabama, in early 1965. SNCC activists had been doggedly conducting a door-to-door voter registration drive in Selma for two years when King and the SCLC targeted the city for a high-profile campaign. The SCLC wanted federal legislation outlawing the practices used by racist officials to keep blacks from registering and voting. The SCLC chose Selma for its campaign because, while the majority of the citizens were black, less than 3 percent of black adults were registered to vote.

On January 18, 1965, King, accompanied by Lewis (who was on the board of directors of the SCLC), kicked off a civil disobedience campaign at the county courthouse that lasted several weeks. Participants would march to the courthouse and announce their intention to register to vote. When denied access to the building, the protesters would remain on the lawn and pray until they were arrested. By February 3, more than 1,500 people had been arrested at the courthouse.

## The SCLC plans march

In early March of 1965 the SCLC planned a fifty-four-mile-long protest march from Selma to the state capital of Montgomery. In Montgomery they would present a list of grievances to the governor. Most SNCC members, resentful of the way the SCLC had come in and taken over, were opposed to the march.

"It was the same old story all over again," wrote Lewis in *Walking with the Wind*. "We dug in early, did the groundwork, laid the foundation, then the SCLC came in again with their headline-grabbing, hit-and-run tactics, doing nothing to nurture leaders among the local community but instead bringing in their own leaders, then leaving after they'd gotten what they needed out of it."

Despite his criticism of the SCLC, Lewis chose to participate in the march. "I grew up in Alabama," Lewis stated at a SNCC meeting. "You know I've been to Selma many, many times. I've been arrested there. I've been jailed there. If these people want to march, I'm going to march with them."

## Marchers meet with violence

On March 7, Lewis and Reverend Hosea Williams (1926– ) of the SCLC marched at the head of a line of 600 people. On the Edmund Pettus Bridge at the edge of the city, the marchers encountered about 200 uniformed officers of the Selma police force and the Alabama state troopers. The officers were holding whips, cattle prods, batons, and rubber hoses wrapped in barbed wire. They were wearing helmets and gas masks, and many were on horseback.

As the marchers knelt to pray, the order was given: "Troopers, advance!" Police fired canisters of tear-gas— intended to induce nausea in its victims—and moved toward the crowd.

"The troopers and possemen swept forward as one, like a human wave, a blur of blue shirts and billy clubs and bullwhips," wrote Lewis in his memoir. "We had no chance to turn and retreat.... I remember ... the clunk of the troopers' heavy boots, the rebel yells from the white onlookers, the clip-clop of horses' hooves hitting the hard asphalt of the highway, the voice of a woman shouting, 'Get em! *Get* the niggers!'"

Lewis, who suffered a fractured skull and a concussion, was among the seventy to eighty marchers badly injured that day. The "Bloody Sunday" beatings were filmed by television cameras and broadcast throughout the United States. Pictures of Lewis, being beaten as he laid on the ground, appeared in newspapers around the world.

The events in Selma convinced President Lyndon B. Johnson (1908–1973) to introduce a voting rights bill in Congress. The Voting Rights Act, signed into law on August 6, 1965, outlawed all practices used to deny blacks the right to vote and empowered federal registrars to register black voters.

## Leaves the SNCC

While the events in Selma had made Lewis a civil rights hero in the eyes of most Americans who supported the movement, they had resulted in a further straining of relations between Lewis and the SNCC. Much of the SNCC leadership saw Lewis as being too close to King at a time when the SNCC was becoming an increasingly separatist organization.

Tensions came to a head at an SNCC leadership meeting in May 1966. Stokely Carmichael (1941–1998, later known as Kwame Toure), who succeeded Lewis as SNCC chairman, blasted Lewis as a "Christ-loving damn fool." The following month Lewis resigned from the SNCC.

"It hurt," wrote Lewis in his memoir. "It hurt to leave my family, so many good brothers and sisters with whom I had shared so much.... My feelings were hurt. I felt abandoned, cast out.... The pain of that experience is something I will never be able to forget."

After leaving the SNCC, Lewis moved to New York City and began working as associate director of the Field Foundation—an organization that funded civil rights and child welfare programs. When Lewis was not working, he mostly kept to himself in his small apartment—resting and recovering from the storm he had weathered the previous six years. One year later Lewis moved back to the South—to Atlanta, Georgia. There he joined the staff of the Southern Regional Council and worked to establish farming cooperatives and credit unions throughout the South.

## Works on Robert Kennedy campaign

In March 1968 Lewis accepted an invitation to work on the presidential campaign of Senator Robert F. Kennedy (1925–1968). Lewis was in Kennedy's hotel suite on June 4, celebrating the candidate's victory in the California primary, when he learned that Kennedy had been shot while delivering a speech in the hotel ballroom. Kennedy died two days later.

"First Dr. King [assassinated on April 4, 1968], then Bobby Kennedy," recalled Lewis, "both shot dead within weeks of each other. It hurt so incredibly much when they were taken away. I knew that what I was feeling was the same thing millions of Americans felt. What could we *believe* in now? How much more of this could we take?"

## Becomes active in electoral politics

Lewis then returned to the Southern Regional Council, where for the next seven years he supervised the registration of tens of thousands of African American voters. In the late 1970s Lewis was appointed by President Jimmy Carter (1924– ) to be director of federally funded community organizing efforts.

Lewis won his first elected political position—a seat on the Atlanta city council—in 1980. Six years later Lewis upset his old friend and civil rights colleague Julian Bond in a race for Atlanta's congressional seat in the House of Representatives. Now in his eighth term as a congressman, Lewis continues to fight for social justice and continues his quest for the "beloved community."

# Sources

## Books

Carson, Clayborne. *In Struggle: SNCC and the Black Awakening of the 1960s*. Cambridge: Harvard University Press, 1981.

Levy, Peter B. *The Civil Rights Movement*. Westwood, CT: Greenwood Press, 1998.

Lewis, John, with Michael D'Orso. *Walking with the Wind: A Memoir of the Movement*. New York: Simon and Schuster, 1998.

Weisbrot, Robert. *Freedom Bound: A History of America's Civil Rights Movement*. New York: W. W. Norton and Company, 1990.

Williams, Juan. *Eyes on the Prize: America's Civil Rights Years, 1954–1965*. New York: Penguin Books, 1987.

## Periodicals

"Freedom Fighter." *People Weekly*. August 24, 1998: 125.

Wilentz, Sean. "The Last Integrationist: John Lewis' American Odyssey." *New Republic*. July 1, 1996: 19+.

# Malcolm X

**Born May 19, 1925**
**Omaha, Nebraska**
**Died February 21, 1965**
**Harlem, New York**

**African American advocate for black nationalism and civil rights and Nation of Islam minister and spokesman**

The life of Malcolm X was a complex journey from rural schoolboy to convicted felon to Muslim preacher to militant political leader. With his gift for fiery oration, Malcolm X inspired African Americans throughout the United States to fight for their rights. He rejected the civil rights movement's premises of nonviolence and integration and instead stressed the need for black people to defend themselves and form their own institutions.

Until the final year of his life, Malcolm X spread the Nation of Islam's message of hatred toward white America and pride in black America. After a pilgrimage through the Middle East in 1964, however, Malcolm X renounced racial animosity. He broke his association with the Nation of Islam and formed his own black nationalist organization, the Organization of Afro-American Unity. Malcolm X was shot and killed while delivering a speech in 1965. Even in death, however, he continued to inspire activists in the struggle for African American rights.

Malcolm X embodied the concepts of black pride and militant action. He powerfully expressed the anger and frustration that African Americans felt about racism.

## Early exposure to violence

Malcolm X was born Malcolm Little in Nebraska in 1925. His father, a Baptist preacher named Earl Little, was a follower of Marcus Garvey (1887–1940; Jamaican black nationalist leader who advocated that all black people return to Africa). When Malcolm was four years old, his home was set on fire by Ku Klux Klan members. (White supremacist Ku Klux Klan groups target minorities and certain religious groups for verbal and physical violence.) After the attack, the Little family moved to Milwaukee, Wisconsin, and then to Lansing, Michigan. When Malcolm was six years old, his father was killed. The suspects were members of a white supremacist group called the Black Legion.

## A difficult youth

Malcolm's mother, living in poverty and suffering from a mental breakdown, was unable to support her eight children. The children were sent to foster homes around the state. Malcolm was sent to East Lansing. An excellent student and class leader, Malcolm aspired to be a doctor or a lawyer. His hopes were dashed, however, when a teacher told him that it was not realistic for an African American child to expect to become a professional. Malcolm lost interest in school and dropped out in the eighth grade.

At the age of fifteen, Malcolm moved to Boston to live with his half-sister, Ella. He found a job shining shoes and learned about life on the city streets, including drugs, gambling, and crime. Three years later Malcolm moved to Harlem, New York, where he earned his money selling marijuana and cocaine, running a gambling game called "numbers," and luring customers into houses of prostitution. He then moved back to Boston and got involved in a burglary ring. At the age of twenty-one, Malcolm was convicted on burglary charges and sentenced to eight to ten years in prison.

## Serves time in prison

While in prison, Malcolm learned about the Nation of Islam (NOI) and its black Muslim leader, Elijah Muhammad (1897–1975). Malcolm was attracted to the NOI's strict regiment of prayer and self-discipline and its message that blacks were superior to whites. The NOI asserted that African Americans could only reclaim their rightful heritage by converting to Islam—their true religion. For Malcolm, whose family had been destroyed and whose aspirations had been crushed by whites, the teachings of the NOI helped him understand these events and provided an outlet for his anger.

Along with Malcolm's conversion to Islam came a desire for learning and self-improvement. He read every book he could find in prison and even copied by hand a dictionary to improve his penmanship. In adherence to his Muslim faith, Malcolm stopped smoking, drinking, and eating pork and kept himself immaculately groomed. He also preached the teachings of Elijah Muhammad to other prisoners.

## Rises to prominence in Nation of Islam

Upon his release from prison in 1952, Malcolm replaced his surname "Little" with "X." He took this step to rid himself of the name that his great-grandparents, who were slaves, had been given by their owners. ("X" was the Muslim designation for the unknown surname of a black American's African ancestors.)

Malcolm X moved to Harlem and began preaching the NOI's message on street corners. He was ordained a minister in the NOI by Elijah Muhammad and assigned his own mosque (Muslim place of worship), first in Detroit and then in Philadelphia. Soon after, Malcolm X was assigned a mosque in Harlem, which he built into the largest in the nation.

From 1952 to 1963 Malcolm X's effectiveness as a preacher earned him the position of national spokesperson for the NOI, making him second-in-command to Elijah Muhammad. He toured widely in the United States during this time, delivering lectures to huge crowds at universities, speaking on radio and television programs, and establishing dozens of mosques. During Malcolm X's years as NOI spokesperson, membership in the organization grew from about 400 to about 10,000 people.

## Clashes with civil rights leaders

In the 1960s, when most civil rights leaders were striving for integration and nonviolence, Malcolm X advocated

Malcolm X (right center) at a Nation of Islam (NOI) meeting. Due to his effectiveness as a preacher, Malcolm X served as the NOI's national spokesperson from 1952 to 1963.
*Reproduced by permission of Archive Photos.*

separatism and self-defense. Malcolm X believed in fighting back against racial violence and seizing self-determination "by any means necessary." He pushed for blacks to create and control their own economy, institutions, and politics. Because of his beliefs, Malcolm X was characterized as dangerous and evil by the media. While he was loved by his followers, he was feared by most whites and many blacks.

Malcolm X did not believe that true integration, where blacks and whites would come together as equals, was possible in a racist society. He argued that if blacks were allowed to enter white institutions, they would be forced to assimilate (become like the whites). Furthermore, Malcolm X believed that integration would only accommodate middle-class blacks, at the exclusion of the black underclass.

Malcolm X was sharply critical of the civil rights movement's emphasis on nonviolence. "If they make the Ku Klux Klan nonviolent, I'll be nonviolent," he once stated. "If they make the White Citizens' Council nonviolent, I'll be nonviolent.... If someone puts a hand on you, send him to the cemetery." (White Citizens' Councils were groups of southern whites, mostly from middle and professional classes, who sought to block the economic and political advancement of blacks.)

## Breaks with Nation of Islam

As Malcolm X's popularity grew, so did tensions between himself and Elijah Muhammad. Muhammad felt his own position threatened by his protégé's rising prominence. At the same time, Malcolm was critical of Muhammad's sexual indiscretions. The final straw came in November 1963, when Malcolm X made a public statement that the assassination of President John F. Kennedy was a case of "chickens coming home to roost." Malcolm later explained that what he meant by the statement was that "the country's climate of hate had killed the president." Muhammad, who was perhaps looking for an excuse to dismiss Malcolm, claimed that Malcolm's statement about the revered American president had alienated too many NOI supporters. He suspended Malcolm from the NOI in December 1963.

## Makes important prayer pilgrimage

In March 1964 Malcolm X made a permanent break with the NOI. Later that spring he conducted a prayer pilgrimage to the Middle East and Africa. On that journey he met Muslims of all races, praying together and living together as equals. Malcolm X realized that people need not be divided because of the color of their skin, which precipitated a fundamental shift in his thinking. He no longer accepted the NOI characterization of white people as "blue-eyed devils." He came to see economic inequality as the true reason for blacks' oppression.

"Since I learned the *truth* in Mecca," wrote Malcolm X in his autobiography, "my dearest friends have come to include *all* kinds—some Christians, Jews, Buddhists, Hindus, agnostics, and even atheists! I have friends who are called capitalists, Socialists, and Communists! Some of my friends are moderates, conservatives, extremists—some are even Uncle Toms! My friends today are black, brown, red, yellow, and *white!*"

Malcolm X and Martin
Luther King Jr. (on left)
were ideological opposites
for many years. Shortly
before his death, however,
Malcolm X attempted to
make amends with
Reverend King (see box).
*Reproduced by permission of*
*AP/Wide World Photos.*

## Forms Organization of Afro-American Unity

Malcolm X's experiences in the Muslim holy land of
Mecca, Saudi Arabia, led him to convert to orthodox Islam and
change his name to El-Hajj Malik El-Shabazz. He returned to
the United States to establish the Muslim Mosque of Harlem
and a black-nationalist group, the Organization of Afro-American Unity (OAAU). The OAAU advocated that African Americans practice self-defense, study African history and reclaim
African culture, aspire to economic self-sufficiency, and
become active in their communities. The OAAU stressed black
pride and supported human rights around the world. The
organization also called upon the United Nations to conduct
an investigation into racial injustices in the United States.

## The death of Malcolm X

After Malcolm X returned from his pilgrimage, hostil-
ities increased between himself and the NOI. Malcolm X's

## Malcolm X and Martin Luther King Jr.

Throughout the 1950s and 1960s Malcolm X publicly criticized Martin Luther King Jr. (1929–1968; see entry) many times. Malcolm X had little use for King's ideals of nonviolence and integration. In 1965, however, both men underwent shifts in their thinking. For different reasons, and through different experiences, both men arrived at a similar conclusion: that racial justice in America would only come about through economic equality.

Shortly before his death, Malcolm X attempted to make amends with King. At the invitation of the Student Nonviolent Coordinating Committee (SNCC; pronounced "snick"; an organization of student civil rights activists), Malcolm X gave a speech in Selma, Alabama, during the voting rights campaign in February 1965. When Malcolm X arrived in Selma, King was in jail as a result of a voting rights demonstration two days earlier. "The white people should thank Dr. King for holding people in check," Malcolm X told an overflow audience in a church. "For there are other [black leaders] who do not believe in these [nonviolent] measures."

Malcolm X later told King's wife, Coretta Scott King, that he had hoped to visit King in jail. "I want Dr. King to know," he explained, "that I didn't come to Selma to make his job difficult.... If the white people realize what the alternative is, perhaps they will be more willing to hear Dr. King."

King was saddened three weeks later when he received the news that Malcolm X had been killed. "Malcolm X was reevaluating his own philosophical suppositions," stated King, "and moving toward a greater understanding of the nonviolent movement and toward more tolerance of white people."

former colleagues in the NOI were disdainful of Malcolm and the OAAU and feared losing their base of support to Malcolm. For his part, Malcolm X criticized Elijah Muhammad for having extramarital affairs and called him a "racist" and a "political fakir."

After receiving a series of death threats, Malcolm's house was firebombed on February 14, 1965. One week later, as Malcolm spoke before a huge crowd in Harlem's Audubon Ballroom, he was shot to death. While three men with ties to the NOI were convicted of the murder, there is speculation

Malcolm X is removed from the Audubon Ballroom after being shot in February 1965. While three men with Nation of Islam ties were later convicted of the shooting, there is speculation that the FBI and other government agencies may have played a role in the murder plot. *Reproduced by permission of Corbis-Bettmann.*

that the Federal Bureau of Investigation (FBI) and other government agencies may have played a role in the assassination plot.

## Black power movement gains momentum

Shortly after Malcolm X's death—and largely due to his influence—the black power movement gained momentum. Favored by young and militant African Americans, black power was synonymous with racial pride. The movement represented the belief that blacks did not have to ask whites for acceptance, but that blacks held the power to create a better society for themselves. It represented the desire of African Americans to hold political, economic, and social power.

## Malcolm X honored with stamp

In 1999 the United States Postal Service honored Malcolm X with a 33-cent stamp as part of its "Black Heritage" series. Malcolm X "was a visionary," stated Postal Service governor David Fineman at the stamp's unveiling, "a man who dreamed of a better world and dared to do something about it."

## Sources

### Books

*African American Biography.* Vol. 3. Detroit: U•X•L, 1994: pp. 487–90.

Malcolm X, and Alex Haley. *The Autobiography of Malcolm X.* New York: Grove Press, 1965.

Levy, Peter B. *The Civil Rights Movement.* Westwood, CT: Greenwood Press, 1998.

O'Reilly, Kenneth. *Black Americans: The FBI Files.* New York: Carroll and Graf Publishers, Inc., 1994

Patterson, Lillie. *Martin Luther King, Jr., and the Freedom Movement.* New York: Facts on File, 1989.

Smallwood, David, et al. *Profiles of Great African Americans.* Lincolnwood, IL: Publications International, Ltd., 1996: pp. 208–11.

### Web Sites

"'Visionary' Activist Malcolm X Given Stamp of Honor." CNN Interactive. [Online] Available http://www.cnn.com/US/9901/20/malcolmx. stamp.ap./index.html (last accessed January 22, 1999).

# Robert Parris Moses

**Born January 23, 1935**
**New York, New York**

**African American civil rights leader and educator**

Robert Moses brought the civil rights movement to Mississippi, initiating a voter registration drive, Freedom Summer, and the Mississippi Freedom Democratic Party.

Portrait: Reproduced by permission of the Library of Congress.

Robert Parris Moses was a soft-spoken, twenty-five-year-old mathematics teacher from New York City when he joined the Student Nonviolent Coordinating Committee (SNCC; pronounced "snick") in 1960. Moses became well known and admired for his courage and commitment, but he believed that a focus on strong leaders detracted from the more important goal of empowering individuals to create their own destiny.

Moses took on the most difficult task the civil rights movement had to offer—registering black voters in Mississippi. In the early 1960s Mississippi was the most segregated state in the nation. It led the South in the number of lynchings, beatings, and unexplained disappearances of African Americans. Moses endured beatings and jailings, and witnessed the killings of his coworkers, to help black Mississippians secure their civil rights.

"There was something about [Moses]," wrote SNCC chairman Cleveland Sellers in 1965, "the manner in which he carried himself, that seemed to draw all of us to him. He had been where we were going. And more important, he had emerged as the kind of person we wanted to be."

## Early life and career

Moses was born in Harlem, New York, in 1935. His grandfather was a Baptist minister, and his father was a janitor. Moses grew up in the four-story Harlem River Projects. He attended Stuyvesant High School, a competitive school to which admittance was based on examination scores. In his senior year Moses was class president and captain of the baseball team.

After graduating from high school in 1952, Moses won a scholarship to the mostly-white Hamilton College in upstate New York. After his junior year Moses participated in a summer workshop sponsored by the Quaker-based peace and justice group, American Friends Service Committee (AFSC), building houses for homeless families in France. The following summer he participated in an AFSC project in Japan.

Moses earned a bachelor of arts degree in 1956, then enrolled in a doctoral program in philosophy at Harvard University. After completing his master's degree in 1957, Moses learned of his mother's death from cancer and his father's mental breakdown. Rather than continue his studies, Moses returned to New York to care for his father. He got a job teaching mathematics at New York's prestigious private Horace Mann High School.

## Becomes interested in civil rights movement

In 1960 Moses was fascinated by news of the student sit-ins in Greensboro, North Carolina. (Sit-ins were a form of civil rights protest in which black students, sometimes joined by white students, would request service at segregated lunch counters, then refuse to leave when denied service.) "Before, the Negro in the South had always looked on the defensive, cringing," Moses recalled in *The Promised Land: The Great Black Migration and How it Changed America*. "This time they were taking the initiative. They were kids my age, and I knew this had something to do with my own life."

Shortly thereafter Moses began volunteering at the New York City office of the Southern Christian Leadership Conference (SCLC), helping staffer Bayard Rustin (1912–1987; see box in Ella Baker entry) prepare for an upcoming visit by Martin Luther King Jr. (1929–1968; see entry).

In June 1960, with Rustin's encouragement, Moses traveled to Atlanta to assist with an SCLC-sponsored voter registration drive. At the time, the SCLC shared its small office with the newly formed SNCC (the national student organization that had emerged from the sit-ins). Moses found that he had more in common with the SNCC, and its group-centered style of leadership, than with the SCLC, with its emphasis on a single leader.

## Begins working in the "closed society" of Mississippi

In August 1960 Moses jumped at the opportunity to travel through Mississippi, recruiting participants for a conference the SNCC was sponsoring that October. Moses began by looking up people on a contact list developed by Ella Baker (1903–1986; see entry) when she served as field organizer for the National Association for the Advancement of Colored People (NAACP).

Moses forged relationships with several local civil rights activists. Key among them was the NAACP leader in Cleveland, Mississippi, Amzie Moore (1900–1969). Moore, whom Moses later called "my father in the movement," explained to Moses his frustrations with the pace of change in Mississippi and requested Moses's assistance in voter registration efforts. In 1960 only 5 percent of all African Americans in the state were registered to vote. Blacks were kept from voting by literacy tests (tests, selectively administered to blacks, that required reading and interpreting a portion of the state constitution), poll taxes (special taxes that blacks were required to pay in order to vote), threats of home eviction and job loss, and violence.

Moses returned to Mississippi in July 1961, after fulfilling the terms of his teaching contract in New York. Together with a handful of other SNCC members, Moses worked on a voter registration drive with Moore, Medgar Evers (the NAACP's Mississippi field secretary who was assassinated in 1963), and other NAACP activists.

Moses and his colleagues quickly discovered the viciousness with which white Mississippians treated civil rights workers. In August 1961 Moses was knifed in the head by Billy Jack Caston, a cousin of the local sheriff. It took eight stitches to repair Moses's wound. That incident was only one of many beatings, arrests, and death threats endured by the civil rights workers that summer. And for all their suffering and efforts, in one year's time they had added very few new black names to voter rolls.

## Two steps forward and three steps back

In the summer of 1961 Moses, along with a new crew of volunteers sent from the SNCC's office in Atlanta, established a voter registration school in Pike County, Mississippi. In three-day classes, prospective voters learned how to fill out registration applications and how to interpret the state constitution. The first three people to complete the class went to the courthouse in Liberty to try to register. Not only were they turned away by the registrar, but one of the applicants was shot.

Moses escorted three more prospective voters to the courthouse shortly thereafter. Again the group was unsuccessful, and that time Moses was beaten and jailed. Moses remained undeterred. After he recovered, he and SNCC volunteer Travis Britt accompanied four African Americans to the courthouse. Moses and Britt were brutally beaten by an angry mob. One white assailant claimed that the pair was being punished for having the nerve to "come down here and teach people to vote."

## Violence escalates

On September 25, 1961, Moses learned that Herbert Lee, a farmer and NAACP member who had assisted him in a door-to-door voter registration effort, had been killed. Lee had been shot in full daylight by a white state representative named E. H. Hurst. Not surprisingly, no charges were filed in the case. The only black witness to the shooting was killed before he could give his statement to the FBI.

Moses and other SNCC members recruited 100 black high-school students and held a march through the streets of McComb, Mississippi. As the marchers knelt to pray on the steps of the city hall, they were arrested. A white mob attacked Robert Zellner (1939– ), the SNCC's foremost white activist, beating him unconscious. After watching the attack, police officers and FBI agents arrested Zellner.

The students who had been arrested were subsequently expelled from school. Moses and SNCC colleague Charles McDew responded to the students' expulsion by creating an alternative school for them called Nonviolent High School. Moses and McDew were soon arrested on the charges of contributing to the delinquency of minors and sentenced to four months in jail. "This is Mississippi, the middle of the iceberg," wrote Moses from jail. "This is a tremor in the middle of the iceberg—from the stone that the builders rejected."

## The Freedom Vote

In the fall of 1963 Moses participated in an SNCC project called the Freedom Vote. The Freedom Vote was a mock election in which blacks, denied participation in the official elections, were able to cast ballots for governor and lieutenant governor. Freedom voters chose between gubernatorial candidates from the Republican Party, the Democratic Party, and the unofficial "Freedom Party." The Freedom Party ran a black pharmacist and head of the Mississippi NAACP named Aaron Henry for governor. Moses, who was interested in racial reconciliation, solicited Edwin King, a white chaplain at the all-black Tougaloo College, to run for lieutenant governor.

Moses enlisted the help of sixty white students from Yale and Stanford universities to help get out the "freedom vote." Volunteers spent two weeks traveling door-to-door through rural Mississippi, talking up the mock election and promoting Freedom Party candidates. On election day, Freedom Vote stations were set up in beauty parlors, barbershops, private homes, and on sidewalks. Ninety-three thousand African Americans cast freedom ballots, and Freedom Party candidates won by a wide margin.

"The freedom vote," Moses was quoted as saying in the *Mississippi Free Press* on October 5, 1963, "is a major step in getting Negroes into the workings of democracy. The next process we have to go through is to prepare people for the day when Negroes run for office."

## Calls for Freedom Summer

Moses and other veterans of civil rights work in Mississippi took note of the decline in violence against civil rights workers during the Freedom Vote. They attributed the relative peace to the presence of white students, whose lives the Justice Department had a stake in protecting. Moses and Dave Dennis, chairman of the Congress on Racial Equality (CORE) in Mississippi, decided to use this reality to their advantage. They put out the call for volunteers to come to Mississippi for Freedom Summer—a massive campaign to register black voters for the upcoming November presidential election. Moses went to Stanford University to recruit volunteers.

Approximately 1,000 people signed up for Freedom Summer. Most of the volunteers were white students from elite northern colleges. Before the volunteers came South, Moses and other SNCC leaders put them through a week-long training session in Oxford, Ohio. Moses talked to the students about the dangers of doing civil rights work in Mississippi and schooled them in techniques of nonviolent action—how to defy authority but not strike back when attacked.

In late June 1964 Freedom Summer volunteers descended upon Mississippi. They conducted door-to-door voter registration drives and established community centers, health clinics, legal clinics, and community feeding sites called "freedom kitchens." Volunteers also founded close to fifty "freedom schools" for African American children, at which they taught reading, math, and African American history. Freedom school students were encouraged to write letters to editors of newspapers about the effects of segregation, short stories about their lives, and poetry.

## Organizes Mississippi Freedom Democratic Party

During Freedom Summer, Moses and a core of volunteers were hard at work laying the foundation of a new political party, the Mississippi Freedom Democratic Party (MFDP). The MFDP was set up as an alternative to the regular Democratic party, which excluded blacks. In about one month's time, the MFDP had signed up 80,000 members. The party held a statewide convention on August 6 at which it elected sixty-eight delegates (four of them whites).

Moses and the rest of the MFDP delegation traveled to the national Democratic Party convention later that month in

Atlantic City, New Jersey. The MFDP claimed to be much more representative of the people of Mississippi than the Democratic Party and insisted on being seated. MFDP delegates also pointed out that they, unlike the regular Democrats, supported the national Democratic Party candidates and platform. (During the civil rights era, the Republican Party was virtually nonexistent in the South. Southern Democrats typically sided with northern Republicans in Congress.)

## Delegates seek recognition

The question of which Mississippi delegation to recognize was put before the convention's credentials committee. Several MFDP representatives testified before the committee. They spoke of the exclusion of blacks from the Democratic party and the overall horrible living conditions for blacks in Mississippi.

Without even taking a roll-call vote of delegates, the credentials committee decided in favor of the regular Democrats. As a consolation, they offered the MFDP two "at-large" seats (not representing the state of Mississippi). The committee also ruled that, in the future, only delegations not tainted by segregationist practices would be seated at national conventions.

Moses, like the vast majority of MFDP delegates, rejected the compromise. He was outraged by the committee's tokenism and felt betrayed by the liberal Democratic establishment. Moses told television reporters, "I will have nothing to do with the political system any longer."

## Withdraws from civil rights activity

After the 1964 Democratic Party convention, Moses began a gradual retreat from both the SNCC and the civil rights movement. That September Moses went on a three-week tour of Africa, funded by singer Harry Belafonte, with a handful of other SNCC activists. Upon his return he helped SNCC director James Forman set up a program in Mississippi called Black Belt, which was a continuation of Freedom Summer using black volunteers. Moses then moved to Birmingham, Alabama, to experience civil rights organizing in an urban environment.

In December 1964, to escape the publicity and the cult of personality that seemed to be forming around him, Moses

## Moses's Opposition to the Vietnam War

Robert Moses was one of the first civil rights leaders to actively oppose the Vietnam War (1954–75). In April 1965 Moses was a keynote speaker at the first national demonstration against the war, sponsored by Students for a Democratic Society (a campus antiwar organization). By the late 1960s many civil rights activists were calling for an end to the war, citing the high proportion of African American casualties and the high cost that took away from social spending.

"The rationale this nation uses to justify the war in Vietnam," stated Moses in a 1965 interview, "turns out to be amazingly similar to the rationale that has been used by the white South to justify its opposition to the freedom movement. For the racist white Southerner, there is a logic in this parallel. He condones murder in Vietnam for the same reason he condones it at home—he sees a threat to his civilization."

changed his surname to his mother's maiden name, Parris. Throughout his tenure in Mississippi people had drawn parallels between Robert Moses and the biblical Moses, pointing out that both had led their people out of bondage. Moses was uncomfortable with that comparison and the fact that his followers, in the words of fellow SNCC activist John Lewis (1940–; see entry), looked upon him as "the all-perfect and all-holy and all-wise leader."

## Flees to Canada

In the fall of 1965, facing criticism that his anti-Vietnam War activities (see box) were stealing attention from the SNCC's civil rights work, Moses resigned from the SNCC. He spent the next several months traveling through Africa. When Moses returned to the United States in the spring of 1966, he learned he had been drafted for military service. Rather than fight in a war he deplored or spend time in jail, he fled to Canada.

While working a variety of odd jobs in Canada, Moses met former SNCC field secretary Janet Jemmott, and the two married. The newlyweds traveled to Africa in 1968. The couple spent the next several years in Tanzania, teaching in a high school and raising a family. For Moses, his time in Africa was an opportunity to heal his nerves after the years of constant tension in Mississippi.

## Initiates the Algebra Project

In 1977, when President Jimmy Carter (1924– ) offered a general amnesty to draft dodgers, Moses and his family returned to the United States. The family settled in Cambridge, Massachusetts, where Moses continued his graduate studies in mathematics. Four years later he was awarded a "genius award" from the MacArthur Foundation. ("Genius awards" are granted yearly to individuals who have made extraordinary contributions to society.) Moses used the money to found the Algebra Project, through which he engaged in community organizing and mathematics instruction for inner-city youth.

In 1992 Moses returned to the Mississippi Delta (flat lands along the banks of the Mississippi River), where he had fought for civil rights three decades earlier, and established the Delta Algebra Project. According to Moses, the Delta Algebra Project is his "version of Civil Rights 1992."

## Sources

### Books

Branch, Taylor. *Parting the Waters: America in the King Years, 1954–1963.* New York: Simon and Schuster, Inc., 1988.

Burner, Eric R. *And Gently He Shall Lead Them: Robert Parris Moses and Civil Rights in Mississippi.* New York: New York University Press, 1994.

Carson, Clayborne. *In Struggle: SNCC and the Black Awakening of the 1960s.* Cambridge: Harvard University Press, 1981.

Dittmer, John. *Local People: The Struggle for Civil Rights in Mississippi.* Urbana, IL: University of Illinois Press, 1994.

Levy, Peter B. *The Civil Rights Movement.* Westwood, CT: Greenwood Press, 1998.

Weisbrot, Robert. *Freedom Bound: A History of America's Civil Rights Movement.* New York: W. W. Norton and Company, 1990.

Williams, Juan. *Eyes on the Prize: America's Civil Rights Years, 1954–1965.* New York: Penguin Books, 1987.

Zinn, Howard. *SNCC: The New Abolitionists.* Westport, CT: Greenwood Press, 1985.

# Leonard Peltier

**Born September 12, 1944**
**Grand Forks, North Dakota**

**Native American activist**

Leonard Peltier, an Obijway-Lakota activist, is currently serving two consecutive life sentences at Leavenworth Federal Prison in northeastern Kansas. In June 1975 Peltier was convicted of killing two Federal Bureau of Investigation (FBI) agents in a shoot-out on the Pine Ridge Reservation. He was one of four Indians charged with the killings; two of the other people accused were acquitted, and charges against the third person were dropped. Peltier's trial was controversial. The evidence against him was scant and inconclusive; in fact, the FBI's main witness later claimed to have been coerced to testify against Peltier, and the FBI employed numerous extralegal tactics to ensure a victory in the case.

Despite his poor health and proclaimed innocence—as well as continuous appeals for clemency (legal pardon) by his numerous supporters—Peltier remains behind bars. Among the organizations that consider him a political prisoner (a person imprisoned for political beliefs and activities rather than the actual crime of which he was been convicted) are Amnesty International, the International Federation of Human Rights, Universal Declaration of Human Rights, and the Human

Activist Leonard Peltier is considered a political prisoner by international human rights organizations.

Portrait: Reproduced by permission of AP/Wide World Photos.

Rights Commission in Spain. Peltier has numerous prominent supporters around the world, including Nobel Peace Prize winner Roberta Menchu, South African archbishop Desmond Tutu, and celebrities Robert Redford, Willie Nelson, and Joni Mitchell.

## Grows up in North Dakota and Montana

Peltier was born in Grand Forks, North Dakota. His maternal grandmother was a full-blooded Lakota (Sioux) and his father was three quarters Ojibway and one quarter French. When Peltier was very young, his large family migrated with the potato harvest every year from Turtle Mountain, in north central North Dakota, to the Red River Valley, on the border of North Dakota and Minnesota.

When Peltier was four years old his parents separated, and he, together with his younger sister, went to live with his paternal grandparents. When Peltier was an adolescent, the foursome moved to Butte, Montana. There Peltier looked for work in the logging camps and copper mines. When he was no longer able to tolerate the racial harassment of his coworkers and supervisors, Peltier moved to the Wahpeton Reservation in North Dakota and enrolled in the Wahpeton Indian School. Shortly thereafter, he went to live with his father on North Dakota's Turtle Mountain Reservation.

## Becomes interested in traditional Indian rites

At Turtle Mountain Peltier became interested in traditional Indian rites, including the sun dance. The sun dance, which for many years was outlawed by the Bureau of Indian Affairs (BIA), involves days of dancing, prayer, and fasting. At the end of the ritual some participants pierce their chests with sharpened sticks in an act of spiritual purification. In 1958, when Peltier participated in his first sun dance, the ceremony was still illegal. Consequently, Peltier and the other sun dancers were arrested and jailed.

## Moves to the West Coast

In 1959 Peltier moved to Oakland, California, to join his mother. Peltier's mother had moved to the West Coast under the auspices of the BIA's relocation program. Through this program the BIA offered financial assistance and job placement services to Indians willing to leave reservations and move to cities. According to critics of BIA policy, the purpose of relocation was to weaken Indian communities and make it easier for outsiders to take over reservation lands.

Peltier learned the basics of machine-tool operation and carpentry from his uncle, who was also living in Oakland. Then Peltier and his cousin, Steve Robideau, found work as welders in the shipyards of Portland, Oregon. At the age of twenty Peltier moved to Seattle, Washington, and became a part-owner of an automobile repair shop.

In Seattle Peltier became involved in the campaign for Indian fishing rights. State authorities in Washington had been attempting to regulate Indian fishing, in violation of treaties that exempted Indians from fishing restrictions. Peltier joined in demonstrations called "fish-ins," in which protesters purposely fished in violation of state fishing laws to assert their treaty rights.

## Joins the American Indian Movement

In the late 1960s Peltier joined the American Indian Movement (AIM), a militant Indian rights group that fought for the return of tribal lands, enforcement of government treaties, respect for Indian human rights, and greater economic opportunities for Indians. Peltier's first action with AIM, in 1970, was the takeover of Fort Lawton, outside of Seattle. Fort Lawton, a deserted army base, had been established on land that was once part of an Indian reservation. AIM staked claim to the land under the terms of an 1868 Sioux treaty, the Treaty of Fort Laramie, which stipulated that abandoned federal installations on former Indian land be returned to Indians.

Peltier joined AIM members from around the country in the Trail of Broken Treaties protest in Washington, D.C., in the fall of 1972. AIM prepared a list of demands for the BIA, including the restoration of tribes' treaty-making status, the return of stolen Indian lands, and the revocation of state government authority over Indian affairs. When BIA officials turned the delegation away at the door, AIM took over the building. Members barricaded themselves inside for six days before accepting a government offer to pay their transportation costs home and consider AIM's demands. Not surprisingly, U.S. officials never conceded a single point on AIM's list.

## Labeled a "key extremist"

After the Trail of Broken Treaties, AIM leaders—including Peltier—were classified by the FBI as "key extremists" and targeted for surveillance under COINTELPRO. COINTELPRO, which stands for Counter-Intelligence Program, was a secret FBI operation in the 1960s and 1970s in which FBI agents, under the guise of combating domestic terrorism, gathered information on and attempted to destroy the anti-Vietnam War movement, the civil rights movement, and militant organizations of people of color.

In November 1972, shortly after the Trail of Broken Treaties, Peltier was beaten by two off-duty policemen in Milwaukee, Wisconsin. Peltier was arrested for carrying an unloaded, broken gun and charged with attempted murder. He spent the next five months in jail. Peltier was finally set free when AIM was able to post bail. Rather than face near-certain conviction in a trial he believed would not be fair, Peltier went underground (hid from the law) and headed for the Dakotas.

## Participates in the siege of Wounded Knee

In February 1973 Peltier joined his AIM comrades and hundreds of Lakota traditionalists (adherents of American Indian cultural practices and religions) in a takeover of Wounded Knee, a village on the Pine Ridge Reservation in South Dakota. Wounded Knee was chosen for its symbolic value. In 1890 the village was the site of a massacre by U.S. military forces of between 150 and 370 Native American men, women, and children.

The 1973 takeover was a protest against the corrupt practices of tribal chairman Richard Wilson, regarded by most Lakota as a BIA "puppet." Demonstrators also drew attention to the brutality of Wilson's police force, the Guardians of the Oglala Nation ("GOONs" for short). The occupation of Wounded Knee lasted ten weeks and attracted about 2,000 Indian participants.

Hundreds of FBI agents, U.S. marshals, and members of tribal and local police forces, all heavily armed, surrounded the Wounded Knee encampment. The army supplied the law enforcement officials with armored personnel carriers, grenade launchers, 600 cases of tear gas, helicopters, and Phantom jets. The protesters and officials reached a negotiated settlement on May 8, and the standoff came to an end. The investigations into conditions on Pine Ridge, which had been promised by the government, never took place.

## Tensions continue to rise

In the two years that followed the occupation, tensions continued to rise on the Pine Ridge Reservation. Traditionalists and AIM members were targeted for revenge by Wilson's GOONs. In 1974 the reservation had twenty-three killings, giving it the highest per capita murder rate in the country. In March 1975 Lakota elders called upon Peltier to protect them from the GOONs. Peltier and six other AIM members responded by establishing a spiritual camp near the village of Oglala.

"The tribal elders sent out an appeal for warriors to come to Pine Ridge," Peltier stated in a 1995 interview with Scott Anderson for *Outside* magazine, "because the GOONs were just taking over—killing people, terrorizing women and children—and the police and FBI were helping them do it. I went to defend my people."

## Charged with murder of FBI agents

On June 26, 1975, two FBI agents came to Pine Ridge Reservation to arrest a nineteen-year-old Oglala Lakota AIM member named Jimmy Eagle. Eagle was wanted for allegedly stealing a white man's cowboy boots. While the details of the event remain unclear, gunfire was exchanged between the FBI agents and Indians. When the shooting stopped, the two FBI agents and a twenty-four-year-old Indian man were dead.

The FBI then began an all-out investigation to find the killer of the agents (the death of the Indian man was never investigated). The reservation was soon swarming with FBI assault teams, armed with fully automatic weapons and lead-

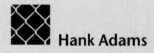

## Hank Adams

Hank Adams (1944– ), an Assiniboine-Sioux Indian from the Fort Peck Reservation in Montana, was a leader of the National Indian Youth Council (NIYC) and a fishing-rights activist in the 1960s. Adams attended the University of Washington from 1961 to 1963. In August 1963 he led a group of Native Americans to the March on Washington for Jobs and Freedom (for more information on the march, see the Martin Luther King Jr. and John Lewis entries). On his return to Washington state, Adams became involved with the NIYC—an action-oriented group of young, mostly urban Indians based in Albuquerque, New Mexico, that called for an end to racist and arrogant U.S. policies toward American Indians.

Adams spearheaded the NIYC's "fish-in" campaign in the Puget Sound area of Washington. Together with members of a local organization, The Survival of American Indians Association, Inc. (of which Adams later became president), Adams and others in the NIYC fished in violation of state laws in order to assert their treaty rights. (Native Americans in that region had treaty rights to fish free from state interference; state officials, however, were attempting to regulate

ing tracking dogs. The agents burst into and vandalized homes, intimidated residents, and trampled upon sacred burial grounds. FBI helicopters flew constantly overhead.

Ten weeks after the shoot-out, the FBI charged Peltier and three other AIM activists—Jimmy Eagle, Bob Robideau and Dino Butler—with the murder of the agents. Rather than face trial in South Dakota, a state known for its extreme anti-Indian racism, Peltier fled to Canada. He later stated that he "realized the possibility of getting a fair trial was very slim."

The FBI was unable to produce hard evidence linking any of the Native Americans with the murders. Robideau and Butler were acquitted by all-white juries (the two key witnesses for the prosecution both admitted that the FBI had bought their testimony). The FBI's case against Eagle was so weak that they dropped the murder charge, preferring to concentrate their energies on finding and convicting Peltier.

**Hank Adams.** *Reproduced by permission of AP/Wide World Photos.*

Indian fishing.) Adams was arrested several times and in 1971 was shot by an unknown assailant and seriously injured.

In the mid 1960s Adams worked with Senator Robert Kennedy and consumer advocate Ralph Nader on Native American rights issues. In the late 1960s he joined the American Indian Movement (AIM). In 1972 Adams participated in AIM's Trail of Broken Treaties protest—a six-day occupation of the Bureau of Indian Affairs in Washington, D.C., during which AIM demanded the restoration of tribes' treaty-making status, the return of stolen Indian lands, and the revocation of state government authority over Indian affairs.

## Arrested and put on trial

In February 1976 Peltier was arrested in Alberta, Canada. At his extradition hearings, the FBI produced a Lakota woman named Myrtle Poor Bear. (Extradition is the legal surrender of a fugitive from the jurisdiction of one state, country, or government to another.) While Poor Bear claimed at the hearing that she had seen Peltier kill the agents, she later recanted her testimony, stating that the FBI had threatened her with the same fate as AIM activist Anna Mae Aquash (1945–1976; see entry) if she did not testify. Aquash, who had also been approached by the FBI to testify against Peltier, had claimed to have no information about the killings. An agent had warned her that she would be "dead within a year" and, indeed, Aquash was found shot to death on the Pine Ridge reservation in February 1976.

Peltier's trial began in March 1977 in Fargo, North Dakota. "The trial of Leonard Peltier," wrote Mark Grossman

in *The Native American Rights Movement,* "can best be characterized as one of the worst miscarriages of justice in American
history." The evidence presented by the prosecution was cir-
cumstantial and inconclusive and included a fabricated murder weapon. There were no witnesses to the murders. The
defense was not allowed to make a case for self-defense and
was prevented from presenting much of its case, including evidence that the FBI had initiated the firefight.

A *Los Angeles Times* reporter broke the story that prosecutors in the Peltier case had "shopped" for a judge, meaning
they sought out and secured a judge known for his anti-Indian
opinions, who was most likely to sympathize with the prosecution. *Washington Post* columnist Jack Anderson wrote on
December 28, 1982, that even though "'shopping' for a
friendly judge is an old, if not particularly honorable, practice
in the American system of justice ... the FBI and federal prosecutors carried it to an unsavory extreme in the murder trial of
American Indian activist Leonard Peltier."

Peltier was convicted of the murders of the FBI agents
by an all-white jury. On June 1, 1977, Peltier was handed two
life sentences to be served consecutively (one after another).

## Exhausts appeals

Peltier's lawyers first appealed his case, unsuccessfully,
before the Eighth Circuit Court of Appeals in December 1977.
In March 1979 Peltier's lawyers attempted to bring his case
before the Supreme Court, but the Court refused to hear it.

In April 1979, while imprisoned in California's Lom-
poc Prison, Peltier learned of a plot to kill him; as a result, he
escaped. Peltier was recaptured and sentenced to an additional
seven years. The penalty for his escape was later overturned by
the Ninth Circuit Court of Appeals.

In 1982, following the revelation of new evidence that
the fatal bullets in the FBI case were not linked to Peltier's gun,
Peltier petitioned for a new trial, but his petition was denied.
Peltier appealed his case two more times—in 1984 and 1987—
and both attempts failed. In 1993, despite the emergence of
new evidence that another man had killed the agents, Peltier
lost his final appeal.

Peltier came up for parole (early release) in 1995. He was turned down despite an admission from U.S. prosecutor Lynn Crooks that "the government doesn't know who killed their [the FBI's] agents." The U.S. Parole Commission claimed that Peltier would have to continue serving his sentence because he had not given a "factual and specific account of (his) actions ... consistent with the jury's verdict of guilt." The commission told Peltier to reappear before them in the year 2009. Meanwhile, the 6,000 pages of documentation the FBI has collected in the case remain sealed on the grounds of "national security."

"You have to understand," Peltier related in his *Outside* interview, "I didn't kill those agents. I didn't order anyone to kill those agents. I'm an innocent man."

# Sources

## Books

Churchill, Ward, and Jim Vander Wall. *Agents of Repression: The FBI's Secret Wars against the Black Panther Party and the American Indian Movement.* Boston: South End Press, 1988.

Grossman, Mark. *The ABC-CLIO Companion to The American Indian Rights Movement.* Santa Barbara, CA: ABC-CLIO, 1996, pp. 293–95.

Malinowski, Sharon, and Simon Glickman, eds. *Native North American Biography.* Detroit: U•X•L, 1996, pp. 274–79.

Matthiessen, Peter. *In the Spirit of Crazy Horse.* New York: Viking Press, 1980.

Olson, James S. *Encyclopedia of American Indian Civil Rights.* Westport, CT: Greenwood Press, 1997, p. 282.

## Periodicals

Anderson, Scott. "The Martyrdom of Leonard Peltier." *Outside.* July 1995.

Ayers, Jane. "Free Peltier!" (editorial). *The Nation.* July 18, 1994: 76+.

Kauffmann, Stanley. "Incident at Oglala" (movie review). *New Republic.* June 8, 1992: 32.

Matthiessen, Peter. "Who Really Killed the FBI Men; New Light on Peltier's Case." *The Nation.* May 13, 1991: 613+.

## Web Sites

International Office of the Leonard Peltier Defense Committee. [Online] Available. http://members.xoom.com/freepeltier/index.html (last accessed February 16, 1999).

## Other

Apted, Michael, director. *Incident at Oglala: The Leonard Peltier Story* (documentary). Miramax, 1992.

# Ed Roberts

**Born January 23, 1939**
**Burlingame, California**
**Died March 14, 1995**
**Berkeley, California**

**Disability rights activist**

Ed Roberts was a pioneer of the disability rights movement in America. (A disability is any physical or mental condition that restricts one or more of an individual's major life activities.) Roberts defied the medical authorities who told him, at age fourteen, that he would have no meaningful life as a quadriplegic (a person with paralysis of all four limbs). He went on to earn a master's degree in political science and to fill the roles of teacher, counselor, director of a statewide agency, husband, father, and founder of two of the world's most effective and influential organizations for people with disabilities. Roberts fought back against a system that relegated people with disabilities to second-class citizen status and helped people with disabilities regain control over their lives.

## Polio leads to paralysis

Roberts was a healthy fourteen year old, living in Burlingame and playing on the McKinley High School football team, when he contracted poliomyelitis. (Poliomyelitis—"polio" for short—is a crippling viral disease, often affecting children, that can lead to permanent partial paralysis and physical deformity.) Within two days Roberts had lost the ability to move all muscles below his neck except two fingers. He could only breathe with the aid of an iron lung (an 800-pound machine the size of a telephone booth that forces air in and out of the lungs).

"I went immediately from being a young aspiring athlete to a helpless cripple," stated Roberts in a 1990 interview with Sandy Kleffman of the *Mercury News*. "Probably the most devastating thing was that people would reiterate what I wouldn't do. Would I ever work? No. Would I ever have sexual relationships? No."

Roberts's doctors told his mother that he would be better off dead, since he could only live as a vegetable. Years later Roberts would joke with his friends that if he had to be a vegetable, he would like to be an artichoke—prickly on the outside and with a big heart. When it happened, however, Roberts's paralysis was no laughing matter. Overcome with despair, Roberts tried to starve himself to death. His weight dropped from 120 pounds to 50 pounds. He was kept alive by force-feeding through a tube. It was only when his private-duty nurse quit and the tube was removed that Roberts snapped out of his depression and regained his will to live.

## Completes high school

Because of his reliance upon the iron lung, Roberts was forced to take his first three years of high school education at home. By his senior year, however, Roberts had recovered to the point that he only needed the iron lung at night. He was therefore able to go to school for some of his classes. Roberts was undeterred by the stares of other students as he wheeled through the hallways, finishing his senior year with straight A's.

When it came time to graduate, the principal told Roberts he would not be receiving a diploma because he lacked the required driver's education and physical education courses. Roberts's parents took his case to the school board, which overrode the principal's decision and permitted Roberts to graduate.

Roberts spent the next two years attending a community college, the College of San Mateo. When he told a guidance counselor that he wanted to study political science, she directed him to the University of California, Berkeley (UCB).

## Attends University of California

Roberts was initially denied admittance to UCB. The reason he was given was that the university had "tried cripples before, and they just don't work out." Roberts continued to press for his admission, and in 1962 the school allowed him to enroll on a trial basis. Roberts became the first quadriplegic to ever attend UCB. "Helpless Cripple Attends UC Classes" stated one headline heralding Roberts's arrival on campus.

The UCB was not an easy place for a wheelchair-bound person to navigate. Very few buildings were wheelchair accessible, and a sidewalk with a cut curb (gentle slope down to the street) was a rarity. Roberts had to live in the university's Cowell Hospital, where an iron lung was provided for his nightly use. He was reliant on other students to carry him and his chair into buildings and up and down flights of stairs. Despite these and other obstacles, Roberts did well in his classes.

Over the next few years UCB admitted a handful of other students with disabilities. Like Roberts, these students lived in Cowell Hospital. The group developed close bonds of friendship and called themselves the Rolling Quads. Together they studied, went to parties, and attended protests against the Vietnam War (1954–75; Berkeley was a major center of anti-war activity in the 1960s). Roberts's involvement in the anti-war movement inspired him to use similar protest tactics to fight for the rights of people with disabilities.

"I began to realize slowly there could be a movement for people like me, people who were disabled," Roberts told Mary Ann Farrell in a 1994 interview for the Knight-Ridder/Tribune News Service. "I began to learn more from the black, women's and Hispanic movements, and I knew that could be applied to persons with disabilities."

## Joins disability rights movement

Roberts began his career as a disability rights activist by taking on the California Department of Vocational Rehabilitation (DVR). The DVR was supposed to assist people with disabilities in their educational and employment pursuits. The DVR counselor at UC-B, however, was anything but helpful. She discouraged students with disabilities from pursuing their studies and cut off funds the DVR had been providing for the students' living expenses. Roberts took the matter to the local media. After unfavorable stories about the DVR made headlines, the students' funding was reinstated.

Roberts then branched out from the university to the community, offering assistance to Berkeley residents with disabilities. Roberts and other members of the Rolling Quads established a peer counseling service and a twenty-four-hour wheelchair repair shop and developed and distributed lists of personal care assistants and wheelchair-accessible apartments. They also successfully pressed the Berkeley city council to make curb cuts and to construct wheelchair-accessible ramps at public buildings.

While working on behalf of the disability community, Roberts continued his education. He eventually earned a bachelor of arts degree and a master's degree in political science. He completed all requirements for a doctorate except his dissertation. While a graduate student in the mid-1960s, Roberts taught courses in political science at UC-B.

In the late 1960s and early 1970s Roberts taught at a series of small, alternative colleges that blossomed during California's countercultural era, including Nairobi College (in East Palo Alto), Venceramos College (in Redwood City), and Common College (in Woodside). Roberts served as a consultant to the U.S. Department of Education in 1969, developing a set of guidelines to assist students with disabilities. In 1970, as a result of the work of Roberts and his colleagues, UC-B established the nation's first Disabled Students Program.

## Founds Center for Independent Living

In 1972 Roberts returned to Berkeley to found the Center for Independent Living (CIL), a program by and for persons with disabilities. The CIL got off the ground with a small federal grant, and Roberts managed to raise $1 million for the organization in ten months. "It was the right idea at the right time," Roberts told Farrell. "We changed things. The whole country was changing."

The underlying philosophy of the CIL was that people with disabilities, with the proper tools, could lead independent, productive lives. The CIL provided assistance with housing, wheelchair repair, and counseling. The organization also organized people with disabilities into a political constituency.

Through the CIL people with disabilities learned to become effective public speakers, how to lobby lawmakers, and how to navigate their way through the political system. CIL members fought to make illegal the discrimination they faced in employment and housing and pressed for the removal of physical barriers in housing and public accommodations (stores, restaurants, buses, etc.). The CIL model caught on nationwide and today the CIL exists in more than 400 cities.

## Heads Department of Vocational Rehabilitation

In 1975 California governor Jerry Brown (whose election campaign Roberts had actively supported) appointed Roberts to the helm of the Department of Vocational Rehabilitation (DRV)—the very department that Roberts had challenged while a student. (Ironically, the same DRV employee who had tried to force students with disabilities off the UC-B campus in the early 1960s was under Roberts's command.)

Roberts found himself in charge of an agency with 2,500 employees and a budget of $140 million. His job was to oversee assistance programs for people with disabilities and to implement independent living programs throughout the state. He also advocated the nationwide establishment of independent living programs.

## Establishes World Institute on Disability

In 1984 Roberts received a "genius award" worth $225,000 from the MacArthur Foundation. ("Genius awards" are granted yearly to individuals who have made extraordinary contributions to society.) With that money Roberts helped establish the World Institute on Disability (WID), an Oakland, California-based international public policy organization that sponsors research into disability issues and promotes the integration of people with disabilities into every aspect of society. Today WID has more than fifty employees and a budget of $3.3 million.

"If I could do it for the whole state," Roberts commented to Farrell, "I could do it for the whole world. This independent living concept works and yet is directly opposite to what the government and legislature thinks. We can do it ourselves. We don't need all the funds, the hospitalization. Just give us the chance and this works."

## WID supports Americans with Disabilities Act

One piece of legislation backed by WID was the Americans with Disabilities Act (ADA), which was signed into law in 1990. The ADA is a broad set of guarantees of equal treatment for people with disabilities. The act bans discrimination against people with disabilities in employment, government-run programs and services, public accommodations, and telecommunications.

"The Americans With Disabilities Act is legislation for the whole world, not just us," claimed Roberts. "First, it acknowledges that we have been discriminated against for all these years. Are we people who don't want to work? No! And yet some 75 percent of us are unemployed at some time. Do we want to be on welfare? No! And yet last year more than $200 billion was spent on people with disabilities."

In his capacity as WID president, Roberts logged over one million miles in his trips to some twenty-five countries. His work was cut short by his death from a heart attack in 1995. "Ed Roberts ... was a major prophet of the new revolution of independence," wrote his friend and colleague Justin Dart in the summer 1995 edition of the CIL's newsletter, *Independent Life.* "Not for nations or groups, but for people as individuals. Ed declared that people with disabilities are fully human; that they have a right and a responsibility to throw off traditional paternalism, to take control of their own lives, to help build a new culture in which they and all people participate fully in the leadership, the labor and the fruits of society."

## Sources

### Books

Kent, Deborah, and Kathryn A. Quinlan. *Extraordinary People with Disabilities.* New York: Children's Press, 1996, pp. 127–32.

### Periodicals

Farrell, Mary Ann. "Quadriplegic Ed Roberts a Pioneer in the Disability Rights Movement." Knight-Ridder/Tribune News Service. July 1, 1994.

Kleffman, Sandy. "Disabled Advocate Ed Roberts Dead at 56" (obituary). Knight-Ridder/Tribune News Service. March 15, 1995.

Shapiro, Joseph P. "Others Saw a Victim, but Ed Roberts Didn't." *U.S. News and World Report*. March 27, 1995: 6+.

## Web Sites

Center for Independent Living. [Online] Available http://www.cilberke-ley.org/ (last accessed on April 30, 1999).

"Ed Roberts Tribute." *Independent Life*. summer 1995. [Online] Available http://www.cilberkeley.org//ed.htm (last accessed April 15, 1999).

# Charlene Teters

**Born April 25, 1952**
**Spokane, Washington**

**Native American activist, artist,**
**educator, and writer**

In 1988 the University of Illinois recruited Spokane Indian Charlene Teters to come to the campus as part of an effort to boost minority student enrollment. Teters, a noted painter, moved her family from Santa Fe, New Mexico, to Urbana, Illinois, to pursue a master of fine arts degree. Her intention was to spend a couple of quiet years as a student, then return to Santa Fe. Instead, she found herself leading a fight to end the use of the school's mascot—a fictitious Indian named Chief Illiniwek.

Teters's one-person campaign to educate the University of Illinois community about the dehumanizing effects of Indian mascots grew into a national movement targeting professional and collegiate sports teams. Today Teters is a spokesperson for the National Coalition on Racism in Sports and Media. Her struggle to stop the exploitative use of American Indian images was documented in the award-winning video *In Whose Honor?,* which was shown in the Public Broadcasting System's *P.O.V.* series in 1997. "Our people paid with their lives to keep what little we have left," said Teters in *In Whose Honor?* "The fact that we even have anything today

> "Our people paid with their lives to keep what little we have left. The fact that we even have anything today speaks to the strength of our ancestors, and that is what I'm protecting."

Portrait: Reproduced by permission of Charlene Teters.

speaks to the strength of our ancestors, and that is what I'm protecting."

## An early interest in art

Teters was born and raised in Spokane, Washington. Her family spent many weekends on the Spokane Indian Reservation, home to most of their relatives. On the reservation Teters learned about native religion, rituals, and culture, and was taught to respect her ancestors.

Teters attended public schools in Spokane and began painting at an early age. She was inspired in her artistic endeavors by her father, who was also an artist. In 1984 Teters and her family (by that time she had two young children) moved to Santa Fe, New Mexico, so that she could attend the Institute of American Indian Arts (IAIA). She earned her associate of fine arts degree in 1986, then enrolled in art school at the College of Santa Fe. Teters received a bachelor of fine arts degree in painting in 1988. Teters and her family then packed up and moved to Urbana, where Teters had been admitted to the University of Illinois (U of I).

## Introduction to Chief Illiniwek

Once Teters settled in at U of I, she could not help but notice an ever-present Indian symbol: Chief Illiniwek, the fictitious Indian mascot of the U of I's "Fighting Illini" sports teams. The chief's head was featured on U of I clothing and literature and in the logos of local businesses. Chief Illiniwek's splashiest appearances, however, were at halftime during U of I basketball and football games. During breaks in play, a white student dressed in buckskin and an eagle feather headdress would dance, generating wild cheers from U of I fans wearing mock war paint.

At first Teters tried to ignore the presence of Chief Illiniwek. She found that was no longer possible, however, after witnessing the "chief" in action at a basketball game in 1989. Teters had taken her two children to the game at their request. "I'd never seen [the chief] before; didn't know at all what he looked like, what he wore," stated Teters in *In Whose Honor?* "I just heard the chief comes out and does what's billed as an 'authentic dance.' And he came out wearing that buckskin ... wearing what looked like real eagle feathers, all the way to the ground. And of course, the fans go into a frenzy. All around us they were yelling 'The Chief! The Chief!' and my kids just sank in their seats. I saw my daughter try to become invisible. My son tried to laugh.... My children know who they are.... They know they're Indian. They have been taught to respect the person who has earned the right to wear an eagle feather headdress. What I saw in my children was a blow to their self-esteem and it still makes me angry."

## Teters speaks out

After witnessing the mockery of Indian traditions at the basketball game, Teters could no longer remain silent. She began speaking out in spite of warnings from the art department that she should just be quiet and complete her degree. "At home we're taught to respect eagle feathers, respect chiefs, respect dance, respect that paint is sacred," explained Teters in *In Whose Honor?* "If you've never been taught to respect those things, it might not bother you.... But if you've grown up within a community where those things have meaning, it's going to have that impact on you.... It definitely was a blow to my kids. Because they saw things they'd been taught to respect being mimicked and reduced to this entertainment event and trivialized. I knew I was probably going to sacrifice my student status by speaking up. But I thought it was worth it."

Holding a sign reading "Indians are human beings, not mascots," Teters staged a lonely vigil in front of the stadium before home basketball games. She quickly discovered the depth of the crowd's attachment to Chief Illiniwek, as well as the depth of their resentment toward her. Students spit on Teters, hurled objects at her, and screamed threats and obscenities in her face. She also received threatening and sexually harassing phone calls at home. The student newspaper ran editorials with titles such as "Bellyachers and Blowhards—Leave Chief Alone" and "Illiniwek Protesters Can Just Put a Feather in It" lambasting Teters and defending the chief.

University of Illinois trustees also trivialized Teters's concerns. "Though they're Native Americans," said trustee Susan Gravenhorst in *In Whose Honor?* "they are not as involved as we are in this situation and perhaps they don't really understand how we're presenting the chief. Perhaps they ought to come to a game. I can't imagine that the Chief, who deports himself ... with such dignity and solemnity ... could be perceived as a racial insult.... To me, it's a compliment."

For her part, Teters compared Indian caricatures to stereotypical symbols of other racial groups. "These images should have gone by the wayside along with Little Black Sambo and the Frito Bandito," stated Teters in *In Whose Honor?* "If it was any other religious practice that was being abused, we would hear about it. We would certainly hear about it if it was some kind of distortion of a Catholic ceremony or Jewish ceremony.... But somehow because it is a Native practice and ceremony and religious items, it is not respected."

## Gains media attention

Teters's crusade came into the media spotlight in October 1989, when she attended a talk on the history and tradition of the mascot. The speaker was Tom Livingstone, the U of I student serving as Chief Illiniwek at the time. As noted in *In Whose Honor?*, Livingstone held up the eagle headdress and stated "Chief Illiniwek is designed to be inspirational, majestic, reverent, moving."

Teters became angered as Livingstone held up the headdress, in her words, "like a trophy." When Teters challenged Livingstone about the portrayal of the Indian mascot, all television cameras and microphones in the room turned her way. "From that point on," recalled Teters, "I had no normal life. I became the focus of media attention."

Teters used the media to educate the American public about why the use of Indian mascots is insulting to Indians. "These symbols do nothing to help us remember Indian people," commented Teters in *In Whose Honor?* "It adds another layer of misinformation. We have to continue to peel away all of these layers of misinformation ... in order for people to see us for who we really are."

## Opposition to Chief Illiniwek grows

A handful of other students began to join Teters in her protests against Chief Illiniwek. In calling on the U of I to dump Illiniwek, students pointed to other universities—such as Dartmouth, Stanford, Marquette, Syracuse, and Oklahoma —that had done away with their Indian symbols since the late 1960s.

In 1990, in response to growing pressure, the university stopped referring to Chief Illiniwek's dance as "authentic" in its literature and made some subtle changes to the chief's costume. At the same time, the U of I board of trustees voted to keep Chief Illiniwek as the school's official symbol.

By the time Teters left U of I in 1991, the issue of Indian mascots had taken on a national scope. The National Congress of American Indians (NCAI), the nation's largest Native American civil rights organization, was receiving daily phone calls from individuals and reporters around the country, asking where the organization stood on the issue. The NCAI hired Teters to field those calls and to help it create a plan of action.

## Founds coalition

In 1991, with her course work completed, Teters headed for Washington, D.C. (She wrote her master's thesis at a later date and received her master's degree in 1994.) She spent nine months putting together a workshop for tribal leaders, to be presented at the NCAI national convention in San Francisco that December. At the conference, attendees responded by passing a unanimous resolution against the use of Indian mascots and nicknames.

While in Washington, D.C., Teters sparked a protest campaign against the Washington Redskins football team. The term "redskin," explained Native American student counselor Dennis Tibbets in *In Whose Honor?*, is "the most blatant racist symbol/term/depiction" that exists for Indians.

Teters and a group of other activists began holding regular pickets in front of the Redskins' RFK Stadium. The group— which included representatives of NCAI, the American Indian Movement (AIM), the National Organization for Women (NOW), the National Association for the Advancement of Colored People (NAACP), the Urban League, and other human rights and antiracism organizations—came together to form the National Coalition on Racism in Sports and Media (NCRSM). NCRSM also drew, and continues to draw, attention to the racist imagery of the Atlanta Braves, the Kansas City Chiefs, the Cleveland Indians, and other teams with Indian mascots or nicknames.

"We believe that [sports teams] very innocently and very sincerely believe that they're really honoring us," stated AIM cofounder Vernon Bellecourt in *In Whose Honor?* "It's what happens when you have these mascots and these names, it triggers all the other ridiculous antics which demean, degrade, and belittle a living people's culture and spiritual way of life."

## Super Bowl protest turns the tide

The NCRSM drew its largest crowd to date at the 1992 Super Bowl in Minneapolis, in which the Washington Redskins played the Buffalo Bills. Two thousand people marched through Minneapolis (the founding site and national headquarters of AIM) the day before the Super Bowl, holding signs and banners reading: "After 500 years it's time for some respect," "Repeal Redskin racism," and "Indians are a people and not mascots for America's fun and games."

There was widespread media coverage of the event, much of it favorable. After the Super Bowl many columnists called for sports teams to drop their Indian logos. And several newspapers—including the *Seattle Times,* the *Minneapolis Star,* and the *Portland Oregonian*—began refusing to print the word "Redskin."

Not only was there talk, there was also action. The following universities decided to drop their Indian mascots: Eastern Michigan, Southern Colorado, St. Johns (in New York state), Marquette, Southern Nazarene (in Oklahoma), Miami of Ohio, and Bradley. The athletic departments of the universities of Iowa, Wisconsin, and Minnesota refused to host any teams outside of the Big Ten conference that used Indian symbols (the U of I, being a Big Ten school, was exempted from the rule). And the school districts of Los Angeles and Dallas threw out all Indian sports team names.

## The Chief Illiniwek saga continues

Even after Teters left Illinois, the debate over Chief Illiniwek continued. In 1994 the U of I inclusiveness committee suggested that the school drop its Indian mascot. There was an immediate backlash from U of I alumni, many of whom threatened to withhold contributions to the school if the chief was removed. As a result, the recommendation was omitted from the inclusiveness committee's final report.

State representative Rick Winkel, a U of I alumnus, cashed in on the publicity surrounding the issue by sponsoring a bill in the Illinois legislature to retain Chief Illiniwek as U of I's official symbol. "We have a rich heritage in this country," Winkel told an interviewer in *In Whose Honor?*, "especially over the past few decades, of protecting minority rights. But minority rights aren't always right." Winkel's bill passed by a large majority but was vetoed by Governor Jim Edgar. Winkle was unable to secure enough votes to override the veto.

In late 1994 a group of Indian students at U of I filed a complaint against the Indian chief mascot with the civil rights division of the Illinois Department of Education. Under pressure from a group of state lawmakers, the civil rights division dismissed the complaint.

In March 1998 the U of I Student/Faculty Senate voted 97 to 29 in favor of removing Chief Illiniwek. Although the ultimate decision about the mascot rests with the board of trustees, the student and faculty vote was an important milestone in the struggle. Teters told the student newspaper *The Octopus* that she was "ecstatic" after the vote.

"Essentially [American Indians] have been invisible in this community," stated Teters in the March 13, 1998, edition of *The Octopus*. "Because we are invisible, who speaks for the American Indian people here? Well, Chief Illiniwek has been speaking for us for a long time, and he is a liar.... What Chief Illiniwek does is dehumanize us. Once you've been dehumanized, you are vulnerable to all kinds of acts of racism. For me ... this brings a little bit of closure. ... But obviously it's not over. Even if the [board of trustees] decide tomorrow that Chief Illiniwek is gone, it's still not over. Chief Illiniwek is just a local definition of a national problem."

## Continues fight for respect

Today Teters and her family reside in Santa Fe, New Mexico. Teters works a professor at the Institute of American

Indian Art and is on the staff of *Indian Artist Magazine*. In her multimedia art installations, of which she has had several shows, Teters draws attention to negative stereotyping and racism against American Indians.

Teters continues to speak out against the use of Indian mascots and nicknames as a spokesperson for NCRSM. She challenges the exploitation of Indian images, religion, and culture, by schools, museums, the media, and corporations. In early 1999 she was interviewed by MSNBC regarding a civil rights complaint filed with the Justice Department. The complaint concerns Irwin High School in Buncombe, North Carolina, which calls its sports teams the "Warriors" and the "Squaws." In March 1999, the Buncombe board of education voted to eliminate the name "Squaws," but let "Warriors" stand.

## Sources

### Periodicals

Pearlman, Jeff. "In Whose Honor?" *Sports Illustrated.* July 14, 1997: 19.

Tilcove, Jonathan. "Symbols of Racism? Movement to Ban Indian Sports Mascots Gains Speed." *The Ann Arbor News.* April 5, 1999: B1-2.

### Web Sites

Charlene Teters biography. [Online] Available http://www.rt66.com/teters/ (last accessed April 30, 1999).

"Chief Illiniwek Issue Not Over Yet." *The Octopus.* March 13, 1998. [Online] Available http://www.octopus.com/1998/mar13/hamlet.html (last accessed January 26, 1999).

*In Whose Honor?* [Online] Available http://www.inwhose.honor.com (last accessed January 26, 1999).

Rolo, Mark Anthony. *The Circle: Native American News and Arts.* [Online] Available http://nnic.com/circle/7.97/MarkMed.html (last accessed January 26, 1999).

### Other

*In Whose Honor?* (videocassette). Champaign, IL: Smoking Munchkin Video, 1997.

Teters, Charlene. Telephone interview with Phillis Engelbert. February 24, 1999.

# John Trudell

**Born 1947**
**Niobrara, Nebraska**

**Native American activist, musician, and actor**

John Trudell has been one of the leading voices for Native American civil rights for thirty years. Trudell's entry into the fight for Indian equality began in 1969, with the takeover of Alcatraz Island by members of the Indians of All Tribes activist group. Soon thereafter Trudell joined the American Indian Movement (AIM); he served as the group's cochairman and national spokesperson from 1973 to 1979. In 1979 Trudell suffered a tremendous personal tragedy when his wife, children, and mother-in-law burned to death in an arson fire. Many people believe that the killings were instigated by law enforcement officials as punishment for Trudell's political activities.

In the early 1980s Trudell made his debut as an actor and a musician. He had major roles in two 1992 motion pictures: *Thunderheart* and *Incident at Oglala*. He has also achieved a measure of fame for his spoken-word style of song. On his two musical recordings, as well as in his live performances, Trudell mesmerizes listeners with his no-holds-barred critiques of the U.S. government's treatment of Native Americans and his defense of the environment.

"The wheel has turned to where all the things we've suffered are now becoming the norm of the average citizen: the lack of representation, the political deception, the ethnic and class discrimination, the loss of jobs and health and property."

## The road to activism

Details about Trudell's early years are sketchy. What is known is that he was born and raised on the Santee Sioux Reservation in Niobrara, Nebraska (in northeastern Nebraska on the border of South Dakota). Trudell never learned the identity of his mother. His father was a Santee Sioux named Thurman Clifford Trudell.

Trudell served in the navy for four years during the Vietnam War (1954–75). He was deeply disturbed by the racism he witnessed in the armed forces, both directed at minority U.S. servicemen and at the Vietnamese people. When Trudell finished his tour of duty, he moved to California. There he married a woman named Lou and had two daughters, Maurie and Tara. He also became involved in the growing Indian rights movement.

**John Trudell on Alcatraz Island during the Indians of All Tribes takeover in 1969.**
*Reproduced by permission of AP/Wide World Photos.*

## Occupies Alcatraz Island

In November 1969 Trudell and his family joined the activist group Indians of All Tribes (IAT) in their takeover of Alcatraz Island, the former penal colony in San Francisco Bay. The occupiers demanded that the island, which had once been populated by Indians, be given back to Indians. They cited the 1868 Treaty of Fort Laramie with the Sioux Indians, which stipulated that abandoned federal properties on former Indian lands were to be returned to Indians. The IAT made plans to convert the island into a spiritual, cultural, and educational center for American Indians.

The Trudell family remained on Alcatraz for the nineteen months of the occupation. During that time Trudell coordinated publicity efforts for the IAT. He spoke at press conferences and hosted a daily radio program called "Radio Free Alcatraz," broadcast on KPFA-FM in Berkeley. John and Lou's daughter, Wovoka, was born on the island. (Wovoka was named after the nineteenth century Paiute spiritual leader and

**Activists at Alcatraz Island.** *Reproduced by permission of AP/Wide World Photos.*

founder of the Ghost Dance religion. Ghost Dance adherents believed they received special protections from white soldiers' bullets.)

In June 1971 the Indians were forced off the island during a raid by federal agents. The U.S. government subsequently annexed Alcatraz to the Golden Gate National Recreation Area. The occupation of Alcatraz thrust the Indian rights movement into the national spotlight. It inspired a generation of Indians to stand up for their rights and touched off a decade-long struggle for the recognition of treaty rights, self-determination, and the return of Indian lands.

## Joins AIM at Mount Rushmore and Plymouth Rock

While on Alcatraz, Trudell became involved with the American Indian Movement (AIM)—a militant Indian rights group, founded in 1968, that fought for the return of tribal lands, enforcement of government treaties, respect for Indian human rights, and greater economic opportunities for Indians. Throughout the 1970s Trudell's life revolved around AIM activities.

In September 1970 Trudell took leave from Alcatraz to help coordinate a demonstration at Mount Rushmore in the Black Hills of South Dakota. Together with AIM activist Russell Means and University of California-Berkeley doctoral student Lee Brightman, Trudell led about fifty Indians to the top of Mount Rushmore. The group demanded that all lands in South Dakota west of the Missouri River, including Mount Rushmore and the rest of the Black Hills, be returned to the Sioux in accordance with the Treaty of Fort Laramie. The demonstration received national news coverage. While Trudell quickly returned to Alcatraz, others in the group remained camped out on the mountaintop until brutal winter storms struck.

In November 1970 Trudell led a group of activists from Alcatraz to a living history museum called Plimoth Plantation (near Martha's Vineyard and the original Plymouth Colony) for an AIM-sponsored Thanksgiving Day protest. AIM had come to Plimoth at the invitation of Wampanoag Indians, whose ancestors had been massacred by the Pilgrims after helping the settlers survive for their first two years on this continent. The descendants of the surviving Wampanoags wanted to publicize their understanding of Thanksgiving—that the holiday had begun as a celebration of the massacre of Indians.

The Indian protesters held a march along the highway to Plimoth Plantation, disrupted the feast underway in the village hall, then took over a replica of the *Mayflower* (the ship on which the original pilgrims came to America) docked at the harbor. Late that night Trudell and a few others scaled the protective fence around the Plymouth Rock monument and bathed the rock in red paint to symbolize the spilled blood of the Wampanoag Indians.

## Participates in the Trail of Broken Treaties

In the fall of 1972 Trudell participated in AIM's occupation of the Bureau of Indian Affairs (BIA) headquarters. The demonstration, called the Trail of Broken Treaties, started out on the West Coast. A caravan of cars, trucks, and buses, picked up Indians at reservations along the way to Washington, D.C. AIM had written to the BIA ahead of time, informing the organization of the coming convergence on Washington and presenting its list of twenty demands. Among AIM's demands were the restoration of tribes' treaty-making status; the return of stolen Indian lands; and the revocation of state government authority over Indian affairs. AIM also asked for the opportunity to address a joint session of Congress.

When the delegation arrived at the BIA, they were turned away at the door. In response, the Indians took over the building and kicked out BIA employees. The occupation lasted six days. During that time protesters destroyed BIA property and smuggled out files containing evidence of BIA corruption.

The siege came to an end when protesters accepted the government's offer of immunity from prosecution, funds for their transportation home, and consideration of AIM's demands. The government later rejected every point on AIM's list.

Throughout the occupation, Trudell served as a spokesperson for the group. As a result of his high-profile position, Trudell came under increased scrutiny from the Federal Bureau of Investigation (FBI)'s Counter-Intelligence Program. (COINTELPRO was a secret FBI operation in the 1960s and

1970s in which FBI agents, under the guise of combating domestic terrorism, gathered information on, and attempted to destroy, the anti-Vietnam War movement, the civil rights movement, and militant organizations of people of color.) In 1986, when Trudell obtained his FBI file under the Freedom of Information Act, he discovered that the FBI had labeled him an "extremely effective agitator." Trudell eventually received 17,000 pages of information the FBI had collected on him between the years 1969 and 1979.

## Becomes co-chairman of AIM

In 1973 Trudell was elected to the co-chairmanship of AIM, a position that he held until 1979. His marriage to Lou Trudell having ended a couple of years earlier, Trudell wed again, this time an activist from the Duck Valley Reservation in Nevada named Tina Manning.

In February 1973 AIM initiated its famed takeover of Wounded Knee. Together with hundreds of Pine Ridge Reservation residents, AIM activists occupied the village of Wounded Knee for seventy-one days to protest the corrupt practices of tribal chairman Richard Wilson. The group also called attention to the brutality of Wilson's police force, the Guardians of the Oglala Nation ("GOONs" for short). Trudell, whose wife was expecting their first child, supported the action from his home in Nevada.

## Helps Peltier

In 1975 Trudell turned his energies to defending fellow AIM activist Leonard Peltier (1944– ; see entry), who had been charged with, and later convicted of, the murders of two FBI agents on Pine Ridge. Peltier had been on the reservation offering protection to Lakota traditionalists (adherents of traditional Indian religion and culture) from attacks by the GOONs when a firefight erupted between FBI agents and Indians.

Peltier was convicted by an all-white jury in a highly controversial trial punctuated by coerced statements from prosecution witnesses, fabricated evidence, and "judge-shopping" (the prosecution manipulated the court system to secure a judge with a known anti-Indian bias). Trudell is among the many people who believe Peltier was framed for the killings.

"FBI agents armed with M-16s came onto the Pine Ridge Reservation to serve a warrant they didn't have," Trudell stated to the press regarding the FBI manhunt in the wake of the shoot-out, "on someone who wasn't there; they were accompanied by over fifty highly trained military marksmen, also with high-powered automatic weapons. These agents opened fire on a small house in which men, women, and children were asleep."

Peltier is presently serving two life sentences at Leavenworth Federal Prison in Kansas. Trudell continues to speak out against the illegality of the FBI presence on the reservation, as well the gross miscarriage of justice in Peltier's trial.

## Family dies in arson fire

In February 1979, when Trudell was in Washington protesting the Peltier case and other abuses against Indians, tragedy struck. An arson fire at Trudell's home (the perpetrator of which was never caught) claimed the lives of his wife Tina, the couple's three children—Ricarda Star, Sunshine Karma, and Eli Changing Sun—and Tina's mother Leah Manning.

Just twelve hours before the arson attack, Trudell had burned an upside-down American flag on the steps of the FBI building and had been arrested. Many people believe that the killing of Trudell's family was orchestrated by the FBI in retribution for the flag burning, as well as for Trudell's years of activism and exposure of FBI abuses on the Pine Ridge Reservation.

After the death of his family, Trudell began writing poetry. He published a book of poems in 1981, entitled *Living in Reality.* In the coming years Trudell would turn some of those poems into songs.

## Shifts focus from AIM

In the 1980s, while continuing to speak out about issues of Indian rights and the environment, Trudell shifted his focus away from AIM. (AIM, weakened by infighting and persistent FBI harassment, had drifted away from its original purpose by the end of the 1970s.) Over the last two decades Trudell has made a name for himself in the music and movie industries.

Trudell's film debut was a cameo appearance in the 1989 Hand Made Films production, *Powwow Highway.* He had larger roles in two 1992 films, both by British director Michael Apted, about events on the Pine Ridge Reservation: *Incident at Oglala: The Leonard Peltier Story* and *Thunderheart.* Trudell was interviewed extensively in *Incident at Oglala,* a documentary about the occupation of Wounded Knee, the shoot-out between Indians and FBI agents, and the conviction of Peltier. And in *Thunderheart*—a fictional portrayal of events on the Pine Ridge Reservation—Trudell played the role of the defiant Indian activist leader.

"[Trudell] was an inspiration to me in making the documentary film *Incident at Oglala,*" stated Apted in a promotional release, "about Leonard Peltier's fight for justice, so much so that I cast him as the charismatic Indian leader in *Thunderheart,* a movie that deals with the government oppression of the contemporary Native American. There wasn't an untruthful moment in his performance. 'Sometimes they have to kill us,' he told me, 'because they cannot break our spirit.' John is one of those rare unbreakable spirits."

## Launches musical career

Trudell launched his musical career in 1979, appearing onstage with Jackson Browne and Bonnie Raitt in a series of concerts that raised funds for environmental and Indian rights causes. Trudell, known in the music industry as a rock-poet, calls his musical style "modern electric song." His songs combine his political convictions and spiritual beliefs and are set to the tempo of traditional Indian chants. His spoken lyrics are accompanied by traditional vocals and instrumentation.

Trudell released his first recording, entitled *aka Graffiti Man,* on the independent label Rykodisc in 1992. His second release, *Johnny Damas and Me,* was released in 1994, also with Rykodisc. Both recordings met with widespread critical acclaim. Trudell continues to promote Indian rights through his onstage performances.

"If people in this country really want to know how to help the Indian people," stated Trudell in a 1992 interview with Timothy White of *Billboard* magazine, "they must learn to help themselves. Because the wheel has turned to where all the things we've suffered are now becoming the norm of the average citizen: the lack of representation, the political deception, the ethnic and class discrimination, the loss of jobs and health and property."

## Sources

### Books

Churchill, Ward, and Jim Vander Wall. *Agents of Repression: The FBI's Secret Wars against the Black Panther Party and the American Indian Movement.* Boston: South End Press, 1988.

Malinowski, Sharon, and Simon Glickman, eds. *Native North American Biography.* Detroit: U•X•L, 1996, pp. 377–79.

Matthiessen, Peter. *In the Spirit of Crazy Horse.* New York: Viking Press, 1980.

Means, Russell, and Marvin J. Wolf. *Where White Men Fear to Tread: The Autobiography of Russell Means.* New York: St. Martin's Press, 1995.

Smith, Paul Chaat, and Robert Allen Warrior. *Like A Hurricane: The Indian Movement from Alcatraz to Wounded Knee*. New York: The New Press, 1995.

## Periodicals

Johnson, Brian D. "Thunderheart" (movie review). *Maclean's*. April 13, 1992: 71.

Sprague, David. "Trudell Inspires Unusual Ryko Promo." *Billboard*. January 29, 1994: 13+.

White, Timothy. "Native American Song, Then and Now." *Billboard*. May 9, 1992: 5.

## Web Sites

Townsend, Lori. "Interview with John Trudell by Lori Townsend of WOJB" (Kyle, South Dakota). February 28, 1998. [Online] Available http://www.dickshovel.com/lsa13.html (last accessed January 14, 1999).

Trudell, John (home page). [Online] Available http://www.planet-peace.org/trudell/index1.html (last accessed January 14, 1999).

## Other

Apted, Michael, director. *Incident at Oglala: The Leonard Peltier Story* (documentary). Miramax, 1992.

Apted, Michael, director. *Thunderheart*. Columbia, 1992.

# Sojourner Truth

**Born c. 1797**
**Ulster County, New York**
**Died 1883**
**Battle Creek, Michigan**

**African American abolitionist, women's rights advocate, and preacher**

S ojourner Truth was born into slavery. After gaining her freedom, she began a quest to end slavery and to assist former slaves. Truth was an early civil rights advocate—she fought the segregation policy of Washington, D.C., streetcars shortly after the end of the Civil War (1861–65). She was also a noted speaker who lectured frequently on the wrongs of racism and sexism and the injustice of denying women the right to vote. A deeply religious woman, Truth rose to prominence at a time when African Americans and women were expected to live in the shadows of society.

## Childhood as a slave

Truth was born Isabella Baumfree in Ulster County, New York, sometime in 1797 (the exact birth and death dates of slaves were not typically recorded). Her father's name was James Baumfree, after his original Dutch owner, and her mother's name was Elizabeth, although she was better known as Mau Mau Bett. Like both her parents, Truth was a slave owned by wealthy landowner Charles Hardenbergh. Prior to Truth's birth, her mother had given birth to eleven other chil-

I am pleading for my people, /A poor downtrodden race, /Who dwell in freedom's boasted land, /With no abiding place.

*Lines from a hymn written by Sojourner Truth*

Portrait: Reproduced by permission of Archive Photos.

dren, all of whom had been sold away from the plantation. The name "Isabella" had been selected by Master Hardenbergh; Truth's parents called her "Belle."

For her first eleven years, Truth lived with her parents, her younger brother Pete, and several other slaves in the master's dank cellar. In the winter the slaves huddled together for warmth. In the summer they slept outside, driven out of the cellar by the heat and foul odor of the humid dirt floor.

Truth's family life was shattered in 1806, when Truth and her brother were taken away and sold at an auction. Truth was purchased, along with a flock of sheep, for $100. Her new masters were an English immigrant couple named Neely. Both Mr. and Mrs. Neely beat Truth mercilessly. One day Truth's father, who was old and crippled but had been freed, came to see her. When he saw his daughter's back, bloodied and scarred from beatings, he sought to help her.

Baumfree convinced a tavern owner named Martin Schryver to purchase his daughter. During her three years with Schryver, Truth was not mistreated and had adequate food, clothing, and shelter. Truth was unaware, however, of the terrible conditions in which her parents were living. She later learned that they had run out of food and firewood and had died.

## Escapes to freedom

In 1810 Truth was sold again, this time to a wealthy landowner in New Paltz, New York, named John Dumont. Dumont arranged for Truth to be married to an older slave named Thomas, so that the couple would bear children (children born to slaves became the master's property). Over a period of ten years, Truth gave birth to five children.

In 1817 Truth was heartened by a new law that required all slaves in New York to be freed on July 4, 1827 (slaves over forty years old were freed immediately). In 1825 Dumont told Truth that if she worked exceptionally hard for the next year, he would grant her and her husband their freedom one year early. He would also give them a log cabin in which to live. Truth held up her end of the bargain, but on the agreed-upon date Dumont went back on his word. Truth had her mind so set on freedom that she could not continue to live as a slave.

Three months later—only nine months before the law would set her free—Truth took her infant daughter, Sophia, and escaped in the early morning hours. She went down the road to a farmhouse, where she had heard Quaker abolitionists lived. (An abolitionist was someone who actively opposed slavery.) The Quaker couple, named the Van Wageners, took Truth in. When Dumont came to the house looking for Truth, the Van Wageners purchased Truth and her daughter. The Van Wageners then granted the mother and daughter their freedom and allowed them to stay on in their house.

Truth soon learned that her son, Peter, had been sold to a wealthy farmer in Alabama. Determined to get her son back, Truth enlisted the help of the Van Wageners and their abolitionist Quaker friends. They informed Truth that Peter's sale had been illegal—New York law prohibited the sale of slaves out-of-state. With the aid of a lawyer, whom the Quakers hired and paid, Truth filed suit and won back her son. Truth's victory in the courts was exceptionally unusual. In the 1820s the legal system rarely worked in favor of former slaves or women.

## Guided by religion

In 1829 Truth moved to New York City with Peter, leaving Sophia with her older daughters. Truth hoped to find a job that would pay enough for her to start a home and provide for all her children (her husband had died a year earlier). In the city Truth found housing in a growing community of free blacks. She was hired to work as a servant and enrolled Peter in a navigational school.

Truth, who had been deeply religious her whole life, began attending services at the Mother Zion African Methodist Episcopal (AME) Church. In church Truth met two of her siblings, who had been sold to different masters before she was born. Truth then learned that another woman with whom she had been friendly in church, and who had recently died, was also her sister.

## Joins commune

Truth became acquainted with a religious and charitable couple named Pierson, who operated a shelter for homeless women. She went to work for the couple on a part-time basis. In 1932 a man named Robert Matthews, who called himself Matthias and claimed he was God, presented himself at the shelter. Matthews was really a con artist, but Truth believed his story. Matthews enlisted Elijah Pierson in a scheme, and the two men established a commune called "The Kingdom." (A commune is a community whose members have common interests and holdings.) The commune drew many believers—including Truth—who had to donate all their worldly possessions to the organization. Truth went to work at the commune as an unpaid cook and maid. Eventually, she caught on to the deceit of the two men and left.

## Changes name and becomes preacher

Truth's experience with the con men did not, however, dampen her religious convictions. She resumed her membership in the Zion AME Church. In June 1843 Truth had a dream in which God told her to "Go East." Truth packed her bags the next morning and headed east into farm country. Along the way she decided to change her name from Isabella Baumfree to Sojourner Truth. She took this new name because she believed it was God's will that she "walk in truth."

That day in June 1843 was the beginning of Truth's life as a traveling preacher. She gave sermons and sang in churches, on street corners, at religious revivals, and in homes. She found food and shelter wherever she could. Sometimes Truth spoke about her life as a slave. "Children, slavery is a [sic] evil thing," Truth told one audience. "They sell children away from their mothers, then dare the mothers to cry. What manner of men can do such a thing?" Truth rapidly gained a reputation as a provocative and inspirational speaker. She was often met with large crowds waiting to hear her speak.

## Dictates memoirs

In late 1843 Truth arrived at a cooperative farm called the Northhampton Association of Education and Industry. At the farm she met several noted abolitionists, among them William Lloyd Garrison (1805–1879) and Frederick Douglass (1817–1895). The cooperative's residents also taught Truth about the antislavery movement and the emerging women's rights movement.

# Harriet Tubman

Harriet Tubman (1821?–1913), an escaped slave, was the most famous of all "conductors" on the Underground Railroad. The Underground Railroad was an elaborate system of safe houses and secret routes through which slaves escaped to freedom beginning as early as the late 1700s. The escape routes stretched from southern slave states (primarily Kentucky, Delaware, and Maryland), to northern states and Canada, where slavery was illegal. "Conductors" were people who ventured into the South to pick up slaves and lead them to freedom.

**Harriet Tubman.** *Reproduced by permission of Archive Photos.*

Tubman was born into slavery around 1821 (there is no record of her exact birth date) in Dorchester County, Maryland. At the age of twenty-five, Tubman married a free black man named John Tubman. Fearing she would be sold and separated from her husband, Tubman escaped in 1849.

During her escape Tubman stumbled across the Underground Railroad and was assisted by abolitionists. She decided to dedicate her life to helping slaves escape. Over the next several years, Tubman returned to the South about twenty times and rescued hundreds of slaves—among them Tubman's elderly parents and ten of her brothers and sisters.

Tubman never lost a passenger. She was known to carry a rifle, which she would threaten to use on any slave who grew fearful and wanted to return to his or her master (a returned slave would be forced to reveal locations of safe houses, and would thus jeopardize the Underground Railroad). Tubman was never captured, despite a $40,000 bounty placed on her head by slave owners.

After the Civil War (1861–65) and the emancipation (freeing) of the slaves, Tubman raised funds and established a nursing home for elderly and homeless ex-slaves. Tubman was considered to be the "Moses" of her people because, like the biblical Moses, she led her people to freedom. She died in 1913.

Olive Gilbert, a feminist and member of the Northampton cooperative, convinced Truth of the need to record her life story. Since Truth was illiterate, she dictated her memoirs to Gilbert. The year 1850 saw the publication of *Narrative of Sojourner Truth: A Northern Slave.*

The same year that Truth's book was published, Congress passed the Fugitive Slave Act. This law gave slave owners or their agents the right to capture runaway slaves, even in states in which slavery was banned. Anyone caught assisting a runaway slave was fined $500—a huge sum in those days. The law encouraged slave catchers to hunt down any black they could find, even if he or she was legally free, and return the person to slavery. The Fugitive Slave Act strengthened the resolve of abolitionists and intensified the debate over slavery, moving the country closer to civil war.

## Gains fame as antislavery lecturer

Truth made her first major appearance on the antislavery lecture circuit in late 1850. Her friend Garrison, who spotted Truth while he was speaking at the podium, invited her to speak. Although Truth had not prepared a speech, she headed to the front of the room.

Standing nearly six feet tall, Truth was a commanding presence. She started her address by singing a hymn of her own composition. The hymn began:

> *I am pleading for my people,*
> *A poor downtrodden race,*
> *Who dwell in freedom's boasted land,*
> *With no abiding place.*

Truth told the story of her life as a slave, the separation of her family, the selling of her son Peter, and how she got Peter back. The audience was moved to tears, and many people bought copies of Truth's book.

Truth then embarked on a national speaking tour. She addressed women's rights conventions and antislavery groups, and often traveled with Garrison and other noted abolitionists. Truth's audiences were not always sympathetic to her message. In some places her opponents burned her effigy in front of the hall where she was to speak; in other places, they disrupted meetings. Truth was clubbed by white

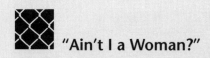

## "Ain't I a Woman?"

In 1851, at the Second Woman's Suffrage Convention in Akron, Ohio, Truth made the speech for which she is most famous. The convention was attended by hundreds of people. In the audience were several people, many of them preachers, opposed to the idea of women's rights. The preachers argued that women were the "weaker sex" and that God had intended for blacks to be subservient. One minister argued that since Jesus was a man, men were intended to be masters over women.

When Truth took the stage, she addressed the ministers' comments. "That man over there says that women need to be helped into carriages, and lifted over ditches, and to have the best place everywhere," stated Truth. "Nobody ever helps me into carriages, or over mud puddles, or gives me any best place, and ain't I a woman?" Truth stood up straight to exhibit her full height. "Look at me!" she said.

Truth then bared her right arm to display the rippling muscles she had developed from many years of hard work. The audience gasped. "Look at my arm!" she implored the audience. "I have plowed. And I have planted. And I have gathered into barns. And no man could head me." In a whisper, which was audible over the hushed crowd, she asked, "And ain't I a woman?"

"Where did your Christ come from?" she asked. "From God and a woman. Man had nothing to do with him."

supremacists in Kansas and was at the center of mob violence in Missouri. Truth refused, however, to let hate-mongers stand in her way.

## Retirement and return to action

In 1857 Truth, then sixty years old, decided it was time to retire. She moved to a spiritual community in Harmonia, Michigan, just outside the city of Battle Creek. Within three years, two of her daughters and their families joined Truth in Harmonia. Truth made her home in a converted barn and one of her grandchildren, Sammy, moved in with her. For a time Truth was content sitting on her porch and telling stories to her grandchildren. But that did not last long.

The Dred Scott decision of 1857 made Truth come out of retirement. Dred Scott (1798?–1858) was a slave from Missouri who had traveled with his owner into Illinois, where slavery had been outlawed. On his return to Missouri, Scott sued for his freedom. *Dred Scott v. Sanford* ended up before the Supreme Court, where Scott's claim was rejected. The court wrote that slaves were not citizens of the United States and had no right to file lawsuits. Chief Justice Roger B. Taney (1777–1864) added insult to injury by claiming that blacks "had no rights which the white man was bound to respect."

After the Dred Scott decision, Truth decided that retirement could wait. In 1859, accompanied by Sammy, she returned to the antislavery lecture circuit.

## Aids black soldiers and freed slaves during Civil War

When the Civil War began in 1861, many blacks enthusiastically supported the Union (Northern) cause. When the Union army began accepting black soldiers in 1862, nearly 180,000 blacks signed up (including Truth's grandson, James Caldwell). Truth supported black soldiers by collecting food and clothing for them and by caring for the wounded. She also supported the idea that black soldiers receive pay equal to that of white soldiers.

Truth was named "counsellor to freed people" by the National Freedmen's Relief Association in 1864 and began a two-year stay in Washington, D.C. Truth's job was to assist newly freed slaves who had poured into Washington, D.C., many of whom were living in squalid refugee camps and slums.

On October 29, 1864, Truth was granted her wish to meet President Abraham Lincoln (1809–1865). At the White House Lincoln told Truth he had known of her for many years before he thought about running for president. Lincoln signed Truth's scrapbook, which she called her "Book of Life."

During her stay in Washington, Truth challenged the city's segregation policy for streetcars. In 1867 Truth was ordered by a driver to sit in the rear of the car. She refused; as a result, the driver slammed her against the door and dislocated her shoulder. Truth sued the driver for assault and battery and won. Thereafter, until the passage of Jim Crow laws, blacks received courteous treatment on Washington streetcars. (The Jim Crow system, which began in 1887 and lasted until the 1960s, dictated the segregation of the races at every level of society.)

## Resumes speaking

Truth began speaking publicly again and selling copies of her book in the late 1860s. In her lectures she combined aspects of Christian religion, mysticism, feminism, and her passion for African American rights.

In 1870 Truth requested that the U.S. government grant tracts of land in the West to ex-slaves. "Our labor supplied the country with cotton," Truth stated before a group of senators. "Our nerves and sinews, our tears and blood have been sacrificed on the altar of this nation's avarice. Our unpaid labor had been a stepping stone to its financial success. Some of its dividends must surely be ours." Truth worked hard for this cause, traveling throughout the country to gather thousands of petition signatures. While her proposal went unfulfilled, Truth succeeded in convincing many freed slaves to homestead in Kansas and Missouri.

## Final years

Truth returned to Harmonia in 1875 to take care Sammy, who had fallen ill. Later that year Sammy died, just shy of his twenty-fifth birthday. Sammy's death sent Truth into a long period of grief and mourning. She believed she would follow Sammy in death, but she survived him for another nine years.

In 1878 Truth set off on a speaking tour of thirty-six cities in Michigan and served as a delegate to a women's rights convention. In early 1883 Truth returned to Battle Creek in poor health. She died on November 26, 1883, at the age of eighty-six. Just before her death, Truth told her family and friends, "I'm going home like a shooting star."

## Sources

### Books

*African American Biography.* Vol. 4. Detroit: U•X•L, 1994, pp. 727–33.

Altman, Susan. *Encyclopedia of African-American Heritage.* New York: Facts on File, Inc., 1997, pp. 250–51.

Giddings, Paula. *When and Where I Enter: The Impact of Black Women on Race and Sex in America.* New York: Bantam Books, 1984.

Mabee, Carleton. *Sojourner Truth: Slave, Prophet, Legend.* New York: New York University Press, 1993.

McKissack, Patricia C., and Fredrick McKissack. *Sojourner Truth: Ain't I a Woman?* New York: Scholastic, Inc., 1992.

Painter, Nell Irvin. *Sojourner Truth: A Life, A Symbol.* New York: W.W. Norton, 1996.

Plowden, Martha Ward. *Famous Firsts of Black Women.* Gretna, LA: Pelican Publishing Co., 1993, 107–28.

Smallwood, David, et al. *Profiles of Great African Americans.* Lincolnwood, IL: Publications International, Ltd., 1996, pp. 176–79.

# Philip Vera Cruz

**Born December 25, 1904**
**Ilocos Sur, Philippines**
**Died June 11, 1994**
**Bakersfield, California**

**Filipino American labor organizer**

Philip Vera Cruz was a skillful and persuasive labor organizer. He represented Filipino American workers in the fields, canneries, hotels, and restaurants of the West Coast. Together with Mexican American labor leader César Chávez (1927–1993; see entry) and other organizers, Vera Cruz was instrumental in founding the United Farm Workers union.

"Through [Vera Cruz's] years of toil as a farm worker, he recognized the importance of worker solidarity and militancy and the capacity of common people to create alternative institutions of grassroots power," wrote Glenn Omatsu—activist, editor, and staff member of the UCLA Asian American Studies Center—in *The State of Asian America*. "Through his work with Filipino and Mexican immigrants, he saw the necessity of coalition-building and worker unity that crossed ethnic and racial boundaries. He has shared these lessons with several generations of Asian American activists."

## Seeks fortune in the United States

Vera Cruz was born on Christmas Day 1904 in the province of Ilocos Sur, on the island of Luzon, Philippines. In

"It is the job of the labor movement to unite all workers regardless of their color, nationality, language, or whatever."

1926, at the age of twenty-two, Vera Cruz left his homeland and traveled 8,000 miles to Seattle, Washington. In the United States Vera Cruz expected to find a well-paying job that would enable him to save money and support his family in the Philippines. Instead, what he found was discrimination and low wages. Rather than return to the Philippines, Vera Cruz chose to stay in the United States and fight for the rights of oppressed workers.

"All the stories we heard were only success stories," said Vera Cruz in a 1992 biography entitled *Philip Vera Cruz: A Personal History of Filipino Immigrants and the Farmworkers Movement*. "So my plan was to finish college in America, get a good job over there, save my money, and then return home and support my family. It was only after I finally got to America that I understood how different reality was for us Filipinos."

## Working in the fields and canneries

From 1926 to 1934 Vera Cruz worked in the canneries of Alaska and restaurants of Washington State. For four of those years—1927 to 1930—Vera Cruz attended Lewis and Clark High School in Spokane, Washington, while working part-time. He then studied for one year at the Jesuit-run Gonzaga University, also in Spokane.

Vera Cruz spent the years 1934 to 1942 in Chicago, Illinois, working in restaurants. In 1942 Vera Cruz received a draft notice and was ordered to report to San Luis Obispo, California, for basic training. Since Vera Cruz was over thirty-eight years old, he received an early discharge.

Vera Cruz then moved to the San Joaquín Valley in central California and found work in the agricultural fields and vineyards. In that region, where agribusiness (also known as "factories in the fields") is a multi-billion-dollar industry, Vera Cruz experienced firsthand the mistreatment of workers by farm managers. Vera Cruz was appalled by the low wages and the living conditions in the worker camps.

"The first camp I lived in had a kitchen that was so full of holes, flies were just coming in and out at their leisure, along with mosquitoes, roaches, and everything else," stated Vera Cruz in his biography. "You didn't have to know much about sanitation not to want flies on your plate. The toilet was an outhouse with the pit so filled-up it was impossible to use."

## Witnesses discrimination

In the towns Vera Cruz witnessed discrimination against Filipino workers. Filipinos, along with other people of color, were made to sit in segregated sections of movie theaters. They were subject to mistreatment by grocery store and bar owners and abuse by police.

Vera Cruz had his first experience on a picket line in the 1940s, when workers in the asparagus fields of Stockton, California, went on strike. It was there that Vera Cruz met Chris Mensalves, a brilliant Filipino American labor organizer. Vera Cruz left during the strike to return to work in the salmon canneries of Alaska, where wages were considerably higher. (At the time, he was helping pay his younger brother's way through law school in Manila.) Nonetheless, Vera Cruz's experience with Mensalves made a lasting impression.

For the next twenty years, Vera Cruz earned his living by doing seasonal work in the canneries (two months per year) and working in the fields the rest of the time. He helped organize several small groups of Filipino American farm workers during this period. In the early 1960s Vera Cruz and other organizers formed the mostly Filipino Agricultural Workers Organizing Committee (AWOC). AWOC conducted numerous strikes in the fields around Coachella and Delano, California.

## United Farm Workers founded

On September 8, 1965, 600 AWOC members went on strike in the grape fields of Coachella. The growers responded by firing the workers and evicting them from their homes. The Filipino workers asked for the support of the mostly Mexican National Farm Workers Association (NFWA) in nearby Delano. Members of the newly formed NFWA were hesitant to risk their livelihoods. Nevertheless, on September 16, 1965, the NFWA voted to join the strike.

In March 1966, when the grape strike was in its second year, the AWOC and NFWA merged to form the United Farm Workers (UFW). The UFW joined the American Federation of Labor-Congress of Industrial Organizations (AFL-CIO), the largest conglomerate of labor unions in the country. Chávez was made president of the UFW, and Vera Cruz was named a vice president. For the next ten years, the UFW engaged in a

Philip Vera Cruz (second from left) and other members of the United Farm Workers union board at the dedication of the Agbayani Village retirement center.
*Photograph by Bob Titch. Reproduced by permission of AP/Wide World Photos.*

series of strikes around the United States to improve working conditions and wages for farm workers.

"When the UFW came along it really changed my life," remarked Vera Cruz in his biography. "It gave me the opportunity to bring my basically philosophical and questioning nature down to earth, and apply it to real everyday issues that actually affect people's lives. As a Filipino it gave me the opportunity to participate in the political struggles of this country, ... as a worker struggling along with my fellow workers for our constitutional rights."

## The Agbayani Retirement Village

One of the UFW projects pioneered by Chávez and Vera Cruz was a workers' retirement home called Agbayani Village. (The village was named for Paolo Agbayani, a Filipino worker who had died of a heart attack while on the picket line in 1967.) Start-up funds for the retirement home were provided through contracts signed between the UFW and large grape growers. The village was designed by a Chicano architect named Luis Peña. It was constructed in 1974 with the volunteer labor of more than 2,000 people from all over the world.

Agbayani Village sits on the forty-acre parcel of land owned by the United Farm Workers, near Delano. It continues to provide low-rent housing for elderly farm workers. Many of the home's residents, ranging in age from seventy to ninety years, worked in the fields all their lives. In the retirement home they have private rooms and bathrooms, as well as air conditioning—luxuries previously unknown to most farm workers.

## Split with UFW

In 1977 a longstanding rift between Vera Cruz and Chávez led to Vera Cruz's resignation from the UFW. One reason for his dissatisfaction was the "cult of personality" that had formed around Chávez. Vera Cruz was a believer in participatory democracy—a system in which every union member has a role in shaping the organization. He felt that the UFW's hierarchical leadership structure, topped by a charismatic leader, was detrimental the union.

"You see, when an individual is built up too much and made to seem like God, then you start defending him when you shouldn't," Vera Cruz stated in his biography. "And you start confusing that person with the union. One person is not a union.... If the leader becomes the most important part of the movement, then you won't have a movement after the leader is gone.... We need truth more than we need heroes."

## UFW ignores undocumented workers

Another point of contention between Vera Cruz and the UFW leadership was the UFW's policy to only support the rights of farm workers who were in the United States legally, while ignoring undocumented workers. Vera Cruz stressed the importance of standing up for the rights of all people. "It is the job of the labor movement to unite all workers regardless of their color, nationality, language, or whatever," Vera Cruz once noted.

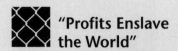

## "Profits Enslave the World"

The following excerpt is from a poem written by Philip Vera Cruz that appeared in his 1992 biography, *Philip Vera Cruz: A Personal History of Filipino Immigrants and the Farmworkers Movement:*

*While still across the ocean,*
*I heard about the U.S.A.,*
*So thrilled by wild imagination,*
*I left home through Manila Bay.*

*Then on my way I thought and*
*    wondered*
*Alone what would the future be?*
*I gambled parental care and love*
*In search for human liberty.*

*But beautiful bright pictures painted*
*Were just half of the whole story...*

*Minorities in shanty towns, slums...*
*Disgraceful spots for all to see*
*In the enviable Garden of Eden,*
*Land of affluence and poverty.*

## Opposes Marcos's regime

The final issue that made Vera Cruz break with the UFW was Chávez's support for Filipino dictator Ferdinand Marcos (1917–1989; ruled the Philippines from 1965 to 1986). Vera Cruz vehemently opposed the corrupt and authoritarian Marcos regime, which prohibited labor unions and had been cited for widespread use of torture against its political opponents.

In 1977 Chávez accepted the Marcos government's invitation to visit the Philippines. There he was presented with a Presidential Appreciation Award. Shortly after returning, Chávez invited the Marcos government's secretary of labor to speak at a UFW convention. Chávez prohibited Vera Cruz from confronting the speaker on the convention floor. "Is César too dumb to see that these U.S. agribusinesses in the Philippines are connected with their counterparts here in California, that [it's] the same economic system that exploits U.S. farm workers for bigger profits?" questioned Vera Cruz.

## Return to the Philippines

Vera Cruz returned to the Philippines in 1987 for the first time in six decades. It was an emotional homecoming for Vera Cruz, who had endured a long separation from his family. During that visit he witnessed the fruits of his labor—the money he had sent home over the years had financed the educations of his younger siblings and their children.

Vera Cruz's trip was paid for by the Philippines' new, democratically elected leader Corazon Aquino (1933– ). Aquino presented Vera Cruz with an award for lifelong service to the Filipino community in the United States. Upon meeting Aquino, Vera Cruz asked why the Filipino government permitted the use of dangerous pesticides that were banned in the

United States and other developed nations. Aquino did not provide a response. Nor did Aquino reply to numerous letters written by Vera Cruz after he returned to the United States, regarding his concerns about human rights in the Philippines.

## Final years

After leaving the UFW, Vera Cruz settled in Bakersfield, California. There he continued to participate in the labor movement and social justice campaigns until his death in 1994. "My life within the union, my life now outside the union, are all one," stated Vera Cruz in his biography. "My continual struggle to improve my life and the lives of my fellow workers. But our struggle never stops. When you are older, like I am now, you do want to sit down and rest a little more, but for me that's the only difference."

## Sources

### Books

Aguilar-San Juan, Karin. *The State of Asian America: Activism and Resistance in the 1990s*. Boston: South End Press, 1994.

"An Interview with Philip Vera Cruz" in *Roots: An Asian American Reader*, edited by Amy Tachiki, et al. Los Angeles: UCLA Asian American Studies Center, 1971.

Scharlin, Craig, and Lilia V. Villanueva. *Philip Vera Cruz: A Personal History of Filipino Immigrants and the Farmworkers Movement*. Los Angeles: UCLA Labor Center, 1992.

Sinnott, Susan. *Extraordinary Asian Pacific Americans*. Chicago: Children's Press, 1993, pp. 70-72.

Vera Cruz, Philip. "Sour Grapes: Symbol of Oppression" in *Roots: An Asian American Reader*, edited by Amy Tachiki, et al. Los Angeles: UCLA Asian American Studies Center, 1971.

### Periodicals

Lyons, Richard D. "Philip Vera Cruz, 89; Helped to Found Farm Worker Union" (obituary). *New York Times*. June 16, 1994: B9.

San Juan, Jr., Epifiano. "From National Allegory to the Performance of the Joyful Subject: Reconstituting Philip Vera Cruz's Life." *Amerasia Journal*. winter 1995/1996: 137-53.

# Index

## A

Abernathy, Ralph 59, 106, 107, 111
Abolitionist (definition) 189
**Abourezk, James G. 1–9**, 1 (ill.), 5 (ill.)
Abscam 4, 5
*Achille Lauro* 7
ACT-UP 77
Adams, Hank 158–59, 159 (ill.)
Addams, Jane 81
*Advise and Dissent: Memoirs of South Dakota and the U.S. Senate* 4, 6–7
AFL-CIO 42, 199
Agbayani, Paolo 200
Agbayani Village 200–01
Agribusiness 198, 202
Agricultural Labor Relations Act 45
Agricultural Workers Organizing Committee (*See* AWOC)
AIDS Coalition to Unleash Power (*See* ACT-UP)
AIM 6, 23, 25, 26, 27, 155, 177, 180–81

"Ain't I a Woman?"
*aka Graffiti Man* 185
Akron, Ohio 193
Alcatraz Island, takeover of 178, 179 (ill.), 180
American Anti-Slavery Society 15, 16
American Civil War 16, 187, 191, 194
American Equal Rights Society 17
American Federation of Labor-Congress of Industrial Organizations (*See* AFL-CIO)
American Field Service 53
American Friends Service Committee 107
American Indian Movement (*See* AIM)
*American West Indian News* 32
American Woman Suffrage Association (*See* AWSA)
American-Arab Anti-Discrimination Committee 1, 5, 6, 7
Americans for Indian Opportunity 9

Bold type indicates main entries and their page numbers.

Illustrations are marked by (ill).

Americans with Disabilities
    Act 167
Anderson, Jack 160
Anthony, Daniel 11, 13
**Anthony, Susan B. 10–22,**
    10 (ill.)
Antislavery movement 15–16,
    190, 191
Apted, Michael 184
**Aquash, Anna Mae 23–30,**
    23 (ill.), 28 (ill.)
Aquash, Nogeeshik 23 (ill.),
    25, 26
Aquino, Corazon 202–03
Arab Americans, racism against 4
*The Arab World* 9
*Asian American Literature: An
    Introduction to the Writings
    and Their Social Context* 99
Asian Americans for Action 120
Atlantic City, New Jersey 36–37
Avery Normal Institute 48
AWOC 41, 90, 91–92, 199
AWSA 15, 18


# B

**Baker, Ella Jo 31–38,** 31 (ill.), 52,
    105, 126, 146
Banks, Dennis 183 (ill.)
Barrio (definition) 55
Baumfree, Isabella (*See* Truth,
    Sojourner)
Baumfree, James 187
Beecher, Henry Ward 18
Bennett, Bruce 85
Bevel, James 66
BIA 25, 154, 155, 181
Birmingham, Alabama 106–07
Black Belt 150
Black power movement 142
"Bloody Sunday" 109, 131
Bond, Julian 124, 133
Bookbinder, Hyman 9
"Book of Life" 194
Boston Indian Council 24
Boxing 56
Brightman, Lee 180
Brit, Travis 147
*Brown v. Board of Education of
    Topeka, Kansas* 33
Browne, Jackson 185

Bureau of Indian Affairs (*See* BIA)
Burnside, John 76
Bush, George 94
Butler, Dino 158


# C

Caldwell, James 194
"Campaign to End Slums"
    110–11
Canaanites 75
Canajoharie Academy 12
Carawan, Guy 82
Carmichael, Stokely 132
Carter, Jimmy 53, 133, 152
Catt, Carrie Chapman 21
Center for Independent Living
    165–66
**Chávez, César 39–46,** 39 (ill.),
    88, 90, 197, 201, 202
Chicano (definition) 55
Chief Illiniwek 170, 171, 172, 173
Circle of Loving Companions 76
"Citizenship schools" 47, 51,
    82–83
Civil disobedience 19
Civil Rights Act of 1964 108–09
Clark, Nerie 49
**Clark, Septima P. 47–54,**
    47 (ill.), 83
Coeducation 16
COINTELPRO 26, 156, 181–82
Commission of Agricultural
    Workers 94
Commission on Wartime
    Relocation and Internment
    of Civilians 121
Communism 73, 85–86
Communist Party 73
Community Service Organization
    (CSO) 41, 90
Congress of Industrial Organiza-
    tion (CIO) 81
Congress on Racial Equality (*See*
    CORE)
Committee for Traditional Indian
    Land and Life 76
CORE 34, 35, 118, 127
Counter-Intelligence Program
    (*See* COINTELPRO)
*Crisis* 32
*A Cross for Maclovio* 57

Crusade for Citizenship 33
Crusade for Justice 55, 56–57, 60
Crystal City, Texas 59, 60
Cuba 8

# D

Daley, Richard 110
"Daughter of the Earth: Song for
    Anna Mae Aquash" 27
Daughters of Temperance 12
"Declaration of Sentiments" 15
De La Cruz, Jesse 93, 93 (ill.)
Delano to Sacramento march
    42–43
Delta Algebra Project 152
Democratic Party national con-
    vention (1964) 36–37, 66–67,
    149–50
Denmark 81
Dennis, Dave 149
Denver, Colorado 58
Denver Democratic Party 56
Department of Vocational
    Rehabilitation 164, 166
Disability (definition) 162
Douglass, Frederick 11, 190
Downstate Medical Center,
    picketing of 118
*Dred Scott v. Sanford* 194
Duck Valley Reservation 182
Dumont, John 188

# E

Eagle, Jimmy 27, 157
*East to America: Korean American
    Life Stories* 96, 97, 98
Eastland, James O. 85
Ebenezer Baptist Church 103,
    105, 113
*Echo in My Soul* 50
Edmund Pettus Bridge 109, 131
*El cortitos* 91
*El Gallo: La Voz de la Justica* 57
El-Hajj Malik El-Shabazz
    (*See* Malcolm X)
Emancipation Proclamation 16
Ethnic Studies 98–99
Evers, Medgar 146

# F

Fabela, Helena 40, 46
"Factories in the fields" 198
Farmer, James 108 (ill.), 127
Farm workers' strike 41–45, 92, 93
Federal Bureau of Investigation
    (FBI) 7, 23, 26, 28, 116, 153
    157–58, 181
Fellowship of Reconciliation
    34, 80
Fernández, Juan 89
Field Foundation 133
Fifteenth Amendment 17–18
*The Fight in the Fields: César
    Chávez and the Farmworkers
    Movement* 90, 93
Fish-ins 155, 158–59
Forman, James 150
442nd Regiment Combat
    Team 117
Fourteenth Amendment 17, 18,
    19, 20
Freedom Farm Cooperative 69
Freedom of Information Act 182
Freedom Riders 118, 123
Freedom Rides 126–29
Freedom Summer 149
Freedom Vote 148
Fugitive Slave Act 192
Fulbright Fellowship 96
Fund for Constitutional
    Government 9

# G

Gandhi, Mohandas 35, 44, 80,
    103, 125
Garrison, William Lloyd 15, 16,
    190, 192
Garvey, Marcus 136
Gilbert, Olive 192
Golden Gate National Recreation
    Area 180
Golden Gloves 56
**Gonzales, Rodolfo "Corky"**
    **55–61**, 55 (ill.)
Grape boycott 42, 92
Great Depression 32, 40, 72
Guardians of the Oglala Nation
    ("GOON squad") 26, 27, 156,
    157, 182
Guthrie, Woody 73
Gutiérrez, José Angel 60

# H

Harlem Parents Committee 117
**Hamer, Fannie Lou** 51, **62–70**,
  62 (ill.), 67 (ill.), 69 (ill.), 83
Hamer, Perry ("Pap") 63, 65
Hamilton, Frank 82
Hardenbergh, Charles 187–88
Harlem, New York 117
**Hay, Harry 71–78**, 71 (ill.)
Hezbollah 8
Highlander Folk School 47, 50,
  79–87
Highlander Research and Educa-
  tion Center (*See* Highlander
  Folk School)
Hijacking 7
*History of Woman Suffrage* 21
Homesteading 195
**Horton, Myles** 50, 52, **79–87**
House Un-American Activities
  Committee (HUAC) 73
Howe, Julia Ward 18
**Huerta, Dolores** 41, **88–95**,
  88 (ill.)
Hull House 81
Hunt, Ward 20

# I

*I am Joaquín* 55, 57
"I Have a Dream" 108
*Incident at Oglala* 177, 184
Indian Child Welfare Act 3
Indian Health Service (IHS) 3
Indian Religious Freedom Act 3
Indian Self-Determination Act 3
Indians of All Tribes 177, 178
Industrial League 32
In Friendship 32
Institute of American Indian
  Art 175
Interior Committee 2
International Bachelors Fraternal
  Order for Peace and Social
  Dignity 74
International Council
  of Women 21
*In Whose Honor?* 169, 171
Iran 8
Israel 4

# J

Jackson, Jesse 46
Japanese American Citizens
  League 121
Japanese Americans, internment
  of 120–21
Jemmott, Janet 151
Jenkins, Esau 51, 83
Jennings, Dale 74
Jerome internment camp 117
Jim Crow laws 84, 194
*Johnny Damas and Me* 185
Johnson, Lillian 81
Johnson, Lyndon B. 56, 67,
  110, 131
Johnson, Zilphia 82
Joseph, Jamal 120
Journey of Reconciliation
  (JOR) 34
"Judge-shopping" 160, 182

# K

Kennedy, Ethel 46
Kennedy, John F. 56, 106,
  107, 128
Kennedy, Robert F. 44, 44 (ill.),
  94, 106, 133, 159
**Kim, Elaine H. 96–101**, 96 (ill.)
King, A. D. 106
King, Coretta Scott 103, 141
**King, Martin Luther, Jr.** 33, 35,
  52, 59, **102–13**, 102 (ill.), 108
  (ill.), 112 (ill.), 124, 140 (ill.),
  141, 145
King, Martin Luther, Jr., assassina-
  tion of 113
King, Martin Luther, Sr. 103
"The Kingdom" 190
Klaver, Ellen 27
Klinghoffer, Leon 7
Kochiyama, Bill 115 (ill.), 117,
  120, 121
**Kochiyama, Yuri 115–122**,
  115 (ill.)
Korean War 2
Ku Klux Klan 136

# L

*La Bamba* 43
La Raza Unida 55, 59–60

Leavenworth Federal Prison 153, 183
Lebanon 2, 4
"Letter from a Birmingham Jail" 107
**Lewis, John Robert** 108 (ill.), **123–34**, 125 (ill.), 126 (ill.), 132 (ill.)
Lincoln, Abraham 16, 194
Literacy test 64–65, 83, 146
Little, Malcolm (*See* Malcolm X)
*Living in Reality* 184
"Living the Legacy" Award 53
*The Long Haul: An Autobiography* 82
Lorraine Hotel 113
Lunch counter sit-ins 105–06, 125

## M

MacArthur Foundation "Genius Award" 152, 166
**Malcolm** X 118–20, 119 (ill.), 129, **135–43**, 135 (ill.), 138 (ill.), 140 (ill.)
Malcolm X, assassination of 141, 142 (ill.)
Maloney, Jake 24
Manning, Robert 7
Manning, Tina 182
March on Washington 34, 107–08, 123, 128
Marcos, Ferdinand 202
Married Woman's Property Act 14
Marshall, Thurgood 49
Martin Luther King Jr. Day 113
Marx, Karl 80
Mattachine Society 74, 75
Matthews, Robert 190
Mau Mau Bett 187
*Mayflower* 181
McCarthy, Joseph 73
McCarthy era 71
McDew, Charles 148
McGovern, George 6
Means, Russell 180, 183 (ill.)
Mecca 139
Medal of Liberty 95
Mensalves, Chris 199
Meshicano 55
Mexican Americans, discrimination against 40
Mexican Independence Day 42
MFDP 36, 37, 37 (ill.), 66–68, 148

Micmac Indians 23, 24
Mississippi Freedom Democratic Party (*See* MFDP)
Monteagle, Tennessee 50, 81
Montgomery bus boycott 33, 84, 103–04
Montgomery City Lines bus company 105
Montgomery Improvement Association 104
Moore, Amzie 146
**Moses, Robert Parris 144–152,** 144 (ill.)
Mother Zion African Methodist Episcopal (AME) Church 189
Mott, Lucretia 13, 15
Mount Rushmore 180
*Moving the Mountain* 34
Moyers, Bill, 9
Muhammad, Elijah 136, 137, 141
Muslim Mosque of Harlem 140

## N

NAACP 31, 32, 48–49, 83
Nader, Ralph 159
Nakahara, Seiichi 116
*Narrative of Sojourner Truth: A Northern Slave* 192
Nashville Student Movement 125, 126
Nation of Islam (*See* NOI)
National American Woman Suffrage Association (*See* NAWSA)
National Association for the Advancement of Colored People (*See* NAACP)
National Chicano Youth Liberation Conference 58
National Coalition on Racism in Sports and Media 169, 173
National Congress of American Indians (NCAI) 173
National Farm Workers Association (*See* NFWA)
National Farm Workers Service Center, Inc. 94
National Freedmen's Relief Association 194
National Indian Youth Council (NIYC) 158
National Urban League 32–33

National Woman Suffrage Association (*See* NWSA)
Nationwide Friends of the Rio Grande 76
Navajos 7–8
NAWSA 15, 21
New Theater League 73
NFWA 41, 91, 93, 199
Nineteenth Amendment 10, 21
Nixon, Ricard M. 2, 106
Nobel Peace Prize 102–03, 108
NOI 135, 136–37, 139
Nonviolence 35, 102, 105, 125, 141
Northhampton Association of Education and Industry 190
Norton, Eleanor Holmes 70
NWSA 15, 18

## O

Odeh, Alex 7
Oglala Sioux Civil Rights Organization 6
ONE Institute Quarterly of Homophile Studies *75*
Organization of Afro-American Unity (OAAU) 118, 135, 140
Outstanding American Award 95
Outstanding Service Award 121

## P

Pacifism 34
Padillo, Gilberto 41
Parks, Rosa 51, 83, 84–85, 85 (ill.), 104, 104 (ill.)
Party of God (*See* Hezbollah)
Pearl Harbor, Hawaii 116
**Peltier, Leonard** 26, 153–61, 153 (ill.), 182–83
Peña, Luis 201
People's Educational Center 73
*Personal Justice Denied* 121
Pesticides, use of 45–46
*Philip Vera Cruz: A Personal History of Filipino Immigrants and the Farmworkers Movement* 198
Philippines 197–98, 202–03
Pilgrims 24, 25, 180–81
Pine Ridge Reservation 1, 6, 25, 153, 184
"Plan of the Barrio" 59

Plimoth Plantation 24–25, 180, 181
Poliomyelitis (polio) 162
Poll tax 65, 146
Poor People's March on Washington 59, 112–13
Port Madison Reservation 28
*Powwow Highway* 184
"Praise Song for Yuri" 120
Presidential Appreciation Award 202
Price, David 28
"Profits Enslave the World" 202
Property rights 12
Puerto Rican Solidarity Committee 37

## Q

Quakers 10, 11, 13, 189

## R

Race Relations Award 53
Radical Faeries 76
*Radically Gay: Gay Liberation in the Words of Its Founder* 77
"Radio Free Alcatraz" 178
Raitt, Bonnie 185
Randolph, A. Philip 34, 108 (ill.), 128
*Ready from Within* 53
*Report from Beirut: Summer of 1982* 8
*Revolution* 17, 18
*The Revolutionist* 57
Riots, Los Angeles (1992) 96, 99–100, 99 (ill.)
**Roberts, Ed** 162–68
Robideau, Bob 158
Robinson, Bernice 51
Rolling Quads 164, 165
Roosevelt, Franklin Delano 32, 34
Rosebud Reservation 2, 28
Ross, Fred 41
Rustin, Bayard 34–35, 35 (ill.), 145

## S

*Sa-I-Gu: From Korean Women's Perspective* 100
San Joaquín Valley 39, 91, 198

Schenley Corporation 42
Schryver, Martin 188
SCLC 31, 33, 47, 52, 66, 102, 105, 110, 130, 145, 146
Second Woman's Suffrage Convention 193
Seeger, Pete 73, 82
Select Seminary for Females 11
Sellers, Cleveland 144
Selma to Montgomery march 109–10, 130–31
Senate Select Committee on Indian Affairs 2–3, 6
Sharecropping 63, 124
Shaw University 69, 126
Short-handled hoe 91, 93
Simmons, J. Andrew 49
Slater, Don 76
Slavery 187–89, 191
SNCC 31, 36, 64, 65, 123, 126, 129, 130, 141, 144, 146, 147
Sons of Temperance 12
Southern California Labor School 73
Southern Christian Leadership Conference (See SCLC)
Southern Regional Council 133
"Spiritual Conference for Radical Faeries" 76
Stanton, Elizabeth Cady 13, 13 (ill.), 14, 15, 21
Stanton, Harry B. 15
Sterilization, of Native American women 3
Stone, Lucy 18
Stonewall Rebellion 71, 74, 76
Student Nonviolent Coordinating Committee (See SNCC)
Student sit-ins 34–35, 64, 125, 145
Student walkouts 58
Students for a Democratic Society 151
Stunts, Joe 29
Sun dance 154
Super Bowl protest 174
Supreme Court 20, 126, 194
The Survival of American Indians Association, Inc. 158
Susan B. Anthony Amendment (See Nineteenth Amendment)
Susan B. Anthony coin 10, 19 (ill.)

**T**

Taney, Roger B. 194
Teaching and Research in Bicultural Education (TRIBES) 25
Teamsters 45
Teatro Campesino 43
Terminal Island 116
**Teters, Charlene 169–76,** 169 (ill.)
Third World Liberation Front 98
"Third World Strikes" 98
Thirteenth Amendment 17
*Through Different Eyes: Two Leading Americans, A Jew and an Arab, Debate U.S. Policy in the Middle East* 9
*Thunderheart* 177, 184
Tibet 8
Tijerina, Reies Lòpez 59
Tlatelolco School 58
Traditionalists 24, 156
Trail of Broken Treaties 25, 155, 159, 181
Train, George 17
Treaty of Fort Laramie 178
Troy Female Seminary 15
**Trudell, John 177–86,** 177 (ill.), 178 (ill.)
Trudell, Lou 178
Trudell, Wokova 178
**Truth, Sojourner 187–96,** 187 (ill.)
Tubman, Harriet 191, 191 (ill.)

**U**

UFW 39, 88, 92, 197, 199
Underground Railroad 12, 191
Undocumented workers 201
United Farm Workers (See UFW)
U.S. House of Representatives 1, 2, 18, 123
U.S. Senate 1, 2
*United States v. Susan B. Anthony* 20
University of California, Berkeley 96, 98, 163, 164
University of Illinois 169, 170, 171, 172

## V

Valdez, Luis 43, 43 (ill.)
**Vera Cruz, Philip 197–203,**
   200 (ill.)
Vietnam War 2, 71, 76, 111, 120,
   151, 178
Voter registration drives 129, 144
Voting Rights Act of 1965 51, 52,
   110, 131–32


## W

*Walking with the Wind: A Memoir*
   *of the Movement* 124, 130
Wallace, Henry 73
Wampanoag Indians 24, 25,
   180–81
War on Poverty 56
"We Shall Overcome" 82
Webster, William 5
Wilkins, Roy 108 (ill.)
Williams, Hosea 131
Wilson, Richard 6, 26, 156, 182
Women's Day Workers 32
Women's Hall of Fame 95
Women's National Loyal
   League 17
Women's Political Council 104

Women's rights conventions:
   New York City 21
   Rochester, New York 15
   Seneca Fall, New York 15
Women's State Temperance
   Society (WSTS) 13
Women's suffrage 13–14, 193
Works Progress Administration
   (*See* WPA)
World Institute on Disability
   (WID) 166
World War II 34, 40, 117
Wounded Knee 23, 25,
   156–57, 182
WPA 32


## Y

Young, Andrew 47, 66, 83
Young, Whitney 108 (ill.)
Young Communist League 34
*Yuri Kochiyama: Passion for*
   *Justice* 115


## Z

Zellner, Robert 147
Zwerg, Jim 127 (ill.)